# MADHUR JAFFREY'S

## Step-by-Step Cookery

# MADHUR JAFFREY'S
# Step-by-Step Cookery

Over 150 dishes from India and the Far East including Thailand, Vietnam, Indonesia and Malaysia

EBURY PRESS
LONDON

First published in 2000

1 3 5 7 9 10 8 6 4 2



First published in the United Kingdom in 2000 by Ebury Press,
Random House, 20 Vauxhall Bridge Road, London SW1V 2SA

www.randomhouse.co.uk

Random House Australia (Pty) Limited
20 Alfred Street, Milsons Point, Sydney,
New South Wales 2061, Australia

Random House New Zealand Limited
18 Poland Road, Glenfield,
Auckland 10, New Zealand

Random House South Africa (Pty) Limited
Endulini, 5A Jubilee Road
Parktown 2193, South Africa

The Random House Group Limited Reg. No. 954009

A CIP catalogue record for this book is available from the British Library.

ISBN 0 09 187527 7

Managing Editor: Janet Illsley
Design: Christine Wood
Special photography: Gus Filgate
Techniques photography: Craig Robertson
Stylists: Penny Markham, Helen Trent
Food stylists: Silvana Franco, Linda Tubby, Joanna Farrow, Julie Beresford

Printed and bound in Portugal by Printer Portuguesa

# ABOUT MADHUR

Madhur Jaffrey is now widely acknowledged as the finest authority on Indian food and cookery. She was born in Delhi, India, and began her career as an actress. She published her first cookery book, An Invitation to Indian Cooking, in 1974 and since then has written several others, including Madhur Jaffrey's Indian Cookery, first aired in 1982, which made her a household name. Madhur has travelled extensively throughout the Far East, and her television series on Far Eastern Cookery in 1989 was highly acclaimed. She now lives in New York.

# COOKERY NOTES

❑ Both metric and imperial measures are given for the recipes. Follow either set of measures, not a mixture of both, as they are not interchangeable.

❑ All spoon measures are level unless otherwise stated. Use measuring spoons, available in metric and imperial, for accurate quantities.

❑ Ovens must be preheated to the specified temperature. Grills should also be preheated. Cooking times in the recipes are based on this assumption.

❑ Use freshly ground black pepper and sea salt unless otherwise specified.

❑ Fresh herbs are used unless otherwise stated. Suggestions for dried equivalents of Asian herbs and other flavourings are detailed in the section on ingredients (see pages 256-264).

# CONTENTS

# INTRODUCTION

The young women stood poised on the craggy black rocks that edge Korea's southernmost island, Cheju, their trim bodies silhouetted against the blue of the sky and the sea. Then, one by one, they dived off and disappeared into the cold waters. Several minutes later they surfaced with a bounty of abalone, oysters and sea-urchins. These briny creatures were not destined to go far! They were prised open, right there on the rocks, dabbed with a heady sauce made of fermented soya beans, chillies and garlic and sold by the women to waiting customers – including this one.

I started travelling to the Far East almost twenty five years ago, marvelling on each trip at how well people ate, at the freshness of their ingredients and at their combinations of cooking techniques and seasonings that produced highly nutritious and delicious foods with such ease. In a market in Indonesia I once bought *gadangan* from a woman with a basket. This was a medley of blanched vegetables tossed lightly with a 'dressing' of grated coconut, red chillies, lime juice, sugar and salt. It was so simple and so utterly glorious. On another occasion I was sitting in a dusty, unpromising office in Vietnam. Some staff members were about to prepare lunch on the premises. Files were cleared off tables and a paraffin cooker lit. Soon an amazing salad emerged. It consisted of raw kohlrabi mixed with very freshly roasted and lightly crushed peanuts, mint, coriander, vinegar, sugar and chilli powder. It could not have been improved upon.

In Japan I have had grilled mushroom caps stuffed with minced chicken and dressed with soy sauce and vinegar. In Thailand I have eaten a superb dish of stir-fried chicken blanketed with crisply fried basil leaves. And in the Philippines I have enjoyed an exquisitely delicate first course of mackerel strips 'cooked' in lime juice. There is so much good food in this region.

You might have sampled Thai, Japanese or Vietnamese dishes in local restaurants and been afraid to try cooking them at home. You should not be put off by the 'foreignness' of some of the ingredients. Just remember that at one time potatoes, tomatoes and corn were 'foreign' (they came from the New World) and so were mangoes, black pepper and cinnamon (they came from Asia). Ingredients, indeed whole dishes, once travelled the world at the cumbersome pace of the mortals who transported them – on foot, by boat or on horseback. Today a chef can eat a dish in Hong Kong on one day, and recreate it in his kitchen in New York the following week. A recipe for a curry from Malaysia can be 'e-mailed' to London and the ingredients for it found in many supermarkets the same day – thanks to air transportation and refrigeration.

For this book I have decided to concentrate on the cooking of Korea, Japan, Hong Kong, the Philippines, Vietnam, Thailand, Malaysia, Indonesia and my homeland, India. The climates of these countries vary from temperate to tropical – Indonesia is actually on the equator – and their cuisines are quite distinct from each other. There are, however, some common elements. What binds all these countries together is their healthy emphasis on grains. Unlike in the West, where the focal point of a meal is usually meat, the place of honour in South and East Asia is given either to wheat, in the form of noodles, pancakes or steamed buns, or to rice.

It is not certain where rice originated, though the latest research seems to point to Thailand. At any rate, rice quickly spread through much of South-east Asia and eventually inched its way north to China and Japan as farming techniques improved. In the entire Far Eastern region, with a few exceptions, rice is synonymous with the meal itself, and an invitation to dine very often translates as 'Come and have rice with me.' In a Chinese dialect, to have a job is to 'have grains to chew', and to have lost it is to 'have broken the rice bowl'. Chinese children are warned that if they leave a single grain of rice in their bowl they will end up with a pockmarked spouse!

While almost all Asians eat rice, they don't all use the same kind. The Chinese generally like a long-grain variety while the Japanese and Koreans frown on anything but their somewhat more glutinous, short-grain varieties. In Bali in Indonesia I have had the fluffiest, lightest rice. In Malaysia I have eaten a pudding made with black rice, while in the Philippines, a cake made with purple rice. In Northern Thailand, following the local custom, I have made small balls out of glutinous rice and eaten them with my pork curry. In India long-grain patna rice or the wonderfully fragrant basmati is eaten.

The soya bean is another ingredient that gives Far Eastern foods their special character and nutritional value. Kilo for kilo, it is richer in protein than red meat, richer in calcium than milk, and contains more iron than ox liver. And it has no saturated fat. But soya beans are hard to digest in their normal state and so need to be processed in some way. This has led to the availability of a host of soya bean products, such as bean curd and soy sauce. Made from the beans combined with wheat, barley or rice, briny fermented soy sauce adds protein, flavour and saltiness to thousands of dishes from Korea to Indonesia.

Soy sauce is not the only flavouring-cum-salting sauce in the region. Fish sauce performs a very similar function in Vietnam, Thailand and the Philippines. Even though this is made from fermented fish, it is neither malodorous nor overpowering. When used properly, as in a Vietnamese dipping sauce that calls for the addition of water, lime juice, sugar and chillies, it is so good as to be almost drinkable.

Then there is that felicitous Chinese creation, the noodle. Originating probably before the start of the Christian era – in fact, as soon as the Chinese were able to grind grains into a fine flour – the noodle quickly made its way into the hearts – and mouths – of the entire Far East. Today there are rice noodles, wheat noodles and buckwheat noodles. These Chinese symbols of longevity may be immersed in soups, stir-fried with meats and put into cold salads. They are as perfect for eating and easy entertaining as Italian pasta.

The one seasoning that is used throughout the Far East is ginger. You probably know it well from Chinese and Indian

cookery. Fifth-century Chinese sailors used to carry it on their ships, embedded in earth to make it last. They knew it was rich in vitamin C and prevented scurvy. They also knew that it had 'heating' properties and, to this day, ginger tea is served after a meal of 'cooling' crabs.

The Chinese have, for centuries, felt that the human body functions best when 'cooling' and 'heating' forces (*yin* and *yang* respectively) are properly balanced. In 1368 Chia Ming, a medieval foodie, catalogued every edible substance, marking its degree of 'hotness' or 'coolness'. He ate carefully himself and lived to be 106! The Chinese, wherever they are – and as well as populating Hong Kong they have spread widely in the Philippines, Thailand, Malaysia and Indonesia – are very aware of this as they cook and eat. I was offered not only ginger tea after a heady meal of many, many roe-filled crabs but also chrysanthemum tea (it is cooling) after we had gorged ourselves on barbecued beef and chicken (they are heating) at a bayside Hong Kong picnic.

An ancient Chinese poem, attempting to entice the soul back to earth, offers it a meal where dishes of 'all flavours' are present, 'bitter, salt, sour, pungent and sweet'. These are still the five flavours the Chinese try to balance at every meal. Koreans took cognisance of a flavour the Chinese seemingly missed – the 'nutty' flavour found in sesame seeds. There is, however, a taste that the Chinese and Koreans were not to know till the sixteenth century – the fire of the red hot chilli.

Chillies came marching into Asia with the Portuguese and conquered the old world for ever, transforming the cuisines of India, Indonesia, Malaysia, Thailand, Vietnam, Korea and some provinces of China such as Sichuan and Hunan. It is hard to say what it is about chillies that causes an addiction. Perhaps it is the exquisite pain they bring that heightens the pleasure of eating, but once you have enjoyed them, there is no turning back: you are hooked forever.

The culinary art of the Far East lies in the magical mingling and balancing of flavours and textures. Western taboos just do not hold: fish and pork strips are thrown together in a fiery stew in Korea; a paste made of minced pork and crab meat is lathered on to triangles of bread before they are fried in Vietnam. The soft, the smooth, the crunchy and the slithery as well as the sweet, salty, hot and sour are all presented in a kaleidoscope of inventive permutations.

The source of meat for much of this region (excepting Japan) has traditionally been the pig. This prolific animal could be raised on scraps while precious grains from the fields could be wisely saved for the growing numbers of humans. Cattle could be saved for ploughing the fields that raised the grains. Changes came to Indonesia, Malaysia and the southern

Philippines with the spread of Islam. Pigs, of religious necessity, were out. Goats and, when the people could afford it, cattle were slaughtered instead. As farming methods improved, more and more cows were raised for slaughter. Today Korea has a few cattle farms that rival those in Texas.

What much of this region thrives on, however, is fresh fish. People demand the freshest of fish and get it. The price of fish drops dramatically if it is a day old. Eels, carp, crabs and octopus, all live, wriggle around in tanks and tubs. Even before dawn, hundreds of prawns are lined up on scrubbed counters like repeating commas. By midday the prawns will have been stir-fried with asparagus in Hong Kong, dipped in batter and fried in Tokyo, and stirred into a coconut sauce in Malaysia.

The demand for freshness extends to vegetables as well. It is said that in China only 60 per cent of the credit for a good meal goes to the person who cooks; 40 per cent goes to the person who shops. Straw mushrooms, it is clear, should be free of spots, and who would buy green beans if they did not snap when they were broken? Vietnam was the poorest country we visited, yet its markets had a fresh herb section that was as verdant as a summer garden.

In Japan the need for freshness is carried a step further. First you buy a very fresh vegetable, then you make it look even fresher. For example, a freshly picked cucumber might be dropped into boiling water for a second, then rinsed in cold water before cutting. The taste is unchanged but its skin turns a lusher green – the cucumber looks even more perfect!

In spite of their many common ingredients and cooking techniques, the individual cuisines chosen for this book are quite distinctive. Let me tell you a little about each of them.

## India

The wealth of India's cuisine lies in its regional cooking. India is a vast country and geography and local produce have played important roles in forming regional culinary traditions. Religion too has played a part, imposing its own restrictions. While strict Hindus do not eat beef, Muslims avoid pork for example. One common denominator in Indian cooking is the imaginative use of spices, especially cumin, coriander, turmeric, pepper, mustard seeds, fennel, cinnamon and cloves. The 'heat' in Indian recipes comes from hot chillies, though not all dishes contain them and not all Indian food is hot. In this book I have gathered together some of my favourite recipes – many of which I learnt from my mother.

## Malaysia

Malaysian cuisine combines the delicacy of Chinese food with the exuberance of Indian spices and the aromas of South-east Asian herbs. This cuisine has developed interestingly. The original Malay diet consisted mostly of rice and fish. The two could be moistened with coconut and flavoured with a host of local seasonings such as shrimp paste (*blachan*), black pepper, ginger, turmeric, shallots, lemon grass and tamarind. But then things began to change.

A look at a map will reveal that peninsular Malaysia, sticking out like a finger into the sea, seems to be a natural meeting point between East and West Asia. It was actually more than that. From the earliest times favourable north-east and south-west monsoon winds literally blew in the ships of Indian, Arab and Chinese traders. By the early fifteenth century Malacca, a southern port, had become a hotbed of commerce, with trade flourishing in silk, jewels and spices. Each group not only traded but also left behind some of its members who settled and intermarried with local women. Starting with its sultan, a slow conversion to Islam also began. As peoples of all three major races – the Malays, Chinese and Indians – commingled and merged, so did their cuisines.

## Thailand

Thai food virtually bursts with contrasting hot, sweet, sour and salty flavours. The Thai people have taken some of the best ideas from the cooking of the Malays, Chinese and Indians, thrown in their own zesty spirit – and their love of the raw, crunchy, aromatic and colourful – and come up with a cuisine that is unmatched in its combination of lightness and seductive earthiness.

Typically, a Thai meal is built around rice. The rice is accompanied by a soup or a soupy stew, a stir-fried dish and a salad-like dish, all served at the same time and eaten either with the fingers or with a fork and spoon, the fork being used only to shove the food into the spoon. Thai foods can be hot – really hot. Generally hot dishes are balanced with mild ones. There are always side dishes of raw vegetables and fruit to nibble upon – forests of mint, lettuce leaves, long beans and bean sprouts. These often look like garnishes but they are meant to be eaten, offering both a change of texture and taste. Meals here tend to end with tropical fruit: in restaurants, the fruit is often carved elaborately into flowers, leaves and other forms. It is quite an art, requiring lethal knives and great patience.

## Indonesia

It is to Indonesia that traders – Indians, Arabs and eventually the Dutch – came for spices. The equator goes right through the island of Sumatra and spices such as turmeric, galangal, ginger, chillies, lemon grass, tamarind, nutmeg and cloves grow abundantly here.

The first time I visited an Indonesian home was during the Muslim holy days that follow Idul Fitri, when everyone keeps glass jars filled with delicacies, such as pineapple pastries, little curry puffs and small Dutch-style cakes for visitors who drop by. I was invited to stay for lunch. A cloth was spread out on the living room floor (I had seen this Muslim custom in India) and all foods placed, in traditional style, in the middle. Food was to be enjoyed communally. A spicy fish curry was set down. So was some rice (the staple), cabbage greens cooked with a red chilli, shallot and garlic paste, some crisp wafers (*krupuk*) and the most renowned dish of the region, beef *rendang*.

Indonesia has no grand cuisine, no special palace dishes. The cuisine is egalitarian: everyone eats the same food. You eat with the right hand and pass food with the left. Food, with the exception of soup, is served at room temperature and is meant to be shared.

## Korea

South Koreans are a rough-tough people of Mongol ancestry who have pushed their country from a developing third world nation into a hive of modern industry. China, which looms further to the north and across the waters to the east, has invaded many times and left a firm imprint. The Japanese were more recent – and much-hated – occupiers. They are rarely mentioned, though their silent mark may occasionally be felt. Today Confucian ideals and modern Mammon are equally revered in a fine balancing act while the Koreans hold on to their unique identity.

Traditionally, Koreans dine seated on the floor around a low rectangular table. Each person has a metal bowl filled with sticky rice (the same sort that is eaten in Japan) and helps themselves to food from the table with thin chopsticks and long-handled metal spoons. Soupy dishes or stews are served alongside grilled and stir-fried foods. Noodles, especially those made of buckwheat and mung beans, are highly popular, too. Some dishes are very hot, others mild. The typical seasonings are soy sauce, vinegar, sesame oil, roasted sesame seeds, sugar, ginger, garlic, red chillies and a family of pastes (*changs*) made of fermented soya beans. It is these pastes and Korean pickles (*kimchee*) that give this cuisine its special character.

## The Philippines

Like most South-east Asian countries, the Philippines has seen waves of Chinese traders and settlers who brought noodles, bean curd, soy sauce, spring rolls and pancakes in their wake. They intermarried with the local Malays to such an extent that much of the country is of Chinese-Malay extraction. Muslims came too, Arabs and Indians, bearing Islam, cumin and coriander. But the people who had the most influence on the country, its religion, customs and food were the ones who followed – the Spaniards and the Americans. The Spanish came in 1521 and introduced a Mediterranean style of eating. The Filipinos were not about to give up their own Chinese-Malay dishes, but they began to add Spanish ingredients to their own recipes and cook *paella* and other Spanish dishes.

Rice, fish and pork have remained the national staples. Rice is eaten from breakfast to dinner and made into thousands of different cakes, noodles and pancakes. This is a nation of 7,000 islands, and fish – fresh or dried – is eaten daily, especially in the villages. It is also made into fish sauce (*patis*) which is used here almost as much as soy sauce in China. A village meal might well consist of vegetables cooked with cockles, fried dried fish and rice. Pork is popular with those who can afford it, and is used in the national dish – *adobo*.

## Vietnam

The Vietnamese people are of mixed Malay and Chinese stock and have a history of foreign influences. The upper part of the country was either occupied or dominated by China for a thousand years, well into the middle of the tenth century. Indians came – somewhat more peacefully – to the south, where they traded their spices. Western powers, looking first for trade and then colonies, followed, starting around the sixteenth century. France had virtually taken over the country by the late sixteenth century. The Americans came last. Each left their mark.

The Chinese influence is quite pervasive. It can be seen in the use of chopsticks, in the small and delicate spring rolls, in the use of bean curd, fermented soya beans, star anise and Chinese medicinal herbs. It is evident in the Vietnamese love of noodles, and in the tasty combination of pork and crab meat for soups and spring roll fillings. The famous Thai noodle soup, *pho* is a glorious breakfast soup, though it can be eaten at any time of the day.

Fresh herbs are used prolifically in Vietnamese food. It is the mixture of these herbs, the flavours of lemon grass, galangal and fried shallots, the taste of crushed, freshly salted roasted peanuts, and the use of salty, hot and sour dipping sauces that make Vietnamese food so wonderfully unique.

## Hong Kong

Big, brash and bustling, this is a modern city with an ancient culture. Those who live there – who use ferries, buses, underground trains and hydrofoils to zig-zag across its many islands at frenzied speed – know how to make money and how to eat. With the sea on one side and fertile sub-tropical country on the other, they have constant access to a rich supply of the fruits of the earth and sea. Spoilt by nature's abundance and fine-tuned by an ancient culinary tradition that is easily one of the world's finest, they demand the best ingredients and are not satisfied unless they get them.

Hong Kong is almost completely encircled by China and its cuisine is very much a mirror of the varying cultural traditions of the mother country. Indeed, half of Hong Kong's food and water is brought from there. The choice in styles of food available in Hong Kong reflects what may be found in China: the fiery cuisines of the western regions of Sichuan and Hunan; Pekinese northern delicacies, such as Lamb with Spring Onions or Peking Duck; and Cantonese food, the local cuisine. Mild and gently seasoned, it is designed, as the Cantonese say, 'to let the ingredients shine through'.

## Japan

The principles of Zen Buddhism – to create order out of chaos, to bring a sense of simplicity and perfection to a confused and entangled world – apply to most aspects of Japanese culture, including its cuisine. Foods are prepared so that their natural flavours remain unmasked and they are served in small, almost austere portions.

The arrangement of food on the plate is always three-dimensional – it may be in little hillocks, or one food may lean against another. In smart restaurants, especially, it is made to resemble 'nature' as far as possible. Tiny long-stemmed mushrooms float in a soup like fresh-fallen flowers in a stream. Bits of skewered and grilled chicken are set on a plate with leaves and end up by looking like small buds in a tree.

It is said that a good Japanese restaurant is rated on three things: a third of the marks go to the cooking, a third to the presentation and the remaining third to the general ambience. Not everyone can rise to the heights of the great Japanese chefs, but the principles hold true even for everyday meals.

# EQUIPMENT

You do not need unusual equipment to prepare the recipes in this book. If you have a reasonably well equipped kitchen, you will probably have everything you need, including good sharp knives, sturdy saucepans and frying pans which distribute heat well, plus the usual utensils, bowls etc. However, it does help to have the following items:

## WOK

This is an all-purpose utensil that may be used for steaming, simmering, stir-frying or deep-frying.

A wok is traditionally a round-bottomed pan. Because of its shape, flames can encircle it and allow it to heat quickly and efficiently. It is most economical for deep-frying as it will hold a good depth of oil without needing the quantity a straight-sided pan would require. It is ideal for stir-frying as foods can be vigorously tossed around in it. As they hit the well-heated wok surface, they cook fast and retain their moisture at the same time. An Indian *karhai* is very similar to a wok.

*Choosing a wok* What kind of wok should you buy? Advances are being made all the time and every year seems to bring new woks on to the market. Traditional woks of good quality are made either of thin tempered iron or carbon steel. The ideal wok is about 35 cm (14 inches) in diameter and fairly deep. (Shallow saucer-shaped woks are quite useless.) A round-bottomed wok works well on a gas hob. A flat-bottomed wok functions more efficiently on an electric hob, although if your cooking fuel is electricity, it is worth considering investing in an electric wok – but make sure it is a good one. Look for one that heats very quickly, becomes very hot and allows foods to be both stir-fried and simmered.

*Seasoning a wok* The iron and carbon steel woks leave the factory coated with oil. This needs to be scrubbed off with a cream cleanser. Then a wok needs to be seasoned. Rinse it in water and set it over a low heat. Now brush it all over with about 2 tablespoons vegetable oil. Let it heat for 10-15 minutes. Wipe the oil off with a piece of kitchen paper. Brush the wok with more oil and repeat the process 3-4 times. The wok is now seasoned. Do not scrub it again; just wash it with hot water and then wipe it dry. It will not have a scrubbed look. It will, however, become more and more 'non-stick' as it is used.

*Wok accessories* When you buy a wok, it is a good idea to invest in one with a tight-fitting lid and a steaming rack or tray. You will also need a curved spatula. On a gas hob, a wok usually needs a stand for stability, and to allow air to circulate underneath. The perfect stand is made of wire. The collar variety with punched holes doesn't seem to permit free circulation of air.

## CAST IRON FRYING PANS

I find a 13 cm (5 inch) cast-iron frying pan ideal for roasting spices and a large one perfect for pan-grilling thin slices of meat. All cast-iron frying pans can be heated without any liquid and they retain an even temperature. Once properly seasoned, they should never be scrubbed with abrasive cleansers.

## BLENDER AND SPICE OR COFFEE GRINDER

In the Far East mortars, pestles and grinding stones of varying shapes, sizes and materials are used to pulverise everything from sesame seeds to fresh hot red chillies. You can, of course, use a pestle and mortar at home and this is invariably the easiest way to grind very small quantities. For normal quantities, I find it much easier to use an electric blender for wet ingredients and an electric spice grinder or clean coffee grinder for dry ones.

## GRATER

The Japanese make a special grater for ginger and horseradish. It has tiny hair-like spikes that are perfect for their purpose. If you ever find one, do buy it. Otherwise use the finest part of an ordinary grater for grating fresh ginger.

## DOUBLE-BOILER

This is simply one pan balanced over another. The lower pan holds boiling water and allows the ingredients in the upper pan to cook very gently. Double-boilers are available from good kitchenware shops but can be easily improvised.

## ELECTRIC RICE-COOKER

Many households in the Far East seem to have one of these small appliances. Its main use is to free all burners on the hob for other purposes and make the cooking of rice an easy, almost mindless task. I do have one and use it only for cooking plain rice. When the water has been absorbed by the rice, the cooker switches itself off, and will then keep the rice warm for some time.

## ELECTRIC DEEP-FAT FRYER

For those who are somewhat afraid of deep-frying, this is a god-send as it is far safer than a large pan of oil on the hob. The temperature of the oil is controlled thermostatically.

## RACKS FOR GRILLING FISH

In Indonesia hinged double racks are used for grilling fish over charcoal. The fish lies sandwiched between the two racks and can be easily turned and basted. Many types of fish racks are available in the West, some even shaped like a fish. I find them exceedingly useful.

# TECHNIQUES

The culinary techniques used in Far Eastern and Indian cookery are not all that different from those used in the West. However, a few general guidelines may be helpful. Specific preparation techniques are described in more detail.

## PREPARING VEGETABLES AND MEAT

Meat and vegetables are frequently cut into strips or dice before they are cooked, so that the pieces cook evenly. This is particularly important for quick stir-frying and for the general look of the food. Aesthetics play a very special role in this region, reaching a pinnacle in Japan where restaurants are judged on the look of their food as much as on its taste.

### To cut vegetable julienne and dice

Each vegetable requires its own cutting technique. In general, you should first cut the vegetable into slices of the required length, then cut these lengthways into strips. (These strips can be cut crossways if small dice are required.)

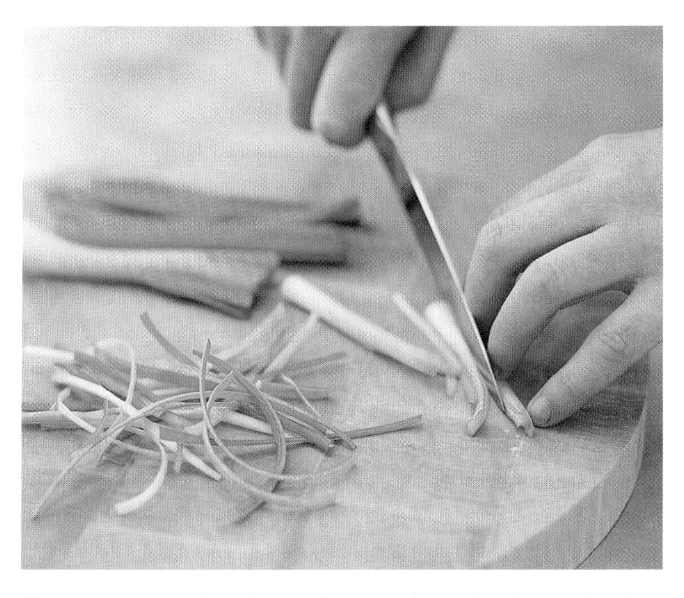

To cut spring onions into julienne strips, trim the ends, then cut into 7.5 cm (3 inch) lengths. Cut each piece lengthwise into very fine strips.

Vegetables, such as mooli and potato, which discolour quickly on exposure to the air should be immersed in a bowl of chilled water as soon as they are sliced or diced unless they are to be cooked immediately. Adding a squeeze of lemon juice to the water further helps to prevent discoloration.

To cut a carrot into julienne strips, trim off the ends, then cut the carrot crossways into 5 cm (2 inch) chunks. Cut each chunk lengthways into slices of the desired thickness. Cut each slice lengthways again, to make the julienne.

To slice chillies, simply cut into fine strips, discarding the seeds, for a less fiery flavour if required. Then cut into fine dice if directed in the recipe. Alternatively, a recipe may call for chillies to be sliced crosswise into fine rings. Make sure you avoid touching your eyes while you are preparing chillies, and wash your hands thoroughly immediately afterwards, as chillies can cause skin irritation.

## To slice meat into thin slices and strips

Recipes of Chinese origin, in particular, often call for lean, tender meat, such as beef or lamb steak to be sliced very finely against the grain. Sometimes these slices are cut into thin strips. It is easier to do this – though not essential – if the meat is partially frozen first.

Use a sharp knife to cut the meat against the grain into very thin slices. Illustrated above: slicing lamb steak.

If strips are called for, stack a few slices together at a time and cut into strips, about 6-7.5 cm (2½-3 inches) long. Illustrated above: cutting beef steak into strips.

## To de-bone a chicken leg

The chicken recipes in this book often call for boneless dark leg meat as it remains moist during lengthy cooking, whereas white meat has a tendency to dry out. Dark meat also has more flavour. De-boning a whole chicken leg is relatively easy.

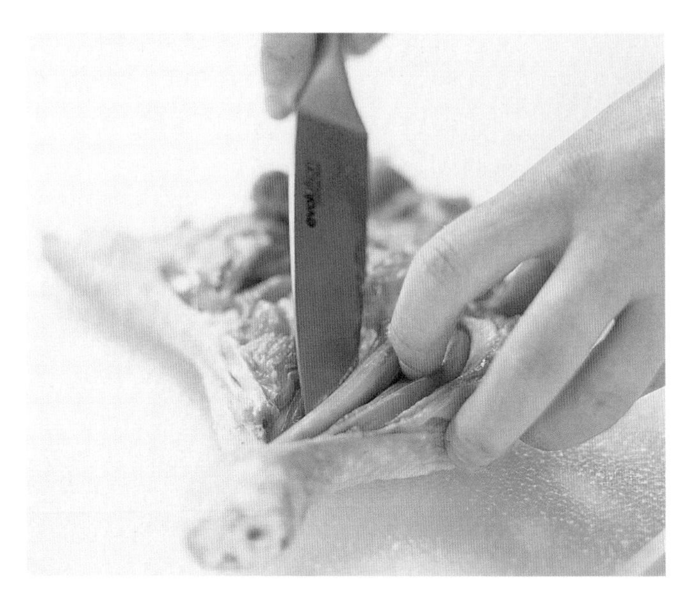

Using a sharp knife, make a deep slit along the length of the bone and drumstick. Free the meat at both ends, cutting at right angles to the bones.

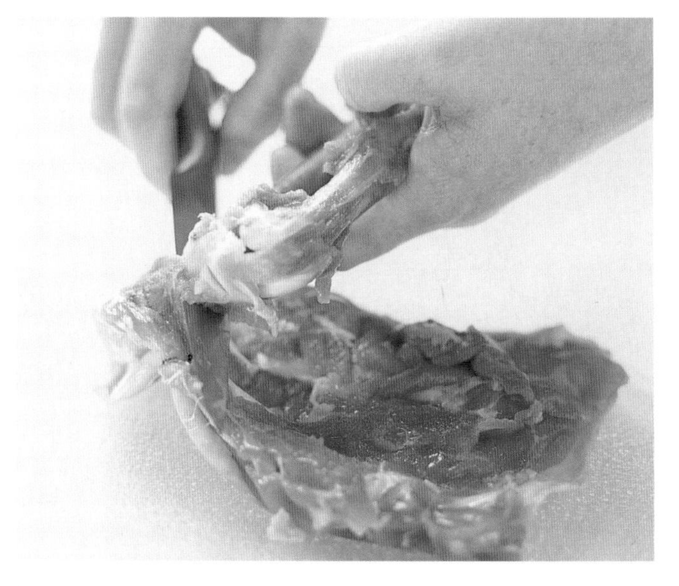

Now cut – almost scrape – the meat off the thigh bone and drumstick, freeing the meat from the middle joint as you do so. The chicken may now be cut into pieces as required.

# PREPARING SHELLFISH

Several recipes within this book call for uncooked, unpeeled prawns, and fresh squid. This is how to prepare them.

## To peel and de-vein a prawn

These instructions apply to the large uncooked prawns known as Pacific or king prawns. These are usually sold frozen and in the shell, but with the heads already removed.

First pull off the tail (unless retaining for decorative purpose). Then peel off the body shell and, with it, the tiny legs.

Make a shallow cut down the back of the prawn and remove the fine, dark, digestive cord that runs the length of it. Alternatively, make a slit in the back and hook out the cord, using a cocktail stick.

## To clean squid

Squid is relatively easy to prepare, but you can buy it ready cleaned from supermarkets and fishmongers if you prefer.

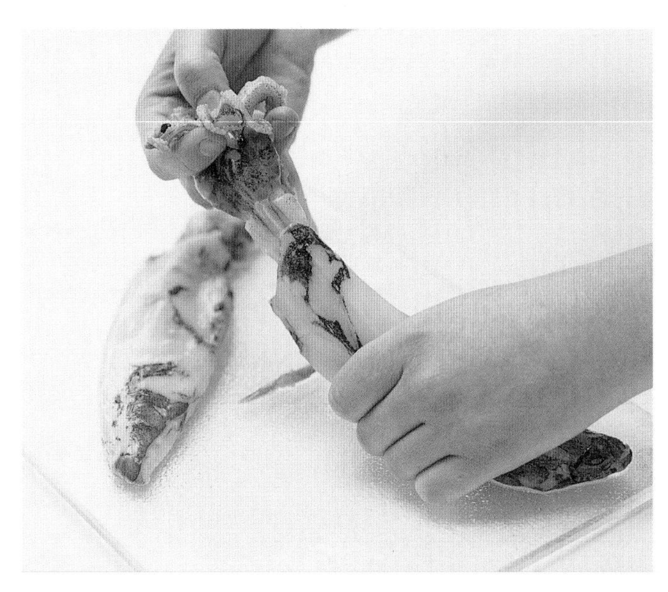

Twist off the head with the tentacles – the inner body sac will probably come away with it. Discard the sac and the hard eye area, which you may have to cut off with a knife. Retain the tentacles. If possible, pull off some of the brown skin on the tentacles. Peel off and discard the brownish skin from the tube-like body.

Carefully pull out the smooth inner cartilage (or pen), then wash the squid. It is now ready to be cut into rings or as the recipe suggests.

# TENDERISING AND FLAVOURING

In their country of origin, Far Eastern and Indian dishes are often prepared with meat and poultry that are tough in comparison to the cuts of meat available here. Ways of tenderising are therefore essential – especially if the meat or poultry is to be cooked relatively quickly. Imparting flavour is equally important.

## Marinating

A good marinade will tenderise tougher cuts of meat and impart all the flavours and aromas of its myriad of ingredients prior to cooking. Poultry and fish are also often marinated. Most marinades are based on oil or something acidic, such as vinegar, lime or lemon juice, or yogurt. Spices and aromatics – such as lemon grass, kaffir lime and garlic – add fragrance as well as flavour.

Meat is usually cut up before placing in a bowl or shallow dish with the marinade. It is important to toss the meat to ensure it is well coated with the mixture. Cover the bowl and leave in a cool place, or refrigerate if marinating overnight. In general, the longer you leave the meat, the more effective the marinade will be.

## Basting sauces

Meat, fish and poultry are often basted with a sauce or liquid during grilling or roasting, to keep them succulent and impart flavour. Sometimes, as in Japan, the basting sauce may contain sugar, to provide a final glaze as well as flavour. In Malaysia, coconut milk is frequently the main ingredient in a basting sauce; it is particularly good at keeping the meat, poultry or fish from drying out.

In Indonesia a practical (and aromatic) brush is made from a stick of lemon grass which is lightly pounded at the end.

## Spice pastes

Most curry-style dishes require that a spice paste be prepared first. Throughout India and the Far East, fresh and dried spices are pounded in a mortar and then fried in oil to get rid of their raw taste. Good quality, freshly pounded spice pastes are sold in most Thai and Malaysian markets.

Commercially prepared spice pastes are available from most supermarkets in this country, but I find the flavour of homemade spice pastes is superior. Using an electric blender (or spice or coffee grinder) takes all the hard work out of preparing spice pastes.

# COOKING TECHNIQUES

Using the appropriate techniques for cooking vegetables, meat and fish is essential. Lean, fine-grained cuts of meat respond well to quick cooking for example, whereas tougher cuts need to be cooked slowly over a longer period of time in order to tenderise them. Fish and vegetables are both easily ruined by overcooking.

## Blanching and refreshing

In order to keep vegetables crisp and their colour bright, they may, once prepared, be plunged very briefly into a large pan of water at a rolling boil – that is, boiling furiously. The reason for using a lot of boiling water is that you do not want the temperature of the water to drop when the vegetables are put into it: this would slow their cooking time and therefore affect both their colour and texture.

The vegetables should be cooked briefly in the boiling water until barely tender; they should retain a slight crispness.

The vegetables are then drained quickly, then immediately either plunged into a large quantity of iced water or rinsed under cold running water. This helps to set their colour and stop the cooking process.

## Braising

This involves cooking foods slowly in liquid but over a long period. Whole birds and fish can be cooked in this way. The liquid is always flavoured: it may be stock or water flavoured with wine, herbs and spices; or as in one recipe in this book, the braising liquid could be tea.

## Cooking with coconut milk

Care must be taken when cooking coconut milk to ensure that it does not curdle. Stir it constantly as it cooks. I often add it only towards the end of the cooking period and then just bring it to a simmer and leave it at that.

Coconut milk may be simmered for a while, but only if it is stirred most of the time.

## Dry-roasting

Spices are often dry-roasted before use. It is best to do this over a medium heat – in a preheated small, heavy cast-iron frying pan. No oil is used: the spices are just stirred around in the pan with a wooden spatula until they brown lightly.

Roasted spices develop a heightened, nutty aroma. They can be stored for at least several months in an airtight jar.

## Grilling

Grilling is very popular throughout the Far East. *Satays* – tiny pieces of meat skewered on bamboo sticks and freshly grilled on charcoal – are sold in the bazaars of Indonesia, Malaysia and Thailand, as everyone loves to eat out.

In Japan one of the most popular dishes is *yakitori* – chicken kebabs basted with a sweetish soy sauce mixture during grilling. The Japanese also pierce fish fillets against the grain with several skewers, then grill it with frequent bastings of sweetish sauces. The skewers are helpful when it comes to turning the fillets over, and they prevent the fish falling apart. If you are using bamboo skewers, they should be soaked in water for 30 minutes beforehand so that they do not burn.

The Koreans cut their meat into strips, marinate it and grill it on their dining tables. Each home is equipped with special portable burners and grills just for this purpose. Although most of the grilled dishes in this book can be cooked under a domestic grill, the taste will be more authentic if you are able to use a barbecue instead. When grilling on charcoal, it is important to get the coals white-hot before you start.

## Poaching

Many recipes require that chicken breasts be poached in sufficient water to just cover. Breast meat is fairly dry and it toughens easily. To poach properly, it is important that the water be barely simmering. If it boils too rapidly, it will toughen the meat.

## Steaming

Steaming is a very popular technique in Far Eastern cooking. Just as every home in the West has a roasting tin, so every home in the Far East tends to have a steamer. It may be used for cooking anything from plain rice to complete dishes, such as Fish Steamed with Lemon Grass (see page 64). Steaming cooks food gently and preserves its flavour.

One of the most satisfactory utensils for steaming is a wok because its width easily accommodates a whole fish, or a large plate of food. Use a wok with a flat base or set a round-based wok on a wire stand. Put a metal or wooden rack into the wok. (If you don't have a rack, you could use a heatproof plate balanced on a small inverted empty can instead.)

Now pour in some water. Bring it to a gentle boil and lower in the food. The water should stay about 2 cm (¾ inch) below the level of the food that is being steamed. Extra boiling water should be kept at hand just in case it is needed to top up the level. Cover the whole wok, including the food, with the wok lid or a large sheet of foil.

## Stir-frying

This is fast cooking over high heat in a small amount of oil. A wok is essential for stir-frying. First the oil is heated in the wok. Then aromatics, such as shallots, garlic and ginger, are usually tossed around in the oil to release their flavours.

Once the flavouring ingredients have released their aromas and started to colour, the cut meat and vegetables are added. These, too, are tossed around quickly until they are cooked.

Finally, herbs and shredded spring onion may be added and stir-fried for a matter of seconds, so that they are heated through, but retain their texture and vibrant colour.

## Deep-frying

This technique involves immersing food in hot oil. The flavour and juices are sealed in and the food cooks quickly. Properly deep-fried foods are not at all greasy; the outside is beautifully crisp while the inside is cooked to perfection. Delicate foods, such as fish, are first coated – usually in some kind of batter – to protect them from the hot oil

You can use a wok, an Indian *karhai*, or a deep-fat fryer. The oil usually needs to be about 5 cm (2 inches) deep in a wok, but significantly deeper in a deep-fat fryer. It is essential for the oil to be heated to the required temperature before the food is added.

Oil that has been used for deep-frying may be re-used. Allow it to cool completely, then strain it through a fine-meshed sieve. Store in a bottle. When you next deep-fry, use half old oil and half fresh oil. Oil that has been used for frying fish should be re-used only for fish.

## Garnishes as flavourings

In Far Eastern cooking a garnish is often an integral part of the dish. For example, crisply fried shallots and crushed roasted peanuts may be sprinkled over a dish at the last minute. They are added because without their flavour and texture the dish would be incomplete.

# recipes

# soups and first courses

# HOT AND SOUR PRAWN SOUP

## *Tom Yam Kung*

*THAILAND*

Serves 6 as a soup, or 4 as a main course

I would definitely classify this as one of the world's greatest soups. I have enjoyed it for some twenty years and have never had quite the same version twice. Traditionally the stock is made only with prawns. Whole prawns that still have their flavourful heads attached to their bodies are boiled in water seasoned with aromatic lemon grass and lime leaves. They are then removed, peeled, and their heads and skins thrown back into the stock pot for added flavour. Since most of us cannot find raw prawns with heads, it is best to use a rich chicken stock instead and add the prawn peelings to intensify its taste.

This soup can be made as fiery hot as you can handle. The amount of both the chilli paste and the hot green chillies can easily be increased. My recipe is for a soup of medium heat, though the fresh green chillies, when bitten into, do carry their own explosive power with them. If you cannot find the Thai chilli paste known as *nam prik pow*, use ¼ teaspoon chilli powder combined with ¼ teaspoon sugar and ½ teaspoon vegetable oil.

*Many Thai restaurants catering to foreigners serve soup as a first course, but in Thai homes it is usually one of several main dishes served with plain rice. All Thai soups – including this stunning hot and sour, lemon grass flavoured broth with its floating prawns and straw mushrooms – are best enjoyed with spoonfuls of plain rice. The neutrality of the soft grain serves to absorb the heat of the soup and accentuate its flavours.*

**450 g (1 lb) uncooked unpeeled prawns**

**2 sticks fresh lemon grass**

**4 fresh or dried kaffir lime leaves, or 1 tablespoon finely grated lemon rind**

**1.2 litres (2½ pints) chicken stock**

**1 tablespoon fish sauce, or salt to taste**

**3 tablespoons lime juice, or to taste**

**1 teaspoon chilli paste (*nam prik pow*; see page 257)**

**425 g (15 oz) can straw mushrooms, or 12 medium fresh mushrooms**

TO GARNISH

**3 fresh hot green chillies**

**3 tablespoons fresh coriander leaves**

■ Wash the raw prawns, then peel and de-vein, saving the peelings. Wash the prawns again, drain and pat dry. Cover and refrigerate.

■ Cut each lemon grass stick into three 5 cm (2 inch) pieces, starting from the rounded bottom end; discard the straw-like top. Lightly crush the 6 pieces with a heavy pestle, a mallet, or the blade of a knife.

■ Combine the lemon grass, kaffir lime leaves (or lemon rind), the stock and prawn peelings in a pan. Bring to the boil. Lower the heat and simmer very gently for 20 minutes. Strain this stock and return to the rinsed-out pan.

■ Add the fish sauce, lime juice and chilli paste. Stir and taste again, adding more fish sauce or lime juice if required.

■ Drain the straw mushrooms and add them to the seasoned stock. If using fresh mushrooms cut into quarters, drop into lightly salted boiling water and boil for 1 minute. Drain and add to the seasoned stock. (The soup may be prepared to this stage several hours ahead if necessary and refrigerated.)

■ Prepare the garnishes shortly before you are ready to serve the soup. Cut the green chillies into very fine rounds and wash and dry the coriander leaves.

■ Just before serving, heat the stock with the mushrooms in it. When it begins to bubble, drop in the peeled prawns. Cook over a medium heat for about 2 minutes or just until the prawns turn opaque. Serve the soup immediately in individual bowls, garnished with the green chillies and whole coriander leaves.

# MUNG BEAN SOUP

## *Mongo Guisado*

*PHILIPPINES*

Serves 4

Here is an easy-to-prepare, delicious and very nourishing soup. Generally it is quite thick and is eaten with rice, but many restaurants now serve it in a somewhat simplified version. Fish sauce, olive oil and lime wedges are usually passed around at the table for those who wish to add a little more seasoning. A common garnish for the soup is pork crackling. If you wish to use it, you will need 1 tablespoon crumbled pork crackling per serving.

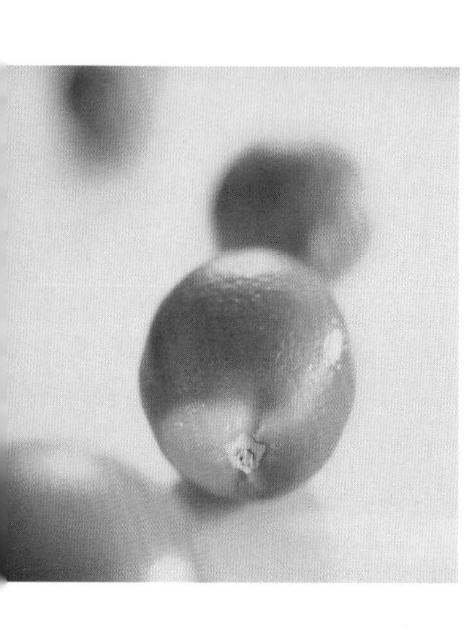

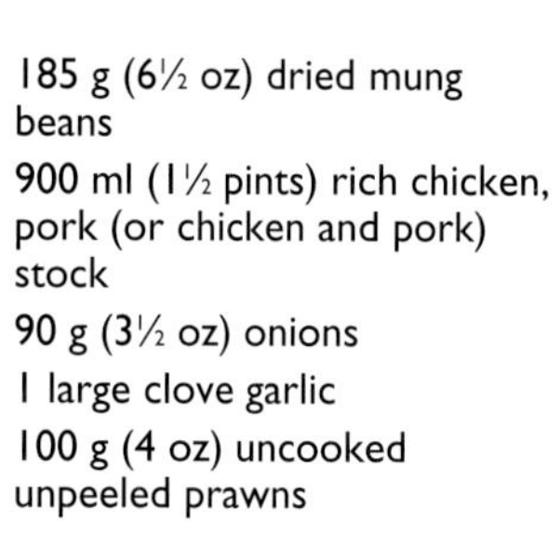

**185 g (6½ oz) dried mung beans**
**900 ml (1½ pints) rich chicken, pork (or chicken and pork) stock**
**90 g (3½ oz) onions**
**1 large clove garlic**
**100 g (4 oz) uncooked unpeeled prawns**
**3 tablespoons olive oil**
**¾ teaspoon salt**
**freshly ground black pepper**

TO SERVE
**lime or lemon wedges**
**fish sauce (optional)**
**extra olive oil (optional)**

■ Pick over the mung beans and wash them in several changes of water. Drain and put them into a medium pan. Add sufficient water to cover the beans by about 5 cm (2 inches) and bring to the boil. Lower the heat and simmer for 2 minutes. Turn off the heat and let the pan and its contents stand for 1 hour.

■ Drain the beans and put them back into the pan. Add the stock and bring to the boil again. Cover loosely, lower the heat and simmer gently for about 1 hour or until the beans are tender. Mash them lightly in the pan.

■ Peel and thinly slice the onions. Peel the garlic and chop it finely. Peel and de-vein the prawns, wash them and pat dry. Cut the prawns crossways into 1 cm (½ inch) segments.

■ Heat the olive oil in a medium frying pan over a medium-high heat. Add the onions and garlic, and stir-fry until they are golden and just beginning to brown.

■ Add the prawn pieces to the pan and stir-fry for about 1 minute until they turn opaque. Empty the contents of the frying pan, including the oil, into the soup pan. Season with the salt and black pepper to taste. Stir to mix.

■ Reheat the soup and serve with lime wedges, and fish sauce and olive oil if you like.

# PORK AND CRAB SOUP

## *Canh Thit Nau Cua*

*VIETNAM*

Serves 4-5

This soup is quite Chinese in its origins, but in Vietnam it is served with a generous squeeze of fresh lime juice and some Red Pepper Sauce (see page 219) for those who want it.

Chinese black fungus imparts a distinctive flavour to this soup, so do try to obtain some (see below).

If you cannot find any dried black fungus, increase the number of dried Chinese mushrooms to 12. If you cannot get those either, use 12 good-sized, flavourful fresh mushrooms (such as chestnut or flat mushrooms) in place of both fungi, cutting them into thin slices and adding to the soup at the same time as you would add dried fungi. The fresh mushrooms will not, of course, need soaking.

8 dried Chinese mushrooms
1 tablespoon small dried black fungus
100-150 g (4-5 oz) lean boneless pork loin
2 teaspoons plus 2 tablespoons cornflour
2 teaspoons sesame oil
1 teaspoon fish sauce, or ¼ teaspoon salt
1 egg
1 spring onion
1.1 litres (2 pints) chicken stock
salt
100 g (4 oz) cooked white crab meat, finely shredded

TO SERVE
lime wedges
Red Pepper Sauce (see page 219; optional)

■ Soak the dried mushrooms in about 250 ml (8 fl oz) hot water for 30 minutes or until they are soft. Soak the black fungus in 250 ml (8 fl oz) hot water for 30 minutes or until soft.

■ Cut the pork against the grain into 3 mm (⅛ inch) slices. Stacking a few slices at a time together, cut the meat again against the grain into long shreds, about 3 mm (⅛ inch) wide. Put the pork in a bowl. Add the 2 teaspoons cornflour, sesame oil and fish sauce. Mix well. Cover and set aside for 20 minutes or longer, refrigerating if necessary.

■ Lift the mushrooms out of their soaking liquid. Strain the soaking liquid through a muslin-lined sieve and set it aside. Cut off the hard mushroom stems and discard them. Cut the caps into 3 mm (⅛ inch) strips.

■ Lift the black fungus out of its soaking liquid and discard the liquid. Feel the fungus for hard 'eyes'. Cut off any you find and discard them. Chop the fungus coarsely.

■ Put the 2 tablespoons cornflour into a small cup. Add 3 tablespoons of the reserved mushroom soaking liquid or water. Mix and set aside.

■ Beat the egg lightly in a bowl and set aside. Cut the spring onion crossways into very fine rounds.

■ Put the stock and any remaining mushroom soaking liquid into a pan. Add the mushrooms and fungus. Bring the stock to a simmer, cover and simmer on a low heat for 5 minutes. Add the pork, stirring and breaking up any lumps as you do so. Simmer until the pork is just cooked through.

■ Taste the soup and add salt if it is needed. Add the crab meat. Give the cornflour mixture a stir, then stir it into the soup. Cook, stirring, over a fairly low heat until the soup is thick and bubbling.

■ Take the soup off the heat. Immediately pour in the beaten egg in a slow steady stream, using a fork to stir the top of the soup in a figure-of-eight pattern to make perfect 'egg drop' slivers. Add the spring onion and stir the soup for a few seconds more to allow the onion to wilt. Serve with lime wedges and Red Pepper Sauce.

*Chinese dried black fungus is also known as wood ears, cloud ears, moer mushrooms or just dried black fungus. Used routinely in Chinese cookery, these 'mushrooms' look like miniature elephant's ears and have a mild earthy taste and a crunchy texture. They are also meant to be very good for the heart! The Vietnamese often use them in their fresh form. In the West, we can obtain them only in their dried form – at Chinese grocers and selected supermarkets.*

# GLORIOUS SEAFOOD SOUP

## *Ama Tito Rey Soup*

*PHILIPPINES*

Serves 4

Seafood is plentiful in the Philippines and is invariably cooked to perfection. This soup combines Spanish techniques with Filipino ingredients in the most delectable way. Needless to say, it should be made only if fresh mussels and clams in shells are available. If you can find only one of these molluscs, use it to replace the other. You can improvise freely here and add seafood that you happen to like. I often put in squid, cut into rings, and cubes of filleted white fish, such as sole. When you are selecting shellfish, avoid mussels or clams that have broken or damaged shells.

**16 mussels**
**8 clams**
**100 g (4 oz) uncooked unpeeled prawns**
**1 cm (½ inch) cube fresh root ginger**
**40 g (1½ oz) onion**
**1.1 litres (2 pints) chicken stock**
**1 teaspoon black peppercorns**
**salt**
**40 g (1½ oz) unsalted butter**
**3 tablespoons plain flour**
**50 g (2 oz) cooked or uncooked white crab meat**
**5 tablespoons thick coconut milk (see page 258)**
**chopped fresh parsley, to garnish**

**1** Rinse the mussels and clams thoroughly under cold running water to help rid them of sand and grit. Scrub them well with a stiff brush under cold running water. Pull off and discard the 'beards' from the mussels.Tap any open molluscs with the back of a knife. If they refuse to close, discard them. Wash the molluscs again; set aside.

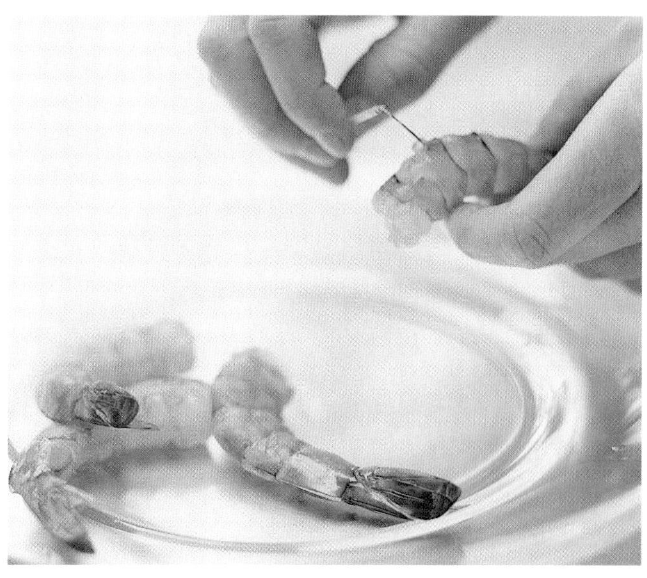

**2** Peel and de-vein the prawns, rinse, then pat dry. Cut each prawn crossways into 3 segments; set aside. Cut the ginger crossways into 4-5 slices. Peel the onion. Combine the stock, ginger, whole onion and peppercorns in a pan and bring to a simmer. Cover and simmer gently for 15 minutes. Strain the stock into a clean pan. Add a little salt – allowing for the saltiness of the shellfish; keep hot.

**3** Melt the butter in a wide heavy pan. Add the flour and cook, stirring, over a low heat for 2 minutes, until bubbling but not brown. Slowly pour in the hot stock, stirring rapidly with a whisk. Simmer gently for 3-4 minutes. (If any lumps appear, strain at this stage.)

**4** Put the mussels and clams into the soup and bring to the boil. Cover, turn the heat to medium and cook for 5 minutes, or until the shells have opened up. (If some have not, cook for another minute, then discard any that remain closed.) Put in the prawns, crab meat and coconut milk. Cook over a low heat for 1 minute. Serve the soup in wide soup plates, garnished with chopped parsley.

# SPICY CHICKEN SOUP WITH MANY FLAVOURS

## *Soto Ayam*

*INDONESIA*

Serves 4

There are probably as many recipes for *soto ayam* as there are families in Indonesia. This soup can be a light and delicate teaser or it can – with the addition of fried potato balls, noodles and hard-boiled eggs – transform itself into a whole meal. I have decided to place my *soto ayam* smack in the middle of its range of possibilities. It is light enough to qualify as a first course and yet it has enough of the titillating additions – bean sprouts, bits of chicken, crisply fried shallot flakes, spring onions and red chilli sauce – to give it its complex Indonesian flavour.

When this soup is made in Indonesia, a whole chicken is first boiled with a few spices. The liquid becomes the stock and the chicken meat is then pulled off the bone, shredded and put back into the stock. I prefer to make a flavoursome stock separately – using necks, backs, wings and odd bones and carcasses – and then lightly poach skinned and boned chicken breast to provide the meat content of the soup.

Making the liquid part of the soup, poaching the chicken and preparing the bean sprouts, red pepper sauce, shallots, potatoes and green seasonings can all be done ahead of time. Just before serving, the bean sprouts can be heated in boiling water and the stock can be brought to a simmer.

**100 g (4 oz) boneless chicken breast, skinned**
**salt**
**350 g (12 oz) fresh bean sprouts**

**FOR THE FLAVOURINGS**
**50 g (2 oz) shallots or onions**
**75 g (3 oz) potatoes**
**vegetable oil for shallow-frying**
**salt**
**1 spring onion**
**1 handful tender celery leaves or stalks**
**½ lime or lemon**

**FOR THE SAUCE**
**50 g (2 oz) red pepper**
**1 tablespoon distilled white vinegar**
**¼ teaspoon sugar**
**½ teaspoon chilli powder**

**FOR THE FLAVOURED STOCK**
**75 g (3 oz) shallots or onions**
**3 cloves garlic**
**15 g (½ oz) candlenuts or cashew nuts**
**1.5 litres (2½ pints) chicken stock**
**salt**

■ First prepare the flavourings. Peel the shallots and slice lengthways into fine slivers. Peel the potatoes and cut into 3 mm (⅛ inch) slices, then into 3 mm (⅛ inch) wide julienne strips.

■ Place a sieve over a bowl on a work surface near your hob. Heat a 5 mm (¼ inch) depth of oil in a frying pan over a medium heat. When the oil is hot, add the shallots and stir-fry until golden brown and crisp. Empty the contents of the pan into the sieve. Drain the shallots well, then spread them out on a plate lined with kitchen paper.

■ Return the strained oil to the frying pan and place over a medium heat. When hot, put in the potato sticks. Stir and fry until they are golden and crisp. Tip into the sieve set over the bowl and drain well, then spread the potatoes out on another plate lined with kitchen paper. Sprinkle them very lightly with salt. Save the oil for the flavoured stock.

■ Cut the spring onion, including the green part, into very fine rounds. Soak in cold water (to make them milder). Coarsely chop the celery leaves. Cut the lime into 4 wedges. Cover and set aside.

■ To make the sauce, deseed the red pepper then place in an electric blender with the vinegar, ¼ teaspoon salt, the sugar and chilli powder. Blend until smooth. Transfer to a small serving bowl, cover and set aside.

■ For the flavoured stock, peel and coarsely chop the shallots and garlic. Coarsely chop the nuts. Put the shallots, garlic, nuts and 4 tablespoons water in a blender and blend until smooth.

■ Put 4 tablespoons of the reserved oil in a medium pan (preferably non-stick) and set it on a medium-high heat. When the oil is hot, add the paste from the blender. Stir and fry for 4-5 minutes until the paste is lightly browned. Add the stock and bring to the boil. Lower the heat and simmer gently for 15 minutes. Add salt to taste, then set aside.

■ Cut the chicken lengthways into 2 cm (¾ inch) wide strips. Place in a pan and cover with about 1 cm (½ inch) water. Add ¼ teaspoon salt and bring slowly to a simmer. Simmer gently for 2-3 minutes or until the chicken turns white all the way through. Lift out and let cool slightly, then tear the chicken into long (not too thin) shreds. Cover with cling film.

■ Trim off the thread-like ends of the bean sprouts if wished, then immerse in a pan of boiling water for 30 seconds. Drain and immediately rinse under cold water. Drain well, cover and set aside. All the elements of the soup are now assembled.

■ To serve, uncover the sauce and put it on the table. Drain the spring onion and pat dry. Arrange the fried shallots, fried potatoes, spring onion, celery leaves and lime wedges on a platter. Heat the flavoured stock. Drop the bean sprouts into boiling water for 10 seconds to heat them through. Drain and divide them between 4 generous soup bowls or plates. Top with the chicken, then ladle the hot stock over the top and take the soup to the table.

■ Diners should help themselves to sauce, lime wedges, shallots, potatoes, spring onion and celery, adding them to their portion roughly in that order.

# SUMMER SOUP WITH PORK AND CUCUMBER

## *Wei Ling Qinggua Rou Jin Jiang* HONG KONG

Serves 4-5

Fresh ingredients and delicate flavours – that is what Cantonese food is all about, and nothing exemplifies it more than this soup. Even though the soup is ideal for summer, you may serve it successfully in winter as well. The cucumber in it, you might be interested to know, does not stay raw. It cooks, however briefly, to turn into a most interesting vegetable. As far as the pork is concerned, you could buy either 225 g (8 oz) of pork tenderloin or 2 pork loin chops weighing about 400 g (14 oz) in total and just cut the meat off the bone.

You can prepare the stock, marinate and parboil the meat, and slice the cucumbers well ahead of time. The soup should be assembled and heated only at the last minute.

**225 g (8 oz) pork tenderloin or 400 g (14 oz) loin chops, boned**
**½ teaspoon cornflour**
**2 teaspoons sesame oil**
**⅔ egg white**
**salt**
**2.5 cm (1 inch) cube fresh root ginger**
**25 g (1 oz) fresh coriander (with stems and roots if possible)**
**1.25 litres (2¼ pints) chicken stock**
**185 g (6½ oz) cucumber**

■ Remove any fat from the pork, then cut the meat into thin slices about 4 x 1 cm x 1.5 mm (1½ x 1 x 1/16 inch). Put the meat in a bowl. Add the cornflour, sesame oil, egg white and ¼ teaspoon salt. Mix well and set aside for 30 minutes, or longer refrigerating if necessary.

■ Peel the ginger and cut into thin slices. Wash the coriander well and pat it dry. Remove the leaves (reserving the stems and roots), cover them with cling film and set aside. Combine the chicken stock, ginger slices and coriander stems and roots in a pan. Bring to the boil, lower the heat and simmer for 20 minutes. Strain and add salt to taste.

■ Pour a 2 cm (¾ inch) depth of water into a medium frying pan and bring to the boil. Add the pork, then turn the heat to low. Stir the pork about until it turns white all the way through. (It is not necessary for the water to come to the boil again.) Remove the pork with a slotted spoon and set aside. Peel the cucumber and cut it into very thin rounds.

■ Just before eating, heat the seasoned stock until it is bubbling. Put in the pork and cucumber slices and let them just heat through; this should take 30-40 seconds. Remove the pan from the heat and add the coriander leaves. Serve immediately, in warmed bowls.

*Korean white radish is very thick, very long and sweet. You may find it sold as mooli or daikon. The one I used here was 4 cm (1½ inches) in diameter. If the only white radish you can find is very sharp, use the sweeter and more commonly available red radishes instead, cutting them in half lengthways. They will lose a little of their red colour in the soup, but that does not matter. You may also substitute young, sweet turnips.*

# BEAN SPROUT AND RADISH SOUP

## *Kongnamul Kuk*

*KOREA*

Serves 4

During my very first stay in Korea many years ago I frequently had this soup for breakfast, along with rice, pickles and barley tea. The thin slices of beef in the soup are cut from the brisket used in Beef Stock (page 254). If you are making Beef Stock especially for this soup, leave out the fish sauce and star anise. If you have made a stock using bones but no brisket, you can prepare this soup without including any meat.

**200 g (7 oz) long white radish (mooli)**
**40 g (1½ oz) sliced boiled brisket from Beef Stock (see page 254; optional)**
**1.1 litres (2 pints) Beef Stock (see page 254)**
**350 g (12 oz) fresh bean sprouts**
**3 spring onions**
**salt**

■ Peel the radish and cut crossways into 5 cm (2 inch) pieces. Cut each section lengthways into ¼ inch (5 mm) wide pieces.

■ If using brisket, cut the meat against the grain into very thin slices. Each slice should be about 4 cm (1½ inches) long.

■ Combine the radish, brisket and stock in a pan and bring to the boil. Cover, lower the heat and simmer gently for 15 minutes. The radish should by now be almost translucent.

■ Meanwhile, wash the bean sprouts and drain. Pull off their thread-like ends you prefer. Cut the spring onions into 5 cm (2 inch) lengths. Quarter or halve the white part lengthways, depending on thickness.

■ Add the bean sprouts and spring onions to the soup and season with salt to taste. Simmer for a further 5 minutes. Serve hot.

# FERMENTED BEAN PASTE SOUP WITH BEAN CURD

## *Miso Shiru*

*JAPAN*

Serves 4

My favourite Japanese breakfast consists of nothing more than a tart preserved plum, so tart that it puckers the mouth and jolts me awake, a hot bowl of this *miso* soup, rice, pickles and tea. Millions of Japanese drink *miso* soup in the morning; those, of course, who have not succumbed to the more modern, fashionable notion of toast and coffee. *Miso* soup may also be served at the beginning or end of a meal.

**1 spring onion**
**100 g (4 oz) bean curd**
**1 litre (1¾ pints) Japanese Soup Stock (see page 255) or light unsalted chicken stock**
**4 tablespoons *aka miso* (the reddish-brown one)**

■ Cut the entire spring onion (including the green section) into very thin rounds. Cut the bean curd into 1 cm (½ inch) cubes.

■ Heat the stock in a medium pan until hot, but not boiling. Take off the heat. Lower a small sieve into the stock so that only its lower half is submerged in the liquid. Put the miso into the sieve and push as much of it through as possible. Discard any lumps that may be left in the sieve.

■ Put the soup back on a medium heat and add the bean curd and spring onion. Bring the soup to a simmer. When the first bubbles appear, remove from the heat and serve.

*Miso is a paste made from fermented soya beans, though it can contain mixtures of other fermented grains as well. It is easy to digest, full of protein and, for vegetarians, a major source of nutrients.*

*There are many different types of miso available in Japan. Shops contain row upon row of wooden tubs, each heaped with miso of a different colour – ranging from white to almost black; a different texture – from coarse grains to a smooth paste; and a different degree of saltiness – from very salty to somewhat sweet. You can also buy low-salt misos. Most of these may be used to make soup.*

*For us in the West, the choice is much more limited. Most of us have access to healthfood shops, which tend to stock three or four varieties. There are nearly always yellowish, brown and reddish-brown misos. Start with aka miso, the reddish-brown one. You may later even decide to mix several misos together, once you get to learn the characteristics of each one.*

# SMALL SPRING ROLLS

## *Nem Ran*

*VIETNAM*

Makes about 50 bite-sized rolls

Called *nem* in North Vietnam and *cha gio* in South Vietnam, these delicious bite-sized crab-and-pork-filled spring rolls are usually wrapped in soft lettuce leaves and dipped into a sauce before being eaten. Fresh herbs such as mint and basil are put into these lettuce bundles as well.

A word about the Vietnamese spring roll wrappers: unlike Chinese spring roll skins, which are made of plain wheat flour, these are made from rice flour. When bought, they look like round translucent sheets of paper with the markings of the cross-woven mats on which they dried firmly imprinted on them. The ideal size is about 10 cm (4 inches) in diameter, but this size is hard to find in the West.

Mrs Vuong, the chef at whose elbow I learned this recipe in Hanoi, used two very thin wrappers, one placed more or less on top of the other, to make each spring roll. Since the wrappers were stiff, she softened them by smearing the outside wrapper with a little caramel-flavoured water.

I find that the wrappers I have managed to obtain at ethnic grocers' in the West are often much larger and coarser in texture, and need repeated brushings with caramel water to soften them. They may also need to be halved or quartered. As they crumble easily, it is best to wet them first, then cut them with a sharp knife. After they have been stuffed, you will need a little flour paste to stick the last end of the wrapper down firmly in place.

You can buy Vietnamese spring roll wrappers in Chinese and Far Eastern food stores – they are usually labelled 'rice paper'. If you cannot get authentic rice paper wrappers, the best substitute is filo pastry, which is widely available.

To use filo pastry, spread one large sheet on a slightly dampened cloth and brush with warm vegetable oil. Cover with another sheet, again brushing with oil. Cut the double sheets into 10 cm (4 inches) squares. As you work with one square, keep the rest covered with a damp cloth. You will not need the caramel water or flour paste. Instead of frying, you can arrange these filo rolls, side by side, on a baking tray, brush with oil and bake in the oven at 200°C (400°F) gas mark 6 for 20-30 minutes, turning them over halfway through the cooking time.

If you cannot obtain dried black fungus, increase the number of dried Chinese mushrooms from 8 to 14.

**2 tablespoons dried black fungus**
**8 dried Chinese mushrooms**
**15 g (½ oz) cellophane noodles**
**½ spring onion**
**40 g (1½ oz) onion**
**100 g (4 oz) cooked white crab meat, shredded**
**100 g (4 oz) lean pork, minced**
**¼ teaspoon salt**
**freshly ground black pepper**
**1 large egg**
**1 large head soft lettuce**
**1 good-sized bunch fresh mint sprigs**
**2 tablespoons plain flour**
**4 tablespoons Caramel Water (see page 219)**
**Vietnamese rice papers**
**oil for deep-frying**

**TO SERVE**

**Fish Sauce Seasoned with Lime Juice (see page 216)**

■ Put the black fungus in a bowl, pour on 300 ml (½ pint) hot water and leave to soak for 30 minutes. Put the dried mushrooms in a separate bowl and soak in 300 ml (½ pint) hot water for 30 minutes or until soft.

■ Soak the cellophane noodles in a large bowl of hot water for 15-30 minutes or until they are soft. Drain and cut them into 1 cm (½ inch) lengths.

■ Lift the fungus out of the water and rinse under cold running water. Feel for the hard 'eyes' and cut them off. Chop the fungus very finely; you should have about 4 tablespoons.

■ Lift the dried mushrooms out of the liquid and cut off the hard stems. Chop the caps finely.

■ Finely chop the spring onion. Peel the onion and chop it finely. Pick over the crab meat to make sure that there are no bits of shell left in it. In a bowl, combine the pork, crab meat, black fungus, mushrooms, cellophane noodles, spring onion, onion, salt, black pepper and egg. Mix well.

■ Wash the lettuce, separating the leaves, and drain. Wash the mint, divide into tiny sprigs, and drain well. Mix the flour with 3-3½ tablespoons water to make a paste. Add 600 ml (1 pint) hot water to the Caramel Water, which should then be warm.

(Step-by-step guide to preparing the spring rolls, overleaf)

**1** To make the spring rolls, brush a piece of rice paper on both sides with the diluted Caramel Water. If it turns soft and pliable, proceed with the next step; otherwise brush again with Caramel Water. If you have the 10 cm (4 inch) rice papers, leave them as they are. If you have the 23 cm (9 inch) papers, cut them into quarters. Work with one quarter at a time.

**2** When the rice paper is soft and pliable, put a heaped teaspoon of the pork-crab mixture roughly in the centre, but closer to the edge nearest you. Spread the mixture into a sausage shape about 4 cm (1¾ inches) long.

**3** Fold the side of the rice paper nearest the filling over it.

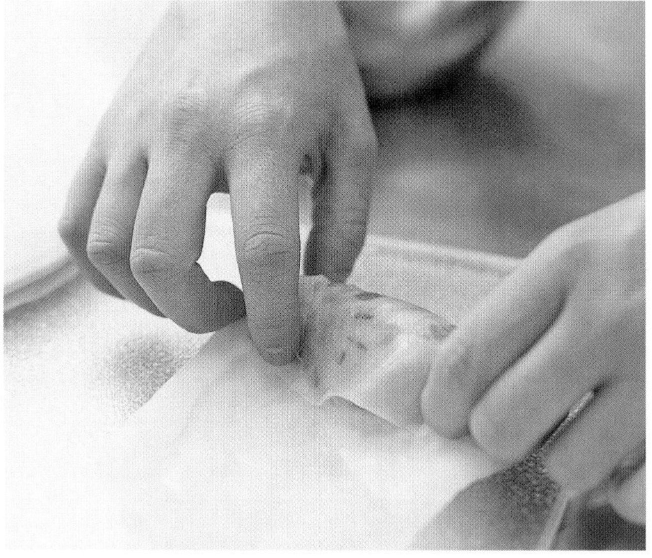

**4** Fold the two adjacent sides over to the centre.

**5** Now roll the parcel away from you to use up the remaining rice paper until you are left with a neat parcel.

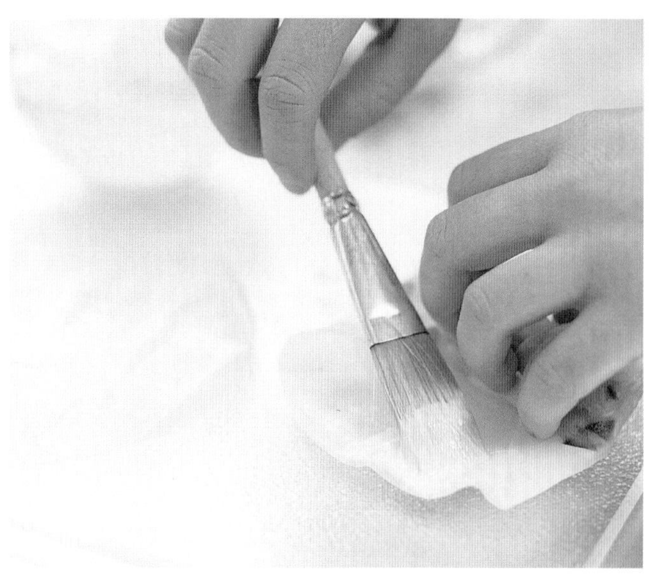

**6** Seal the edge with a little flour paste. Make all the spring rolls in this way and set them aside on a plate. (If you find that the rice paper is too thin and unmanageable, use 2 papers, one on top of the other.)

**7** Heat the oil in a wok or deep-fat fryer over a medium heat. When the oil is hot, put in as many spring rolls as will fit easily in one layer. Fry them until they are golden.

**8** Remove them with a slotted spoon and drain on kitchen paper. Continue until you have fried all the spring rolls in this way. Arrange the spring rolls on a plate. Arrange the lettuce leaves and mint sprigs on another plate. Put a small bowl of the dipping sauce near each diner, or place a bowl between 2 diners for them to share. To eat, take a lettuce leaf, or part of one, and put a spring roll and a few mint leaves on it; roll it up and dip it into the sauce.

# SAVOURY PORK AND CRAB TOASTS

## *Banh Mi Chien*

*VIETNAM*

Makes about 32

Here is another pork and crab combination that the Vietnamese do so well. These toasts are simple to prepare in advance. All you need to do just before you serve them is to fry them – usually for less than 2 minutes per batch.

If you are using frozen crab meat make sure that you defrost it completely and squeeze out all the moisture. If you are mincing the pork yourself, put the garlic and shallots into the mincer along with the meat.

**2 large cloves garlic**
**15 g (½ oz) shallot or onion**
**75 g (3 oz) cooked crab meat, finely shredded**
**100 g (4 oz) lean pork, very finely minced**
**1 small egg**
**freshly ground black pepper**
**1½ teaspoons sugar**
**1½ teaspoons fish sauce, or salt to taste**
**8 medium slices white bread, about 5-7.5 mm (¼-⅓ inch) thick**
**vegetable oil for frying**

■ Peel the garlic and shallot and mince or chop them finely. Combine the garlic, shallot, crab meat and minced pork in a bowl. Beat the egg in a separate bowl. Add 2 tablespoons of the beaten egg to the pork-crab mixture. (Use the remaining egg for another dish.) Add also a generous amount of black pepper, the sugar and fish sauce. Mix well to form a paste. (This mixture may be made ahead of time, covered and stored in the refrigerator until needed.)

■ Stacking a few slices of bread together at a time, cut off the crusts. Now cut the slices in half diagonally, making large triangles, then cut these triangles in half again to make small triangles. Using a knife, spread the prepared paste over one side of each triangle to a thickness of 3 mm (⅛ inch).

■ Pour the oil into a large frying pan to a depth of just under 1 cm (½ inch) and set over a medium-low heat. (To test whether the oil is hot enough, drop in a cube of bread – it should begin to sizzle immediately.)

■ Add as many bread triangles to the hot oil as will fit in a single layer, placing them meat-side down. Cook for 1½ minutes or until the meat is golden brown. Turn the bread triangles over and cook on the second side for 30-60 seconds or until golden. Remove them with a slotted spoon and drain on kitchen paper. Fry all the triangles in this way. Serve hot.

*These delicious toasts may be served as a savoury at the end of a meal or as a first course. When I invite people over for drinks I find that these are the perfect nibble to pass around. They are rather like the prawn toast triangles you might have eaten in Chinese restaurants, though I prefer this Vietnamese topping of minced pork and shredded crab meat.*

# PRAWN WAFERS

## *Krupuk Udang* — *INDONESIA*

*Krupuk* are wafers which, rather like the Indian poppadums, add a pleasing crunch to a meal. They may be found sitting neatly at the edge of a plate of *Gado-Gado* (page 184), their crispness balancing nicely with the blanched vegetables, or on a plate of *Nasi Goreng Istimewa* (Special Fried Rice with Beef and Prawns, page 196). They nearly always appear at festive banquets, are amazingly good with drinks – try them with a dip of *Sambal Terasi* (page 219), and may be eaten on their own as a snack or appetiser.

There are many, many varieties of *krupuk*. They may be flavoured with prawns, made of cassava or of nuts. One of my favourites, found only in the hills of Western Sumatra, is made of cassava and comes thinly smeared with a sweet and hot red chilli jam.

*Krupuk udang*, made of prawns and starch, come in many sizes and colours, some rather startling. I have seen bright blue, pink, green and yellow *krupuk* gracing many a table. *Krupuk* need to be fried quickly – passed through hot oil, you might say – before they are served. To ensure crispness, the wafers must be bone dry before they hit the oil. Indonesian housewives routinely put *krupuk* in the sun for a brief period first. You could place them in a warm oven for 10 minutes. Once they are in the hot oil, they expand quite a bit and assume a lighter, airier texture. Ideally they should be cooked shortly before they are eaten. If you cannot manage that, store them in an airtight container after they have been cooked. Uncooked *krupuk* should also be stored in tightly lidded jars.

*General method for preparing krupuk*

■ Put enough oil into a wok or other wide, deep pan to give a depth of at least 4 cm (1½ inches) in the centre. Heat until it is very hot, registering about 185°C (365°F) on a deep-frying thermometer.

■ Drop in 2 or 3 small *krupuk* (fewer if they are large). They will sink, rise almost immediately and greatly expand in size. If you are using a wok, spoon oil over them during the few seconds that they take to cook. Do not let them brown. Adjust the heat if necessary.

■ Remove the wafers with a slotted spoon and transfer them to a plate lined with kitchen paper. Cook as many *krupuk* as you need in this way.

# CHICKEN, PRAWN AND FRUIT SALAD

## *Yam Polamai*

*THAILAND*

Serves 6 as a first course, or 4 as a main course

Who, first of all, would think of putting such disparate ingredients together – shredded chicken, prawns, grapes, oranges, fried garlic, fried shallots and roasted peanuts – and then of dressing them with lime juice, sugar, salt and green chillies? Only the Thais. Yet this salad is so good that, when I serve it, my guests cannot stop marvelling – or eating.

There is such exuberance about Thai salads. Not only are meat, fish and fruit all put together, but they also are seasoned quite brilliantly with hot, sweet, sour and salty flavours as well as with crisp-fried slivers of shallots and garlic.

In Thailand the fruit in the salad can include such exotic fare as pomelo, water chestnuts, mangoes, rose apples, mangosteens and lychees, all of which should be diced. Do use these fruit if you can find them. The amount of sugar, salt, lime juice and chillies will vary not just according to your taste but also according to the natural flavours of the fruit. Taste as you mix the salad and make your own adjustments. If you do not want tiny explosions of 'heat' as you eat, leave out the green chillies and use chilli powder instead. You may use cooked instead of uncooked prawns, in which case you will not need to poach them.

This salad does have several parts to it but each takes very little time, and can be prepared several hours ahead. The salad should, however, be mixed only at the last minute so that the texture is crisp.

salt
I large, firm, sour dessert apple (such as Granny Smith)
150 g (5 oz) red or black grapes (preferably seedless)
150 g (5 oz) green grapes (preferably seedless)
I medium orange
5 cloves garlic
90 g (3½ oz) shallots or onions
oil for deep-frying
100 g (4 oz) boned chicken breast, skinned
8 medium or 16 small uncooked unpeeled prawns
4 tablespoons Roasted Peanuts (see page 223)
I teaspoon sugar
3 tablespoons lime or lemon juice
2-3 fresh hot green chillies
2 tablespoons fresh coriander leaves

■ Pour 600 ml (I pint) cold water into a bowl and add I teaspoon salt. Peel and core the apple, then cut into 7.5 mm (1/3 inch) dice, adding the apple pieces to the salted water as you do so. Set aside.

■ Halve the grapes lengthways and remove the seeds if necessary. Put the grapes into a bowl. Peel the orange and cut into segments, removing the white pith and membrane. Cut each segment crossways at 7.5 mm (⅓ inch) intervals. Lay the orange pieces over the grapes. Cover and set aside.

■ Peel the garlic, slice thinly, then cut the slices into fine slivers. Peel the shallots, halve lengthways and slice thinly.

■ Pour the oil into a medium frying pan or wok to a depth of 2.5 cm (I inch). Place over a medium-low heat. Set a sieve over a bowl on a surface near to the hob. Spread some kitchen paper over a large plate. When the oil is hot, add the garlic slivers and stir-fry until they turn golden. Pour the oil and garlic into the sieve; once the garlic has drained, spread it out over one half of the kitchen paper.

■ Pour the oil back into the frying pan and set it over a medium heat. Replace the sieve over the bowl. When the oil is hot, add the shallots and stir-fry until they are golden brown and crisp. Empty the contents of the pan into the sieve. Once the shallots have drained, spread them out on the remaining kitchen paper. (Save the flavoured oil for another purpose.)

■ Cut the chicken into long thin strips and put these into a clean medium frying pan. Add sufficient water to cover and ¼ teaspoon salt. Bring to a simmer. Simmer gently for about 5 minutes or until the chicken is just done. Remove the chicken with a slotted spoon and tear into shreds 2.5 cm (I inch) long, or cut it into 7.5 mm (⅓ inch) dice. Reserve the cooking water.

■ Peel and de-vein the prawns. Bring the chicken poaching water to a simmer and add the prawns. Turn the heat to medium-low. Stir and poach the prawns for 2-3 minutes or until they are just cooked through; drain. Cut the prawns into 7.5 mm (⅓ inch) dice. Combine the chicken and prawns, cover and set aside.

■ Crush the peanuts lightly – put them into a polythene bag and hit them gently with a mallet or rolling pin; set aside. In a small bowl, mix I teaspoon salt with the sugar and lime juice in a small bowl; set aside. Cut the chillies into very fine rounds. Wash and dry the coriander. Cover and set aside.

■ Just before serving, drain the apples and pat dry. Set aside a little of the fried shallots and coriander for garnishing, then toss all the other ingredients together in a large bowl. Check the seasoning. Bring the salad to the table on individual plates, garnished with the reserved shallots and coriander.

# STIR-FRIED PRAWNS WITH TAMARIND AND CHILLIES

## *Sambal Udang*

*MALAYSIA*

Serves 4

Hot, sour and simple to prepare, this is yet another delicious way to cook prawns. For a mildly spiced dish, use 2 chillies; 10 chillies will make a very hot one.

**2-10 dried hot red chillies**
**6 candlenuts or 8 cashew nuts**
**90 g (3½ oz) shallots or onions**
**1 teaspoon shrimp or anchovy paste**
**450 g (1 lb) uncooked unpeeled prawns**
**8 tablespoons vegetable oil**
**2 tablespoons tamarind paste (see page 264), or 4 teaspoons lime or lemon juice**
**½ teaspoon salt**
**2 teaspoons sugar**
**fresh coriander sprigs, to garnish**

■ Crumble the chillies into a cup, then add the nuts and 5 tablespoons water. Set aside for 1 hour. Peel the shallots and chop them coarsely.

■ Transfer the soaked chillies and nuts to a blender with their soaking liquid. Add the chopped shallots and shrimp or anchovy paste. Blend to a smooth paste, adding up to 3 tablespoons water if needed.

■ Peel and de-vein the prawns; wash them and pat dry.

■ Put the oil in a wok or large frying pan over a high heat. When it is hot, add the paste from the blender. Stir-fry for 1 minute. Turn the heat down to medium, and continue to stir-fry for 2-3 minutes.

■ Turn the heat up again and add the prawns. Stir-fry for 1 minute. Lower the heat to medium and add the tamarind (or lime or lemon juice), salt and sugar. Stir-fry for 3-5 minutes or until the prawns are cooked. Check the seasoning. Serve garnished with coriander.

*The Malaysian climate is tropical and eating out is a pleasure. There are restaurants, of course, but food can be enjoyed even more as one takes the breeze. From breakfast until dinner, obliging hawkers sell an infinite variety of scrumptious snacks. On the way to the office, workers may stop to pick up a nasi lemak. At its simplest, this banana leaf packet might contain some rice cooked with coconut milk, fried whitebait, a couple of tamarind-flavoured prawns, a few cucumber or pineapple slices and a dollop of fiery chilli sauce made with roasted shrimp paste and pounded red chillies.*

# PACIFIC KING PRAWNS ON COCKTAIL STICKS

## *Tali Hui Jhinga*

*INDIA*

Serves 4

Speared on to cocktail sticks, these spicy prawns make an excellent appetizer to serve with drinks. Alternatively, you can double the quantities and serve the prawns – without cocktail sticks – as a main dish.

**5 cloves garlic**
**2.5 cm (1 inch) cube fresh root ginger**
**675 g (1½ lb) uncooked Pacific king prawns**
**3 tablespoons vegetable oil**
**3 tablespoons tomato purée**
**½ teaspoon ground turmeric**
**1 tablespoon lemon juice**
**¾ teaspoon salt**
**⅛-¼ teaspoon cayenne pepper**

■ Peel and chop the garlic and ginger. Put them into an electric blender with 3 tablespoons water and blend to a smooth paste.

■ Peel and de-vein the prawns. Wash well and pat them dry. Cut each prawn into 3 sections. Set aside.

■ Heat the oil in a 25-30 cm (10-12 inch) frying pan over a medium heat. When hot, pour in the paste from the blender and fry, stirring constantly, for 2 minutes.

■ Add the tomato purée and turmeric. Fry and stir for a further 2 minutes. Add 4 tablespoons water, the lemon juice, salt and cayenne pepper. Cover and simmer gently for 2-3 minutes. (This much preparation can be done in advance.)

■ Five minutes before serving time, lift off the cover, put in the prawns and turn the heat to high. Stir and fry the prawns for about 5 minutes or until they just turn opaque.

■ Transfer to a serving platter and stick a cocktail stick into each prawn piece. Serve hot, with pappadums if you like.

*Pappadums are traditionally served with drinks at cocktail parties or before a meal. Both plain and spiced pappadums are available from selected supermarkets and delicatessens. The spiced ones have a liberal sprinkling of crushed black pepper. To serve, you simply shallow-fry the pappadums in oil — they will turn golden, puff up and crisp within seconds. Drain well on kitchen paper to remove excess oil. Do not fry pappadums too far in advance though, as they soften and turn limp on contact with moisture in the air.*

# SQUID IN CHILLI AND GARLIC SAUCE

## *Sotong Dan Chilli Dan Bawang Putih*

*MALAYSIA*

Serves 4

In Malaysia the sauce for this dish is made with fresh red chillies. When these are unobtainable, I use a mixture of dried chillies and paprika; the dish still tastes very good. For a mild dish, use fewer chillies; the maximum number will make a very hot one.

**2-4 fresh or 4-9 dried hot red chillies**
**½ teaspoon paprika**
**½ teaspoon shrimp or anchovy paste**
**450 g (1 lb) squid, cleaned (see page 15)**
**3 cloves garlic**
**100 g (4 oz) onions**
**5 tablespoons vegetable oil**
**½ teaspoon salt**
**½ teaspoon sugar**
**1 teaspoon lime or lemon juice**

■ If using dried chillies, crumble them into a cup. Add 4 tablespoons warm water and set aside for 30 minutes. Put the fresh or dried chillies (and soaking liquid if appropriate) into an electric blender and blend until smooth. Return the mixture to the cup and add the paprika and shrimp or anchovy paste. Stir to mix.

■ Wash the squid and pat it dry. Cut the tubular body of the squid crossways into 2 cm (¾ inch) rings. The tentacles may be left clumped together or separated into 2-3 clumps. Peel the garlic and chop finely. Finely slice the onions.

■ Place 3 tablespoons of the oil in a frying pan over a high heat. When it is hot, put in the garlic. Stir and fry for about 30 seconds or until the garlic is golden. Add the squid. Stir and cook for 3-4 minutes or until the squid has turned opaque all the way through. Empty the contents of the frying pan into a bowl and set aside.

■ Wipe the frying pan clean with kitchen paper. Put in the remaining 2 tablespoons oil and set the pan over a medium-high heat. When the oil is hot, put in the onions. Stir-fry for about 3 minutes or until the onions are soft. Add the paste from the cup, the salt, sugar and lime juice. Stir and cook for 1 minute. Add the squid and all the juices in the bowl. Toss to mix, heat through and serve.

# CUCUMBER AND PRAWN SALAD

## *Ebi To Kyuri No Sunomono* — *JAPAN*

Serves 4

In Japan a *sunomono* is a 'vinegared thing', a salad which is usually served in small portions at the start of a meal. I have used Japanese rice vinegar here; it is milder and slightly sweeter than distilled white vinegar. If you are unable to obtain some, substitute 3 teaspoons distilled white vinegar mixed with 1 teaspoon water and a pinch of sugar.

It is best to use small prawns for this dish. Buy raw ones if available and drop them into a pan of simmering water for a minute or two, then lift out, cool slightly and peel and de-vein. Larger prawns should be cut into 1 cm (½ inch) pieces.

**200 g (7 oz) cucumber**
**salt**
**4 teaspoons Japanese rice vinegar**
**2 teaspoons Japanese soy sauce (*shoyu*)**
**½ teaspoon sugar**
**2 teaspoons Japanese Soup Stock (see page 255) or unsalted chicken stock**
**½ teaspoon sesame oil**
**100 g (4 oz) small cooked peeled prawns**

■ Peel the cucumber only if the skin is coarse. Slice the cucumber crossways into very thin rounds and place in a bowl. Add a very scant ½ teaspoon salt and toss. Set aside for 30-45 minutes. Squeeze as much liquid as possible out of the cucumber slices and pat them dry with kitchen paper.

■ Mix the vinegar, soy sauce, sugar, Japanese Soup Stock and sesame oil in a small bowl.

■ Just before serving, drain the cucumber slices again, pat them dry and put them in a bowl. Add the prawns and the vinegar dressing. Toss to mix.

■ Put the salad into the centre of each of 4 small individual plates or bowls, heaping it up to form little hillocks.

*Many years ago my husband and I were taken to one of the better eating establishments on one of the uglier outskirts of Kyoto city. The day was hot and miserable, the city congested and the traffic a nightmare. But the minute we entered the restaurant, our world changed. Our private room was cool and serene. We were seated facing the one large window. All we could see from it was a hill, a stream and an exquisitely proportioned tree. The window frame had been ingeniously placed to crop out all vulgarity and disarray. Japanese food is meant to serve the same purpose – to create order, and to bring a sense of simplicity and perfection. Presentation is important, and food is essentially prepared so that the natural flavours of the ingredients are enhanced, not masked.*

# MACKEREL 'COOKED' IN LIME JUICE

## *Kilawing Tanguigue*

*PHILIPPINES*

Serves 4

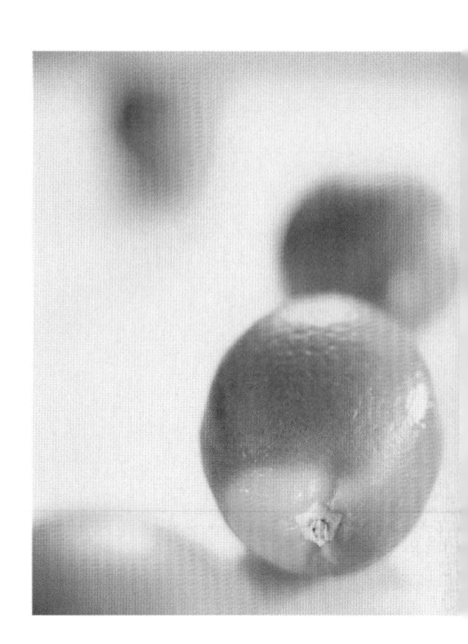

This startlingly good and refreshing first course is particularly suitable for the summer. The mackerel is actually not cooked at all, yet it doesn't taste in the slightest bit raw. That is because it is marinated in lime juice, which firms the flesh and turns it opaque – in essence doing to the fish what cooking would do to it, only with less effort on your part. If you have never eaten raw fish, you simply must try this. It is sour and gingery and best served as a first course over a bed of salad greens.

You may prepare this mackerel dish a day in advance. Keep it well covered and refrigerated.

**250 g (9 oz) mackerel fillets, skinned**
**4-5 tablespoons lime juice**
**2.5 cm (1 inch) cube fresh root ginger**
**40 g (1½ oz) carrot**
**½ teaspoon salt**
**25 g (1 oz) onion**
**freshly ground black pepper**

■ Mackerel fillets that are supposedly boned invariably have a few bones left in them. Feel for them with your hands and pull them out either with your fingers or with a pair of tweezers. Cut the fillets into 1 cm (½ inch) cubes and put these into a non-metallic bowl. Add the lime juice and toss well. Cover the bowl and set aside for 1 hour.

■ Meanwhile, peel the ginger and cut it into very thin slices. Stacking a few slices together at a time, cut the slices into very thin strips, then halve the strips. Peel the carrot and cut into thin slices, then into minute dice. Peel the onion and chop it very finely.

■ Drain the fish carefully and add to it the ginger, carrot and onion. Season with the salt and some black pepper. Toss well. Cover and refrigerate for at least 2 hours. Serve cold.

*Kilawing tanguigue is not all that different from the Latin American ceviche and was probably brought to the Philippines by the Spaniards, who most likely picked it up in Central or Southern America. It is now very popular in the northern province of Ilocos Norte, where it is made with a very special local vinegar.*

# STUFFED MUSHROOMS

## *Shiitake Nikozume*

*JAPAN*

Serves 6

A yakitori bar in Japan produces not just tantalising tit-bits of grilled chicken on skewers (see page 88), but also a whole range of snacks that may be served with drinks or as a first course at a somewhat formal dinner. These mushrooms, for which I must confess a passion, are one such example. They are simple enough to make.

Mushroom caps are stuffed with ginger-flavoured minced chicken and then cooked on a hot, lightly oiled surface. What gives them a heady lift is the final dousing they get in a tart sauce of soy and vinegar. A little mustard is served on the side to add further piquancy. A serving in the yakitori bars I frequented consisted of three mushrooms – four is considered an unlucky number. You may, of course, serve as many as you please.

**2.5 cm (1 inch) cube fresh root ginger**
**1 medium egg**
**275 g (10 oz) skinless boned chicken, minced (dark or light meat, or a mixture)**
**freshly ground black pepper**
**2-3 blades fresh chives or 1 spring onion (optional)**
**18 large well-formed mushrooms**
**1 tablespoon vegetable oil**
**6 tablespoons Japanese soy sauce (*shoyu*)**
**2 tablespoons distilled white vinegar or 3 tablespoons Japanese rice vinegar**
**English mustard, to serve**

■ Peel the ginger and grate it finely. Collect it all on your fingertips, hold over a bowl and squeeze out as much juice as you can. Discard the grated ginger, retaining the juice.

■ Break the egg into the same bowl and beat it lightly. Add the minced chicken and pepper to taste. Finely chop about 2 teaspoons chives or spring onion and add to the stuffing. Mix gently.

■ Gently break off the mushroom stems. Wipe the mushroom caps with damp kitchen paper. Stuff each mushroom cavity with a heaped teaspoon of the chicken mixture, flattening off the top.

■ Put the oil into a large non-stick frying pan and set it over a medium-high heat. When it is hot, put in the mushroom caps, stuffed-side down. Cook for 4-5 minutes or until lightly browned. Turn the caps over, turn the heat down to medium, cover the pan and cook for 3-4 minutes.

■ Meanwhile, mix the soy sauce and vinegar together in a bowl.

■ Arrange the mushroom caps, stuffed-side up, on individual plates. Spoon on the sauce and serve hot, with the mustard handed separately.

*As you become more familiar with Japanese cooking, it is apparent that the seasonings and sauces are made of careful permutations of the same few ingredients. The most important of these are Japanese soy sauce (shoyu), rice wine (sake), sweet rice wine (mirin), sugar, stock made from fish and kelp (dashi), and the juice of various sour citrus fruits (especially lime). The aromatic Japanese pepper (sansho) is occasionally used too.*

# WHOLEWHEAT MEAT SAMOSAS

## *Samosas*

*INDIA*

Serves 8-10

Samosas are deep-fried patties, filled with ground meat and/or vegetables, such as potatoes and peas. This is my version. The samosas can be cooked in advance and reheated in the oven at 150°C (300°F) gas mark 3.

FOR THE DOUGH
225 g (8 oz) plain wholemeal flour
½ teaspoon salt
3 tablespoons vegetable oil, plus a little extra for brushing

FOR THE KHEEMA STUFFING
3 onions
4 tablespoons vegetable oil
2.5 cm (1 inch) cube fresh root ginger
1 medium tomato
2 bay leaves
7.5 cm (3 inch) cinnamon stick
6 whole cloves
5 cloves garlic, crushed
1 tablespoon ground coriander
1 tablespoon ground cumin
1 tablespoon ground turmeric
2 tablespoons yogurt
900 g (2 lb) lean minced lamb or beef
½ teaspoon ground mace
½ teaspoon ground nutmeg
1 teaspoon salt
¼-½ teaspoon cayenne pepper (optional)

TO SERVE
vegetable oil for deep-frying
Fresh Coriander and Yogurt Chutney (see page 224)

FIRST MAKE THE STUFFING

■ Peel the onions; halve and thinly slice one of them. Heat the oil in a large heavy-based frying pan over a medium heat and fry the halved onion rings for about 5 minutes until dark brown, but not burned. Remove with a slotted spoon and drain on kitchen paper; set aside.

■ Finely chop the other 2 onions. Peel and finely chop the ginger. Peel and chop the tomato. Put the bay leaves, cinnamon and cloves in the hot oil. When the bay leaves begin to darken and the cinnamon starts uncurling slightly, add the chopped onions, ginger and garlic. Fry, stirring, for 10-12 minutes, until the onions are browned.

■ Lower the heat and add the coriander, cumin and turmeric. Fry for about 2 minutes, stirring all the time. Add the yogurt and cook, stirring, for 1 minute. Add the tomato to the pan and fry, stirring for a further 2-3 minutes.

■ Add the meat. Increase the heat to medium (medium-high if the meat is watery) and fry, breaking up all the lumps with the back of a slotted spoon, for about 7-8 minutes. Stir in the mace, nutmeg, salt, cayenne and 150 ml (¼ pint) water. Bring to the boil, cover, lower the heat and simmer for 1 hour; stirring every 10 minutes or so.

■ The filling should be quite dry. If necessary, remove the lid and increase the heat to medium for the last 10 minutes of the cooking time to drive off excess liquid. Mix in the browned onion half-rings and remove the cinnamon.

TO MAKE THE SAMOSAS

**1** Put the flour and salt in a mixing bowl, add the oil and rub together using your fingertips. Gradually mix in approximately 250 ml (8 fl oz) water, a little at a time, until you have a firm dough. Knead the dough well for 7-10 minutes, until smooth. Form into a ball. Brush with a little oil, and cover with a damp cloth. Set aside until ready for use. If any fat has accumulated on the surface of the cooked *kheema*, it should be discarded.

**2** Divide the dough into 28 equal balls. (Each ball makes 2 samosas, so you'll end up with about 56.) Flatten each ball and roll out on a floured surface to a 9-10 cm (3½-4 inch) round. Cut each round in half.

**3** Taking one semi-circle at a time, moisten half the length of the cut edge with a finger dipped in water. Form a wide cone with the semi-circle, using the dampened section to overlap by 5mm (¼ inch), and hold it closed. Fill the samosa three-quarters full with the stuffing.

**4** Moisten the inside edges of the opening and close. Seal by pressing this edge with the tip of a fork. Repeat to make the rest of the samosas; keep covered with cling film.

Heat a 7.5-9 cm (3-3½ inch) depth of oil in a wok, karhai or other pan for deep-frying on a medium heat. To check the temperature, drop in a samosa: it should sizzle immediately. Fry the samosas in batches for 2-3 minutes, or until lightly browned. Remove with a slotted spoon and drain on kitchen paper. Serve hot or warm with the chutney, as a dip.

# SPICY VEGETABLE FRITTERS

## *Pakoris*

*INDIA*

Serves 6-8

*Pakoris* are similar to Japanese *tempura*. They are generally eaten with tea, but there is no reason why they cannot be served with drinks.

I have specified potatoes in this recipe, but cauliflower florets, onion rings and pepper quarters are equally good.

Fresh Coriander and Yogurt Chutney is the perfect dip to serve with *pakoris*, though if you're feeling lazy, you could serve Chinese duck sauce, tomato ketchup, or a combination of soy sauce, white vinegar and grated fresh ginger with a dash of Tabasco instead.

**BATTER**

**115 g (4 oz) chickpea flour (besan)**

**¼ teaspoon salt**

**¼ teaspoon ground turmeric**

**¼ teaspoon ground cumin**

**¼ teaspoon bicarbonate of soda**

**⅛ teaspoon freshly ground pepper**

**⅛ teaspoon cayenne pepper (optional)**

**FILLING**

**3 medium potatoes, peeled (or other vegetables, see above)**

**vegetable oil for deep-frying**

**salt**

**freshly ground black pepper**

**TO SERVE**

**Fresh Coriander and Yogurt Chutney (see page 224)**

■ To make the batter, sift the chickpea flour into a bowl. Gradually mix in about 200 ml (7 fl oz) water until you have a fairly thick batter – thick enough to coat the vegetables. Add the other batter ingredients and mix well.

■ Cut the potatoes into thin rounds, 1 mm (1/16 inch) thick, and immerse them in a bowl of cold water.

■ Pour sufficient oil into a wok, karhai or other deep frying pan to give a 6.5-7.5 cm (2½-3 inch) depth in the middle. Place over a low heat until hot but not smoking.

■ Take a few potato slices at a time, wipe them dry, and dip them in the batter. Now drop them into the oil in a single layer. Fry slowly for 7-10 minutes on each side, until they are golden brown and cooked through. Remove with a slotted spoon and drain on kitchen paper. Sprinkle with salt and pepper and keep hot while cooking the rest of the *pakoris* in the same way.

■ Serve the *pakoris* while they are crisp and hot, with the Fresh Coriander and Yogurt Chutney as a dip.

*A karhai is very similar to a Chinese wok. It has a rounded base and is almost semi-circular in shape. It is particularly good for deep-frying as it allows you to use a relatively small amount of oil to obtain a good depth in the middle of the pan, to submerge foods in the oil.*

# SPICY MEAT KEBABS

## *Seekh Kabab*

*INDIA*

Serves 8-10

This version of the ground meat kabab is excellent to serve with drinks and to take out on picnics. The meat should be very finely minced – if you are preparing it yourself, pass it through the mincer three times. The mixture can be prepared a day in advance, covered and refrigerated overnight.

- ½ onion
- 4 cloves garlic
- 2.5 cm (1 inch) cube fresh root ginger
- 20 black peppercorns
- 10 whole cloves
- seeds from 8 cardamom pods
- 1 fresh hot green chilli, sliced (optional)
- ½ teaspoon ground nutmeg
- ½ teaspoon ground cinnamon
- 3 tablespoons lemon juice
- 4 tablespoons chickpea flour (besan)
- 1.25 kg (2½ lb) finely minced lamb or beef
- 1 teacup (loosely packed) chopped fresh green coriander leaves
- 1 teaspoon ground cumin
- 1 teaspoon ground coriander
- 1-1½ teaspoons salt
- ½ teaspoon cayenne pepper, or to taste (optional)
- 1 egg, beaten
- 5 tablespoons melted butter

TO SERVE

Fresh Coriander and Yogurt Chutney (see page 224)

■ Peel and chop the onion, garlic and ginger. Put the onion, garlic, ginger, peppercorns, cloves, cardamom seeds, green chilli, nutmeg, cinnamon and lemon juice in an electric blender and blend to a smooth paste.

■ Heat a small cast-iron frying pan over a medium heat. Add the chickpea flour and 'roast', stirring, until it is slightly darker. Remove from the heat.

■ In a large bowl, combine the meat, chopped coriander, the spice paste, cumin, coriander, salt, cayenne and roasted chickpea flour. Mix thoroughly, using your hands. Cover and refrigerate for several hours (or overnight if required) to allow the flavours to mingle. Take the meat out of the refrigerator 45 minutes before ready to grill.

■ Preheat the grill. Add the beaten egg to the spiced meat and mix well.

■ Line a 25 x 38 cm (10 x 15 inch) baking tray with foil and brush it with half of the melted butter. Spread the meat mixture in the tray: it should be approximately 1 cm (½ inch) thick. Brush the top with the rest of the melted butter.

■ Place under the grill, 7.5-10 cm (3-4 inches) from the heat. Grill for 15-20 minutes, until golden brown. Remove any liquid that may accumulate, with a bulb baster or kitchen paper.

■ Cut the meat into 4-5 cm (1½-2 inch) squares. Serve hot, or cold, with Fresh Coriander and Yogurt Chutney.

# fish and seafood

# GRILLED FISH WITH SWEET SOY SAUCE

## *Sake No Teriyaki*

*JAPAN*

Serves 4

You may cook mackerel or salmon fillets in this way. All you need is Sweet Glazing Sauce and some skewers. The Japanese like to skewer their fish before it is grilled. The reason is simple and practical: it is much easier to turn the fish over with the help of skewers. If you want both sides browned and glistening with the glaze of the sauce, there is no better way to do it. And it is the only way to make the skin crisp.

There are a few pointers here which might prove useful. In order to prevent the fish from falling off the skewers while it is being cooked, the skewering must always be done against the grain. Push the skewers into the flesh just under the skin. Also, let the skewers fan out so that the handles are all close together but the tips are quite separated. This way you will be able to hold all the handles with one hand when the fish needs to be turned.

The Japanese also like to salt fatty fish before setting it to grill. This draws out excess water and firms up the flesh.

You may grill this fish over charcoal outdoors or cook it indoors under your grill.

**750 g-1 kg (1½-2 lb) mackerel or salmon fillets, with skin**
**2 tablespoons coarse sea salt**
**Sweet Glazing Sauce (see page 222), cooled**
**a little vegetable oil**

TO SERVE
**Ginger Shreds in Sweet Vinegar (see page 222)**

■ Lay the fish fillets on a clean surface and sprinkle with half of the salt from a height of about 30 cm (12 inches) – this ensures an even sprinkling. Turn the fish over and sprinkle with the remaining salt. Set aside for 15 minutes.

■ Wash the fish to remove the salt, pat dry and place in a large bowl. Pour on the glazing sauce and toss to coat both sides of the fish. Leave to marinate in a cool place for 1 hour.

■ Preheat the grill or an outdoor charcoal grill. If you can control the heat, keep it at medium-high. Lift the fish pieces out of the marinade, reserving the liquid. Push 3-5 skewers into each piece of fish, depending on size, going against the grain and keeping the skewers just under the skin.

■ Lightly oil the grill rack to prevent sticking and position it about 13 cm (5 inches) from the heat source. Grill the fish, skin-side down, until it is lightly browned.

■ Turn the fish over carefully and grill until the skin is light brown. Brush with some of the remaining marinade and continue to grill until the skin is crisp and brown.

■ Turn the fish over very carefully, brush with marinade and grill until the flesh is glazed and brown. Lift the fish very carefully on to a serving plate and hand the Ginger Shreds round separately.

*Although meat has become more popular in recent years, fish still predominates in the Japanese diet. The basic Japanese stock (dashi) used in everything from soups to sauces is made from shavings of dried bonito (a large mackerel-like fish) and dried kelp. Fish may be grilled simply with just a sprinkling of salt or basted as it grills with a thicker sauce of soy and sweet rice wine (mirin). It may be tossed with rice wine (sake), steamed and then served with a sauce of lemon and soy. It may also be dipped in batter and fried, making the glorious tempura.*

*The Japanese delight in raw fish too, in the form of sashimi – thin fish slices eaten with a dip of horseradish-flavoured soy sauce; or sushi – sliced raw fish of all sorts put together with small portions of lightly seasoned rice and eaten as canapes might be.*

# FISH FILLETS WITH BLACK BEAN SAUCE

## *Doushi Yi*

*HONG KONG*

Serves 3-4

Here is southern Chinese food in its simplest and most divine form. I love salted black beans whenever they make an appearance, but have always had trouble stir-frying delicate fish fillets as they have a frightening tendency to disintegrate. I no longer worry: having learnt the tricks from Chinese masters, I realise how easy the technique really is.

When the fish is put into a marinade containing egg white and cornflour, there must be sufficient cornflour to hold the fish together when it is cooked. The fish also has to be allowed to marinate for at least 2 hours. I frequently leave it to marinate in the morning and cook it in the evening.

The fish also needs to be pre-cooked, very briefly, in water. This has to be done tenderly, just before it is put in its sauce. For those who like fish, I cannot recommend a better way to prepare it. The dish is light, delicate and full of flavour.

400-425 g (14-15 oz) flat white fish fillets, such as flounder or sole

FOR THE MARINADE

¼ teaspoon salt

1 tablespoon Chinese rice wine or dry sherry

freshly ground black pepper

1 egg white

4 teaspoons cornflour

2 teaspoons sesame oil

FOR THE SAUCE

1 teaspoon cornflour

120 ml (4 fl oz) chicken stock

2 teaspoons Chinese rice wine or dry sherry

¼ teaspoon salt

2 tablespoons sesame oil

freshly ground black pepper

1 dried hot red chilli

YOU ALSO NEED

1½ tablespoons salted black beans

2 cloves garlic

2.5 cm (1 inch) cube fresh root ginger

2 spring onions

3 tablespoons vegetable oil

■ To marinate the fish, halve each fillet lengthways, then cut crossways into 5 cm (2 inch) wide strips. Put the fish strips in a wide bowl and add the salt, rice wine and black pepper. Stir gently to mix.

■ Beat the egg white lightly (not to a froth) and add to the bowl with the cornflour and sesame oil. Toss to mix. Cover the bowl with cling film and refrigerate for 2 hours, or longer if required.

■ Now make the sauce. Put the 1 teaspoon cornflour in a cup. Slowly stir in the stock, then add the rice wine, salt, sesame oil and black pepper. Crumble in the dried red chilli. Set aside.

■ Rinse the black beans and chop them coarsely. Peel the garlic and ginger and chop them finely. Cut the spring onions crossways into very fine rounds along their entire length, including the green part; set aside.

■ Just before serving, heat a 2 cm (¾ inch) depth of water in a large frying pan (preferably non-stick). Bring to the boil, then turn the heat down to a bare simmer. Put the fish into the water, separating the pieces very gently and spreading them in the pan. Even before the water comes to a simmer again, the fish pieces will turn nearly white. Carefully remove them with a slotted spoon and place on a plate. Discard the water in the frying pan and wipe the pan dry.

■ Put 2 tablespoons of the oil in the frying pan and set it over a medium-high heat. When the oil is hot, put in the garlic, ginger and black beans. Fry, stirring once or twice, until the garlic turns golden. Take the pan off the heat, stir the sauce and pour it in. Put the pan back on a medium-low heat and stir gently until the sauce thickens.

■ Add the fish and gently spread it out in the pan. Spoon the sauce over the fish and cook briefly until just tender, carefully turning the pieces over just once.

■ Transfer the fish mixture to a warm serving plate. Scatter the spring onions on top. Quickly heat the remaining 1 tablespoon of oil in a small pan, then pour it over the onions to wilt them slightly and make the fish glisten. Serve immediately.

*There is a restaurant and a street in Hanoi, Cha Ca Street, which is named after this famous dish. Here chunks of fresh, firm, river fish are marinated in a mixture of turmeric, galangal, shrimp paste, lime juice and tamarind, then grilled over charcoal or wood. The fish is then brought to the table where a frying pan set over a portable stove awaits. The diners take over and cook the fish briefly in lard and fish sauce, then smother it with a blanket of fresh dill and spring onions. As soon as the herbs wilt, the fish is devoured, with noodles, peanuts and deliciously sour dipping sauces.*

# MONKFISH WITH DILL

## *Cha Ca*

*VIETNAM*

Serves 4

At the suggestion of Vietnamese friends living in the West, I have used monkfish as a substitute for the fish normally used for this recipe in Vietnam. It is traditionally eaten with fresh thin rice noodles, which can be found here at some Chinese and Far Eastern grocers – look for rice vermicelli noodles.

Ground dried galangal, better known as laos powder, is also used in this recipe. If you do not have any, I suggest that you take a little dried sliced galangal and whiz it to a powder in a clean coffee grinder.

To eat this dish, you prepare one mouthful at a time. First put a few noodles in your bowl. Then add a piece of fish – which you may dip first in the anchovy-lime sauce or fish sauce with lime juice if you like. On top, sprinkle some fresh mint or coriander, white spring onion, and some peanuts. Add a drizzle of either sauce, and/or a squeeze of lime juice if you wish. Eat this delicious combination with chopsticks.

**500 g (1¼ lb) monkfish fillet**
**½ teaspoon ground turmeric**
**1 teaspoon anchovy paste**
**3½ tablespoons lime juice**
**½ teaspoon vinegar**
**½ teaspoon ground galangal (laos powder)**
**1 tablespoon tamarind paste (see page 264), or ½ tablespoon lime juice mixed with ¼ teaspoon sugar**
**225 g (8 oz) dried fine rice noodles (such as rice vermicelli)**
**50 g (2 oz) fresh dill**
**8-10 spring onions**
**several fresh mint sprigs**
**several fresh coriander sprigs**
**10-12 tinned anchovy fillets**
**2-3 tablespoons vegetable oil**
**1 tablespoon lard**
**1-2 tablespoons fish sauce**

TO SERVE

**Fish Sauce with Vinegar and Lime Juice (see page 217)**
**Roasted Peanuts (see page 223)**
**lime wedges**

■ Wash the fish and pat dry. Cut into 2.5 cm (1 inch) chunks. In a shallow dish, mix together the turmeric, anchovy paste, 2 tablespoons of the lime juice, the vinegar, ground galangal and tamarind paste. Add the fish chunks, toss to mix and rub the mixture well in. Cover and refrigerate for 2-3 hours.

■ Put the noodles in a bowl, add cold water to cover and leave to soak for 2 hours.

■ Wash the dill and pat dry. Trim away all coarse stalks, retaining only the very fine sprigs; set aside on a large plate. Separate the green and white parts of the spring onions. Cut the green parts into 5 cm (2 inch) lengths and put these on the plate alongside the dill.

■ Cut the white spring onions into very fine rings and put into a small bowl. Wash the mint and coriander sprigs, pat dry and place in separate bowls.

■ Next make the anchovy-lime sauce. Wipe the oil off the anchovies and put them in a blender, together with the remaining 1½ tablespoons lime juice. Blend until smooth. (Or pound the anchovies, using a pestle and mortar, then mix in the lime juice.) Transfer to a small bowl.

■ Drain the noodles and immerse them in a pan of boiling water for 1 minute or less, until they are just tender. Rinse under cold running water. Drain again and put them into a serving bowl.

■ Arrange the bowls of mint, coriander, white spring onion and anchovy-lime sauce on the table. Set out the cold noodles, the Fish Sauce with Vinegar and Lime Juice, the Roasted Peanuts and lime wedges as well.

■ Preheat an indoor grill or outdoor charcoal grill. When hot, brush the fish lightly with the oil and cook about 13 cm (5 inches) from the heat source for 4-5 minutes on one side. Turn and cook for 3 minutes on the other side.

■ Heat the lard in the frying pan. When hot, add the fish, stir once, then pile in all of the dill and green spring onion. Moisten with a tablespoon or so of fish sauce and stir.

■ The fish is now ready to be eaten with the various herbs, sauces and seasonings as described (above left).

*It was a warm day. A fire of coconut shells had been lit under a spreading star fruit tree to grill the fish. I was in the seafront town of Padang in Western Sumatra but the fish we were to eat was gurami, a freshwater creature. It had already been bathed in two marinades – one of lime juice and salt and the other of coconut milk and hot spices. Then it was put between the twin racks of a hinged grilling contraption and cooked slowly about 15 cm (6 inches) above the fire with frequent and lavish bastings of the marinade. The basting brush was unusual: a stick of lemon grass whose bulbous end had been lightly crushed, so that it basted the fish and flavoured it at the same time.*

# WHOLE GRILLED FISH, SOUR AND SPICY

## *Ikan Panggang*

*INDONESIA*

Serves 2-3

This fish may be grilled either outdoors over charcoal or indoors. If you are grilling indoors, it is important to keep the fish far enough from the heat so that it cooks without charring on the outside. Alternatively, you could brown the fish on both sides under the grill, then place in the oven at 180°C (350°F) gas mark 4, for 10-15 minutes to cook through.

Whether grilling in- or outdoors, a hinged double-racked 'holder' makes it much easier to turn the fish. Mine is rectangular and can hold two medium fish. Such gadgets are available from kitchen shops, but if you cannot obtain one, just oil your grill rack well and lay the fish directly on it. The quantities in this recipe may easily be doubled.

**500 g (1¼ lb) whole fish, such as small salmon, trout, salmon trout, bass, sole or turbot, scaled and cleaned**
**¾ teaspoon salt**
**3 tablespoons lime or lemon juice**
**2-3 dried hot red chillies**
**1 stick fresh lemon grass**
**1 cm (½ inch) cube fresh galangal**
**1 cm (½ inch) cube fresh root ginger**
**3 cloves garlic**
**50 g (2 oz) shallots or onions**
**90 g (3½ oz) red pepper**
**¼ teaspoon ground turmeric**
**200 ml (7 fl oz) coconut milk (see page 258)**
**2-3 tablespoons vegetable oil**
**lime wedges, to serve**

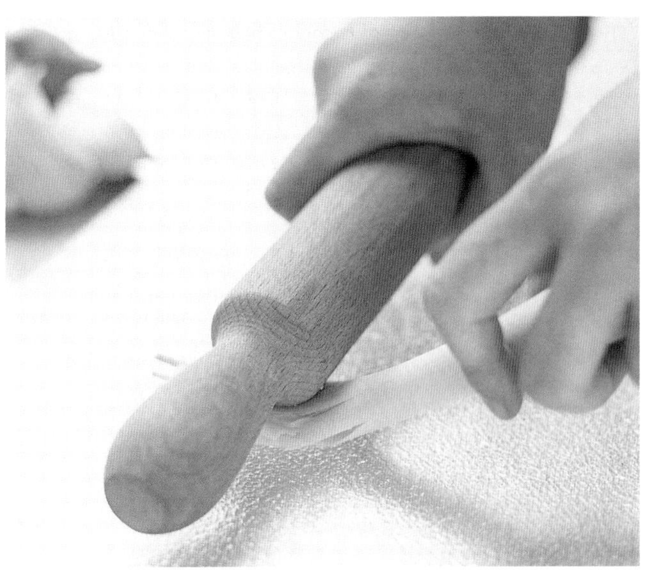

**1** Cut 3 or 4 deep slightly diagonal slits across both sides of the fish. Rub ½ teaspoon of the salt and 1 tablespoon of the lime juice over the entire fish, working the mixture well into the slits and the stomach cavity. Set aside for 20-30 minutes. Put 2 tablespoons water in a small bowl. Crumble in the dried red chillies and set aside for 20-30 minutes.

**2** Cut about 5 mm (¼ inch) off the base of the lemon grass, then lightly crush about 2.5 cm (1 inch) of the bulbous bottom to open it up like a brush. Peel and coarsely chop the galangal, ginger, garlic and shallots. Coarsely dice the red pepper, discarding the core and seeds.

Put the chillies and their soaking liquid, shallots, red pepper, ginger, garlic, galangal, turmeric, remaining 2 tablespoons lime juice and ¼ teaspoon salt in a blender and blend until smooth.

**3** Preheat the grill or an outdoor charcoal grill. Put the spice paste into a wide shallow dish large enough to hold the fish. Add the coconut milk and stir to mix. Put the fish into the dish. Spoon some marinade over it, making sure that it penetrates all the slits and cavities. Set aside for 10 minutes, turning the fish from time to time.

**4** Brush a hinged wire fish rack or your grill rack with oil to help prevent sticking. Lift the fish from the marinade and place in the holder or on the grill rack, 13-15 cm (5-6 inches) from the heat source. Cook for about 20 minutes until the fish is cooked through, turning every 5 minutes and basting frequently and generously with the marinade, using the lemon grass brush. The fish should be brown on the outside, but soft and tender inside. Don't baste for the last 5 minutes to allow a spice crust to form. Serve with lime wedges.

# FISH POACHED IN AROMATIC TAMARIND BROTH

## *Kaeng Som*

*THAILAND*

Serves 3-4

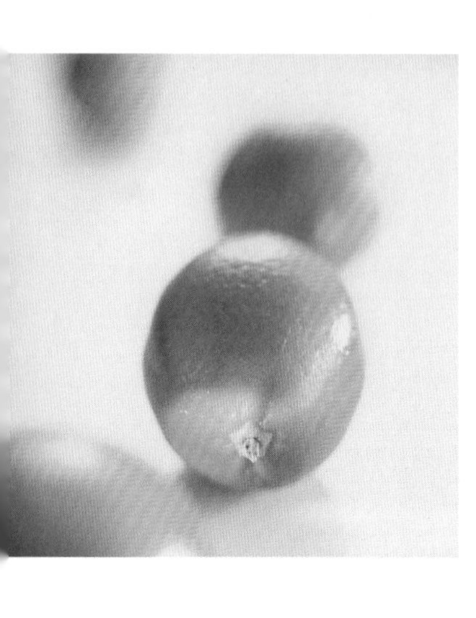

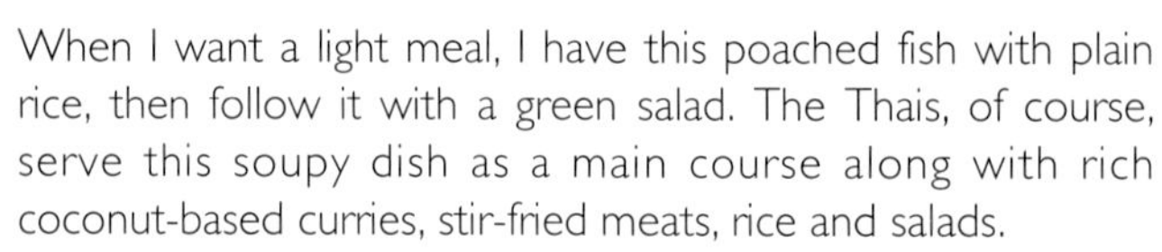

When I want a light meal, I have this poached fish with plain rice, then follow it with a green salad. The Thais, of course, serve this soupy dish as a main course along with rich coconut-based curries, stir-fried meats, rice and salads.

You could buy almost any filleted fish that you fancy. Moderately priced fillets, such as cod, halibut and haddock, are perfectly suited to this dish, though you could also use sole, bass or turbot. It is important to buy thick fillets or the thicker end of large fillets as they hold their shape best; about 2.5 cm (1 inch) is a suitable thickness.

**25 g (1 oz) shallots or onion**
**4 cm (1½ inch) cube fresh root ginger**
**about 50 g (2 oz) fresh coriander (preferably with roots still attached)**
**1 teaspoon shrimp or anchovy paste**
**750 ml (1¼ pints) chicken stock**
**1 tablespoon tamarind paste (see page 264), or 2 teaspoons lime juice**
**1 teaspoon dark brown sugar**
**¼-½ teaspoon salt**
**450 g (1 lb) thick white fish fillets**
**1 spring onion**
**lime wedges, to serve**

■ Peel the shallots and chop them coarsely. Peel the ginger and chop two thirds of it coarsely; cut the remaining third into very fine julienne strips and set these aside. Wash the coriander well and pat dry. Cut the roots off the coriander and chop them coarsely.

■ In an electric blender, combine the chopped coriander roots, chopped shallots, chopped ginger, shrimp paste and 3 tablespoons water. Blend until you have a purée.

■ Put the stock into a medium frying pan. Add the puréed mixture from the blender, the tamarind paste (or lime juice), sugar and salt. Bring to a simmer, and simmer gently for 5 minutes. Taste and adjust the seasoning, if necessary.

■ Meanwhile, cut the fish into 7.5-10 cm (3-4 inch) squares. Add to the poaching liquid in a single layer. Bring the liquid back to a simmer and cook gently for 1 minute. Turn the fish pieces over carefully. Cook gently for another 5-8 minutes, basting the fish frequently with the cooking liquor, until it is cooked through.

■ In the meantime, cut the spring onion crossways into very fine rounds. With a fish slice, carefully pick up the fish pieces and put into a wide serving bowl. Pour the poaching liquid over the fish. Scatter the sliced spring onion and reserved ginger julienne over the top and serve, with lime wedges.

# FISH BRAISED IN TEA

## *Ca Kho*

*VIETNAM*

Serves 4 as a first course, or 2 as a main course

Oily fish, such as mackerel and sardines, are amazingly good when they are gently braised. Their flesh turns meltingly tender but does not fall apart, while the braising juices add extra flavour. Teabags are needed here. It is best to use a plain, dark tea that is not too aromatic with added seasonings.

This mackerel is served either at room temperature or cold with some of its juices poured over. You may eat it with a green salad flavoured with fresh herbs such as basil, coriander and mint. Alternatively, it can be served on toast with sliced tomatoes, or arranged over salad greens as a first course.

**750 g (1½ lb) mackerel, cleaned, gills removed**
**2.5 cm (1 inch) cube fresh root ginger (unpeeled)**
**1 tablespoon Chinese dark soy sauce**
**2 tablespoons fish sauce**
**2 teabags**
**1 tablespoon sugar**

■ Cut the mackerel crossways into 7.5 cm (3 inch) sections. (The head may be left on the fish or discarded if preferred.) Wash the mackerel pieces and put them into a medium pan.

■ Cover with about 1 litre (1¾ pints) water and add all the other ingredients. Bring to the boil, turn the heat down to medium-low and simmer, uncovered, for 1½ hours. At this stage there should be about 150 ml (¼ pint) of sauce remaining. Leave the fish to cool in the sauce.

■ When you are ready to serve, lift the fish out of its liquid. Skin it, if you like, and open the pieces like a book, removing the centre bone. Pour just a little sauce over the top.

# FISH STEAMED WITH LEMON GRASS

## *Tom Som Pla*

*THAILAND*

Serves 2-4

I am sure you must have eaten Cantonese-style steamed fish. Cooked with a fine julienne of ginger and sliced spring onions, it is light, succulent and delicious. The Thais, influenced by the Chinese, keep to the same basic concept but add some of their own aromatic seasonings – galangal, kaffir lime leaves, fresh coriander leaves and lemon grass. Fish sauce replaces soy sauce and fresh green chillies are added if a little heat is required. No oil is called for, so this dish is perfect for dieters. If you cannot get lemon grass use 1 tablespoon finely grated lemon rind, scattering it over the fish as you would the lemon grass, just before steaming.

Almost any whole fish can be used, such as sole, flounder, mullet, trout or even small sea bass or salmon, as long as it is very fresh. It should be gutted and its scales, gills and fins removed. In the Far East the head is always left on a steamed whole fish, but if you cannot bear to look at it you could ask your fishmonger to remove it. The fish should be of a size that can fit into your wok or steaming pan. The fish is laid out on a large heatproof serving plate – to catch the precious juices – and the plate is then balanced on a rack over boiling water. The water level should be 2 cm (¾ inch) below the plate. The pan or wok is then covered and the fish steams, lying happily on its plate, until it is done. Any desire to lift the lid and peep inside is best resisted as precious aromas can vanish with the steam. (For suggestions on steaming equipment, see page 18.) If you do not wish to cook a whole fish, you may cook fillets or steaks by the same method.

How long do you steam the fish? This depends largely on its thickness. Steaks or fillets about 1 cm (½ inch) thick can be done in 7-10 minutes; those which are 2 cm (¾ inch) thick may take 10-13 minutes. A whole flat fish, such as sole, weighing 750 g (1½ lb) will take about 15 minutes, while a 750 g (1½ lb) sea bass should be allowed 20 minutes because of its thickness.

You may, of course, peep at the fish towards the very end of the cooking. Look quickly, deep down into one of the cut slits, if the fish is whole. If it is white all the way through, it is ready. For a fillet or steak, poke the flesh gently with the point of a sharp knife. If it is white all the way through, it is done.

**2 cm (¾ inch) cube fresh galangal**
**2.5 cm (1 inch) cube fresh root ginger**
**25 g (1 oz) shallots or onion**
**1 stick fresh lemon grass**
**1 fresh hot green chilli (optional)**
**25 g (1 oz) fresh coriander leaves**
**750 g (1½ lb) whole fish, cleaned and scaled (see left), or 450 g (1 lb) fish fillets or steaks, such as sole, haddock, cod, salmon or halibut**
**4 teaspoons fish sauce, or salt to taste**
**4-5 fresh or dried kaffir lime leaves**
**1 fresh hot red chilli**

■ Peel the galangal, ginger and shallots, then cut into fine slivers. Cut off and discard the straw-like top from the lemon grass, leaving about 15 cm (6 inches) at the base end. Hit the bulbous bottom with a mallet or other heavy object in order to crush it lightly.

■ Cut the green chilli into very fine rounds. Wash the coriander leaves, pat dry and chop coarsely. Set aside a generous tablespoon for the garnish; the rest is for steaming.

■ If you are preparing a whole fish, wash it well and pat it dry. With a sharp knife, cut deep slightly diagonal slits across the body on both sides of the fish. These slits should be made 4 cm (1½ inches) apart and go three quarters of the way down to the bone.

■ On an oval or rectangular heatproof plate large enough to hold the fish and fit inside your steaming pan, scatter a third each of the galangal, ginger, shallots, green chilli and coriander. Place the fish on top.

■ Scatter with the remaining galangal, ginger, shallots, green chilli and coriander, and add the lemon grass. Sprinkle with the fish sauce. Tear the fresh kaffir lime leaves in half, remove the central vein and place on top of the fish.

■ Bring sufficient water to the boil in a wok or steamer to come 2 cm (¾ inch) below the plate holding the fish. Protecting your hands with oven mittens, place the fish plate on the rack in the steamer. Cover and let the steam build up over a high heat for 2 minutes. Turn the heat to medium-high and cook for a further 5-18 minutes, depending on the fish (see left), until it is just done.

■ Meanwhile, cut the red chilli into fine long slivers. Again protecting your hands with oven mittens lift the fish plate carefully out of the pan, holding the plate level so that the precious juices do not spill. Sprinkle the fish with the red chilli slivers and the reserved coriander leaves. Serve at once.

# SEA BASS IN GREEN CHUTNEY

## *Hare Masale Wali Macchi*

*INDIA*

Serves 2

Here is my version of a very popular dish in which a whole fish is smothered in green chutney and then cooked in banana leaves. When I haven't any banana leaves handy, I use foil, which seems to work perfectly well. Serve the fish with plain basmati rice. Tomato and Onion Relish (see page 224) is an ideal accompaniment.

**750-900 g (1½-2 lb) whole sea bass, with head and tail, cleaned**
**2.5 cm (1 inch) cube fresh root ginger**
**5 cloves garlic**
**2 tablespoons vegetable oil**
**½ teaspoon black mustard seeds**
**2 whole hot dried red peppers (optional)**
**½ teaspoon ground turmeric**
**1 teacup chopped fresh green coriander leaves**
**2 tablespoons lemon juice**
**½ teaspoon salt**

■ Wash the fish thoroughly inside and out under cold running water. Pat dry, inside and out. Preheat the oven to 200°C (400°F) mark 6.

■ Peel and coarsely chop the ginger and garlic. Place them in an electric blender with 3 tablespoons of water and blend to a smooth paste.

■ Heat the oil in a frying pan over a medium-high heat, add the mustard seeds and stir for a few seconds until they begin to expand and pop. Add the red peppers, and stir them once. Pour in the paste from the blender, add the turmeric and fry, stirring, for about 2 minutes.

■ Pour the contents of the frying pan into the blender. Add the coriander, lemon juice and salt. Blend again to a smooth paste, adding up to 2 tablespoons of water if necessary.

■ Line a large baking dish with a sheet of foil, large enough to enclose the fish. Lay the fish on the foil and cover with the coriander paste, inside and out. Fold the foil over the fish to enclose it completely. Bake in the oven for 30 minutes.

■ Carefully unwrap the fish and lift on to a warm platter. Spoon any green chutney in the foil on to the fish to serve.

*Inevitably, the fish available in Indian seas and rivers are quite different from those found in our cooler waters. In my family, pomfret is easily the most popular fish. It is a flat salt-water fish on average 20-23 cm (8-9 inches) long, with a skeletal structure designed to make filleting easy. Its flesh is tender, but firm – flaking delicately when cooked. Pomfret is often cooked in green chutney and banana leaves for special occasions. Unfortunately it isn't available here, but sea bass is an excellent substitute.*

# CODFISH STEAKS IN YOGURT

## *Dahi Wali Macchi*

*INDIA*

Serves 2

This is one of my favourite fish dishes. At home in Delhi, the river fish – *rahu* – is often cooked in this way. I have chosen to use cod because it has a similar texture, though you can use other thick-cut fish steaks, such as haddock or halibut.

I like to serve these steaks with plain boiled rice and a green salad with an oil and vinegar dressing, but you could choose any other rice dish and green beans, cauliflower, peas or okra.

**2 cod steaks, each about 200 g (7 oz) and 2 cm (¾ inch) thick**
**¼ teaspoon ground turmeric**
**½ teaspoon salt**
**3 medium onions**
**6-8 cloves garlic**
**150 ml (¼ pint) yogurt**
**freshly ground black pepper**
**¼ teaspoon cayenne pepper (optional)**
**pinch of sugar**
**6-8 tablespoons vegetable oil**
**6 whole cardamom pods**
**two 5-6 cm (2-2½ inch) cinnamon sticks**

■ Wash the fish steaks, removing any scales that adhere to the skin. Pat the steaks as dry as possible. Sprinkle both sides with the turmeric and ¼ teaspoon salt, rubbing the seasonings in gently.

■ Peel the onions. Finely chop two of them and set aside. Coarsely chop the other one and place in an electric blender. Peel and chop the garlic cloves. Put them into the blender with the yogurt, remaining ¼ teaspoon salt, black pepper, cayenne and sugar. Blend to a smooth, thin paste.

■ Heat 5 tablespoons of the oil in a large frying pan over a medium heat. Add the fish steaks and fry gently for about 3 minutes on each side, turning them over carefully; don't allow to brown or crisp.

■ Using a spatula, transfer the fish to a plate. Pour the oil from the frying pan into a small bowl, leaving any sediment behind. Wash and dry the frying pan. Measure the oil and return to the clean frying pan, adding more if necessary to make up to 5 tablespoons. Place on a medium heat.

■ When hot, add the chopped onions, cardamom pods and cinnamon. Fry, stirring, for about 5 minutes until the onions are light golden brown.

■ Turn the heat down to low and pour in the thin paste from blender. Simmer gently on a low heat for 10 minutes, stirring from time to time; do not boil. Transfer half of the sauce to a small bowl.

■ Spread the sauce in the frying pan evenly. Place the fish steaks in the pan, then pour the reserved sauce on top of them, spreading it evenly. Cover and simmer on a low heat for about 10 minutes or until the fish is cooked through. Serve with plain boiled rice and a salad or vegetable.

# STEAMED FISH WITH GINGER AND COCONUT MILK

## *Ca Loc. Happy*

*VIETNAM*

Serves 3-4

Here is another steamed fish with deliciously contrasting tastes. There is oyster sauce and coconut milk, fried garlic and fresh ginger, spring onions and mushrooms, all lending their flavours to the fish. You may, of course, eat the fish with plain boiled rice, but I prefer to serve it the traditional Vietnamese way (as illustrated). For this you will need:

■ A plate containing cucumber slices, sprigs of fresh mint, basil and coriander, and whole lettuce leaves.

■ A plate of halved sheets of rice paper (see page 263) and a bowl of water. (If you cannot get rice paper, simply use lettuce leaves alone to wrap the fish.)

■ Fish Sauce Seasoned with Vinegar (see page 217).

Each diner assembles their own packages. A piece of rice paper is dipped into a bowl of cold water immediately before assembling the 'package'. This will soften the rice paper and make it more malleable. To eat, you lay a lettuce leaf on a piece of rice paper – it should protrude on one side. Then, with chopsticks, take pieces of fish and cucumber and sprigs of herbs and put them on the lettuce. Wrap up or roll up the bundle and dip it into the sauce.
(For general steaming directions see page 18.)

**750 g (1½ lb) whole fish, such as sole, or small salmon trout, cod, haddock or mullet, cleaned**
**½ teaspoon salt**
**freshly ground black pepper**
**1 teaspoon dark brown sugar**
**3 cloves garlic**
**90 g (3½ oz) onions**
**vegetable oil for shallow-frying**
**2.5 cm (1 inch) cube fresh root ginger**
**2 spring onions**
**4 mushrooms**
**1½ tablespoons oyster sauce**
**6 tablespoons coconut milk (see page 258)**
**4-5 tablespoons Roasted Peanuts (see page 223), crushed**

■ Wash the fish and pat it dry. Using a sharp knife, cut deep slightly diagonal slits across the body of the fish on both sides, about 4 cm (1½ inches) apart.

■ Put the fish on an oval or rectangular heatproof plate of a size that will fit into your steaming utensil. Rub the fish inside and out with the salt, pepper and sugar.

■ Peel the garlic and cut into fine slivers. Peel and finely slice the onions. Heat a 1 cm (½ inch) depth of oil in a frying pan over a medium-low heat. Set a sieve over a bowl near the hob. Line a large plate with kitchen paper and place nearby.

■ When the oil is hot, add the garlic slivers and stir-fry until golden. Empty the oil and garlic into the sieve. Spread the drained garlic over part of the kitchen paper. Return the strained oil to your frying pan and heat it again on a medium heat. Set the sieve back on the bowl.

■ When the oil is hot, add the onion slices and fry, stirring, until golden brown and crisp. Empty them into the sieve to drain, then spread on the other part of the kitchen paper.

■ Peel the ginger and cut it into fine slivers. Cut the spring onions crossways into very fine rounds along their entire length. Slice the mushrooms thinly.

■ Mix the oyster sauce with 2 tablespoons of the coconut milk and drizzle over the fish. Scatter the ginger, spring onions, mushrooms, fried garlic and half of the fried onions on top.

■ Bring some water to the boil in a wok or steamer, remembering that it will need to come 2 cm (¾ inch) below the plate holding the fish. Protecting your hands with oven mittens, place the fish plate on the rack in the steamer. Cover and let the steam build up over a high heat for 2 minutes. Turn the heat down to medium-high and steam for a further 18 minutes or until the fish is just done.

■ Remove the cover and spoon some of the sauce from the fish into a bowl. Carefully lift the fish plate out of the steamer. Add the remaining 4 tablespoons coconut milk to the sauce in the bowl. Mix well and pour it over the fish.

■ Scatter the crushed peanuts and remaining fried onions over the fish to serve.

# FISH, SHELLFISH AND BEAN CURD STEW

## *Saengsun Chigae*

*KOREA*

Serves 4

This is one of my family's favourite stews. It has a bit of everything in it and is deliciously spicy to boot. You can put in almost any fish that you like. The ideal combination includes a whole white-fleshed fish, cut into 3-4 pieces (with the head if you wish); a few molluscs, such as clams or mussels; chunks of bean curd (which happily absorb the sauce); dried mushrooms, sliced courgettes; and a few slices of beef for a more complex flavour. The stew is generally served with rice.

There is one seasoning ingredient in this dish that is hard to find but very easy to improvise. It is Hot Fermented Bean Paste *(kochu chang)* and contains, among other things, fermented soya bean powder and chilli powder. To make a rough equivalent at home I combine Japanese-style red or brown *miso* – available from most healthfood shops – with chilli powder, paprika and a little sugar (see page 218). Hot Fermented Bean Paste is very hot. My paste is relatively mild, though you could add extra chilli powder to it for a more fiery dish.

**10 dried Chinese mushrooms or fresh mushrooms**
**100 g (4 oz) lean tender beef**
**175 g (6 oz) courgettes**
**2 cloves garlic**
**1 tablespoon Japanese soy sauce (*shoyu*)**
**1 teaspoon sesame oil**
**4 tablespoons Hot Fermented Bean Paste (see page 218)**
**4 spring onions**
**25 g (1 oz) green pepper**
**25 g (1 oz) red pepper**
**10-11 oz (275-300 g) bean curd**
**8 small clams**
**750 g (1½ lb) whole white fish, such as mullet, trout or small haddock or cod, scaled, cleaned and cut crossways into 3-4 pieces, or 450 g (1 lb) fish steaks**
**2 teaspoons vegetable oil**
**few celery leaves, to garnish**

■ Put the dried mushrooms in a bowl and pour on 300 ml (½ pint) hot water. Leave to soak for 30 minutes or until the mushrooms are soft. Drain the mushrooms, cut off the hard stems and slice the caps into 3-4 pieces. If using fresh mushrooms, trim the ends off the stalks and wipe the caps with damp kitchen paper, then slice the mushrooms thickly.

■ Cut the beef into very thin slices, about 2.5 x 5 cm (1 x 2 inches). Trim the courgettes and cut into 7.5 mm (⅓ inch) thick slices. Peel and finely chop the garlic.

■ In a bowl, combine the mushrooms, beef, courgettes, garlic, soy sauce, sesame oil and Hot Fermented Bean Paste. Mix well and set aside.

■ Cut the spring onions into 5 cm (2 inch) lengths. Cut the peppers into 1 cm (½ inch) squares. Cut the bean curd into 2.5 cm (1 inch) cubes.

■ Scrub the clams well with a stiff brush under cold running water. Wash the fish and pat dry.

■ Heat the oil in a large, wide, flameproof casserole (that can be brought to the table) over a medium-high heat. When hot, add the meat mixture and fry, stirring, for 2 minutes. Pour in 900 ml (1½ pints) water and bring to a simmer, scraping up the sediment on the base of the casserole.

■ Put in the fish pieces, spring onions and peppers. Bring to a simmer, cover and simmer for 5 minutes. Add the bean curd and clams, scattering them about and submerging them in the liquid as gently as possible. Bring to a simmer again. Cover and cook on a medium-low heat for a further 5 minutes or until the clams open.

■ Meanwhile, coarsely chop the celery leaves. Scatter them over the stew and serve.

*In Korea, the pots used for cooking these stews (or chigaes) are made of heavy clay and are taken directly from the fire to the table. They retain their heat for a long time, so the stew stays hot. I use a heavy casserole dish instead.*

*Koreans save the water from the second washing of raw rice to use in this stew. Because it is not from the first washing, it is clean. It adds a little flavour and the starch in the water helps to thicken the sauce very slightly.*

# SPICY PRAWN AND CUCUMBER CURRY

## *Gulai Labu*

*MALAYSIA*

Serves 4-6

This curry is actually made with bottle gourd – a pale green vegetable, shaped like a bowling pin. You can easily use cucumber instead as its taste is similar when cooked. The origins of this Malay dish probably lie in India – the use of ground coriander and fennel seeds as well as the final popping of seasonings in hot oil all testify to that. What I find fascinating here is the use of white pepper. The original recipe calls for 1 tablespoon finely ground white pepper. This may sound unusual – and excessive – in the West. But if you travel in the regions where pepper has grown for thousands of years, such as Kerala in South India, you will find that the use of such large amounts is not at all uncommon. It makes the dish decidedly peppery. What must be kept in mind is that red chillies arrived in this part of the world only in the late fifteenth century.

*I remember once attending a gathering of the Penang Women's Institute, where a dozen women had collected in one of their homes to prepare a Malay-style meal. Shoes had been left at the front door, as is the custom, and the Muslim Malay ladies, in their long-sleeved, ankle-length dresses and head scarves, were padding around happily, pounding chillies, slicing shallots and squeezing coconut milk. Hasna Abu Baker was to make a prawn and bottle gourd curry. She boiled the ground spices – cumin, coriander, fennel, pepper and chillies – in water, then added the prawns, the gourd and coconut milk. When they were cooked, she heated a little oil, browned shallots, garlic and fennel seeds in it, and then threw the oil and seasonings into the curry as a final flavouring. I had never seen this last step done anywhere except in India. The dish was a miraculously good hybrid.*

**350 g (12 oz) uncooked unpeeled prawns**
**275 g (10 oz) cucumber**
**100 g (4 oz) shallots or onions**
**6 cloves garlic**
**2 tablespoons ground coriander seeds**
**1 tablespoon ground fennel seeds (see note)**
**½-1 teaspoon ground white pepper, or to taste**
**1 tablespoon ground cumin seeds**
**1 teaspoon ground turmeric**
**3-4 dried hot red chillies**
**¾-1 teaspoon salt**
**1 teaspoon sugar**
**400 ml (14 fl oz) thick coconut milk (see page 258)**
**4 tablespoons vegetable oil**
**1 teaspoon whole fennel seeds**

■ Peel and de-vein the prawns. Rinse and pat them dry. Peel the cucumber and cut crossways into 1 cm (½ inch) thick rounds.

■ Peel the shallots and finely chop three quarters of them; finely slice the rest. Peel the garlic cloves. Chop four of them very finely; cut the other two into fine slivers. Combine the sliced shallots and slivered garlic and set these aside.

■ In a medium pan, combine the chopped shallots, chopped garlic, ground coriander, ground fennel, white pepper, cumin, turmeric and 450 ml (¾ pint) water. Crumble in the red chillies. Stir and bring to the boil. Boil, uncovered, on a fairly high heat for about 5 minutes.

■ Add the cucumber rounds and bring to a simmer. Cover and simmer gently for 5 minutes. Add the prawns, salt and sugar. Bring to a simmer again and simmer gently for about 1 minute, stirring the prawns around in the sauce. Give the coconut milk a good stir and pour it in. Bring the mixture to the boil, then lower the heat and simmer for 1 minute, stirring now and then.

■ Put the oil in a small frying pan and set over a medium-high heat. When hot, add the slivered shallots and garlic and stir-fry until they turn golden. Add the whole fennel seeds, stir once, then quickly pour the contents of the pan (oil and seasonings) into the pan containing the curry. Cover the curry pan immediately to trap all the aromas. Serve with rice.

NOTE If you cannot get ground fennel seeds, simply grind whole seeds in a clean coffee grinder.

*On the island of Sumatra, spices and flavourings, such as galangal, ginger, turmeric, chillies, lemon grass and tamarind grow in kitchen gardens, alongside aubergines, basil and mint. To see these flavourings used in everyday cooking, I watched a fish curry (gulai ikan) being prepared in a family home – a beautifully carved minangkabau house, with its roof curving up at the ends like a water-buffalo's horns. The fish was alive shortly before, swimming in the family tank – it has been mercifully dispatched and cut into steaks. A daughter was grinding the spices on a stone slab set in the counter: red chillies, shallots, ginger, galangal, fresh turmeric and candlenuts (so called because they can actually be lit). The spice mixture (or bumbu) was combined with the fish, coconut milk and herbs, such as the leaves of turmeric and mint, and then left to cook. The curry looked spectacular and tasted wonderful.*

# WEST SUMATRAN FISH CURRY WITH COCONUT MILK

## *Gulai Ikan*

*INDONESIA*

Serves 4

For this recipe you need steaks from a firm-fleshed white fish such as cod, haddock or bass. Salmon steaks are also ideal. The souring agent used in Western Sumatra is not regular tamarind but *asem candis*, something that I knew in India as *kokum*. This is the dried sour skin of a mangosteen-like fruit. It is generally added whole or in segments to a dish where it slowly imparts its sourness. If you can obtain this seasoning, put in about 3 pieces when you add the fish. Tamarind paste or lime juice make a good substitute.

**1.2 litres (2 pints) coconut milk**
**8-12 dried hot red chillies**
**15 g (½ oz) candlenuts or cashew nuts**
**2 sticks fresh lemon grass**
**100 g (4 oz) shallots or onions**
**4 cm (1½ inch) cube fresh galangal**
**2.5 cm (1 inch) cube fresh root ginger**
**3 cloves garlic**
**100 g (4 oz) red pepper**
**½ teaspoon ground turmeric**
**1 teaspoon paprika**
**4 fish steaks, each about 200 g (7 oz) and 2.5 cm (1 inch) thick**
**1 teaspoon salt**
**2½ tablespoons lime or lemon juice**
**4 tablespoons vegetable oil**
**4-5 fresh kaffir lime leaves**
**10 fresh curry leaves, or 3 dried bay leaves**
**15-20 fresh mint leaves**
**8-10 cherry or very small tomatoes**

■ Leave the coconut milk to stand for a while until the cream has risen to the top.

■ Crumble the red chillies into a small bowl. Add the nuts, then pour on enough water just to cover and leave to soak for 1 hour.

■ Cut off a sliver from the base of the lemon grass sticks, then trim to 15 cm (6 inch) lengths, discarding the tops. Crush the bulbous bottoms lightly with a hammer or other heavy object and set aside.

■ Peel and coarsely chop the shallots, galangal, ginger and garlic. Core, deseed and coarsely chop the red pepper.

■ Into a blender, put the soaked chillies and nuts together with their soaking liquid, the shallots, galangal, ginger, garlic, red pepper, turmeric and paprika. Blend thoroughly to a fairly smooth paste, adding another 1-2 tablespoons water to mix if necessary.

■ Rub the fish steaks with ½ teaspoon salt and 1 tablespoon lime juice; set aside.

■ Thick coconut cream should have risen to the top of the coconut milk: spoon it off into a bowl and set aside. Add enough water to the remaining thin coconut milk to make it up to about 1.5 litres (2½ pints).

■ Put the oil in a large frying pan (preferably non-stick) and set it over a medium-high heat. When the oil is hot, put in the paste from the blender. Stir and fry until the paste turns dark red and separates from the oil. (Turn the heat down a little, if necessary, while you do this.) Pour in the diluted coconut milk and add the lemon grass stalks. Bring to the boil, scraping up any sediment stuck to the bottom of the pan. Turn the heat to low and simmer gently for 15 minutes. Remove the lemon grass and set aside.

■ Empty the contents of the pan into a sieve set over a bowl and push the sauce through. Return all but 4 tablespoons of the sieved sauce to the frying pan and bring to a simmer. Return the lemon grass to the pan and add the lime leaves, curry leaves, mint, remaining 1½ tablespoons lime juice and the remaining ½ teaspoon salt. Stir well.

■ Lay the fish steaks in a single layer in the pan and bring to a simmer over a medium-low heat. Cook gently for about 10 minutes or until the fish is done, spooning the hot sauce over the steaks frequently.

■ Stir the reserved thick coconut cream well, then gradually mix in the reserved 4 tablespoons sauce. Pour this over the fish. Halve the tomatoes and add to the pan. Check the seasoning, heat through, then serve.

# PRAWN AND VEGETABLE FRITTERS

## *Tempura*

*JAPAN*

Serves 4

The Japanese may have learned the technique of making deep-fried fritters from Portuguese missionaries in the late sixteenth century, but by now they have made this dish their own. Only the freshest fish and vegetables are used, the batter is exceedingly light, and the dipping sauce a glorious, almost drinkable mixture of stock, soy sauce, sweet sake and grated white radish.

In Japan the best way to eat *tempura* is at a tempura bar. You sit at a counter behind which the chefs prepare the *tempura*. One item at a time is dipped in batter, fried and placed in your paper-lined basket. You eat it immediately while it is still crunchy and hot, dipping it quickly either into its dipping sauce or into the tiny bowls of salt and lemon juice which also sit on the counter. Warm sake or cold beer flow freely.

On one of my visits to Osaka, Professor Shizuo Tsuji, one of Japan's leading food authorities, arranged for me to have what he regarded as the best *tempura* in Japan. That the restaurant was in another town did not worry him at all. He had me driven to Kobe, but only after making sure that a certain fresh prawn from the local seas was available. Two of his leading chefs accompanied me to extend his hospitality and to make sure that all my questions would be answered.

I have had *tempura* all over Japan – in Tokyo, where the batter is golden yellow; in Osaka, which is famed for its pale, almost white, batter; and in the markets of Kyoto, where the food is enclosed in a more-than-generous layer of batter. According to Professor Tsuji, 'The common man goes for the crunch more than for the food it covers'.

However, the *tempura* in Kobe just could not be improved upon. The wild prawns we were served had been bought live from the market, where the restaurant has first choice. The prawns were selected for their size and colour, and had a very fresh sea flavour. We also had rolled white fish *(kisu)* fillets, minnows (all lumped into a ball), a moss-eating trout *(ayu)*, octopus pieces, sea eels, baby prawns and vegetables – such as baby aubergines, lotus root slices, mushroom caps and green chillies. We ended with a *miso* soup, rice and pickles, to be followed by an exotic (and expensive) fruit – sweet prickly pears from Columbia.

*Tempura*, for the average person, is a simpler affair: one or two prawns (they are very expensive in Japan), a few green beans and a few slices of sweet potato, aubergine and lotus root. A small Japanese salad is generally served beforehand and soup, rice and pickles at the end. All in all, it is very satisfying and good.

While I consider prawns essential, you can add almost any other seasonal vegetable or leaf. Kyoto specialises in serving red maple leaves in the autumn. You might serve mint in the summer. Among the vegetables that can be dipped in batter and fried are cauliflower florets, sliced onions, potatoes, green pepper, asparagus, mushrooms and broccoli sprigs.

The batter must be mixed only at the last moment, though all the ingredients for it may be measured and kept in readiness some time beforehand. It is important that the batter be left lumpy and not be over-mixed. The flour and water are measured by volume here. After you have fried a batch of *tempura*, clean the oil of all debris using a slotted spoon. (In Japan this debris – little droplets of batter – is usually saved. It is then rinsed off and put into soup as tiny dumplings.)

If you are using *dashi-no-moto* instead of Japanese Soup Stock, use 2 tablespoons soy sauce in the dipping sauce.

75 g (3 oz) onions
about ½ medium sweet potato
75 g (3 oz) green pepper
about 16 green beans
8 medium mushrooms
12 uncooked unpeeled prawns

FOR THE BATTER
1 egg yolk
250 ml (8 fl oz) ice-cold water
250 ml (8 fl oz) plain white flour, plus extra for dusting

FOR THE DIPPING SAUCE
250 ml (8 fl oz) Japanese Soup Stock (see page 255), or light unsalted chicken stock
2½ tablespoons Japanese soy sauce (*shoyu*)
3 tablespoons sake
2 teaspoons sugar

TO SERVE
90 g (3½ oz) white radish (mooli)
salt
6 tablespoons lemon juice
vegetable oil for deep-frying

(Step-by-step tempura method, overleaf)

**1** Prepare all the foods that are to be fried. Peel the onions and cut in half lengthways. Lay cut-side down and insert cocktail sticks at 5 mm (¼ inch) intervals, pushing them right the way through. Cut the onion halves into slices downwards between the cocktail sticks. The sticks will hold the onion slices together.

**2** Peel the sweet potato and cut into slices, each about 3 mm (⅛ inch) thick. Put the slices straight into a bowl of cold water to prevent discoloration. Cut the green pepper lengthways into 1 cm (½ inch) wide strips. Trim the green beans, but leave them whole. Wipe the mushrooms clean with damp kitchen paper.

**3** Peel the prawns but leave their tails on. The tails have a little water in them, which must be pushed out. To do this, cut the very tip off each tail and then press the water out by pulling the blunt side of a knife along the tail.

**4** De-vein the prawns. Make a few strokes crossways on the underbelly of each prawn so that it does not curl up.

**5** Next make the dipping sauce. Combine the stock, soy sauce, sake and sugar in a small pan and simmer gently for 1 minute or until the sugar dissolves. Divide the sauce among 4 bowls and keep them warm. Peel the radish and grate it finely. Put one small hillock of grated radish on to each of 4 tiny saucers or into 4 tiny bowls. Prepare also a tiny bowl of salt and a tiny bowl of lemon juice for each diner.

**6** To make the batter, in a large bowl, beat the egg yolk lightly. Add the cold water and mix lightly. Sift the flour, then add it all at once to the bowl. Stir lightly with a fork or chopsticks. Do not over-mix – the batter should be lumpy and floury-looking.

**7** Heat the oil in a wok or deep-fat fryer to a temperature of 180-190°C (350-370°F). Drain the sweet potato and pat all the foods dry. Put the dusting flour on a plate. Dip the pepper strips first in the dusting flour, shaking off any excess, then dip them in the batter.

**8** Fry as many pieces as your wok or pan will hold easily in one layer for 2-3 minutes until golden, turning once or twice. Remove with a slotted spoon, drain on kitchen paper and serve (or keep hot). Fry all the vegetables this way, removing the debris from the oil with a slotted spoon between each batch. Stir the batter lightly occasionally. Fry the prawns last.

Diners usually put some or all of the grated radish into the dipping sauce. They dip the tempura into the sauce or into the lemon juice and salt before eating.

# PRAWNS WITH ASPARAGUS

## *Xian Lusun Chad Xiaqiu* — *HONG KONG*

Serves 3-4 as a main course, or 6 as a first course

I serve this elegant Cantonese dish both as a main course and, in small portions, as a first course.

**300 g (10 oz) uncooked unpeeled prawns**
**1 small egg white**
**2½ teaspoons cornflour**
**2 teaspoons sesame oil**
**salt**
**225 g (8 oz) fresh asparagus (untrimmed weight)**
**5 tablespoons vegetable oil**
**2 cm (¾ inch) cube fresh root ginger**
**1 clove garlic**
**1½ teaspoons oyster sauce**
**1 teaspoon Chinese light soy sauce**
**2 teaspoons Chinese rice wine or dry sherry**
**¼ teaspoon sugar**

■ Peel and de-vein the prawns, leaving on the tail shells. Rinse well, pat dry and put them in a small bowl. Beat the egg white lightly and add to the bowl along with 2 teaspoons cornflour, 1 teaspoon sesame oil and a pinch of salt. Mix well, cover and set aside for 30 minutes or longer, refrigerating if necessary.

■ Trim and discard the woody bases of the asparagus spears. Peel the lower third of the spears, then cut them slightly on the diagonal into 4 cm (1½ inch) lengths. Bring about 750 ml (1¼ pints) water to a rolling boil in a medium pan. Add salt and 1 tablespoon of the vegetable oil to the water. Add the asparagus and boil rapidly for 2-3 minutes or until it is just cooked but still crisp and bright green. Drain and refresh under cold running water. Drain again and set aside.

■ Peel and finely chop the ginger and garlic, keeping them separate. In a small bowl, combine the oyster sauce, soy sauce, remaining 1 teaspoon sesame oil, the rice wine, sugar and 2 tablespoons water. In a cup, mix the remaining ½ teaspoon cornflour with 1 tablespoon water.

■ Just before you are ready to eat, heat the remaining 4 tablespoons vegetable oil in a wok or large frying pan over a high heat. Add the prawns and fry, stirring, for about 3 minutes or until they just turn opaque. Immediately remove the prawns with a slotted spoon and set aside.

■ Pour off all but 1 tablespoon of the oil from the wok and place over a medium heat. When hot, add the ginger, stir once, then add the garlic. Stir once or twice, then put in the prawns and asparagus. Stir briefly, then add the oyster sauce mixture. Stir a few times and take the wok off the heat.

■ Give the cornflour mixture a good stir, pour it into the centre of the wok and stir to mix. Put the wok back on a low heat and cook briefly, stirring, until the sauce has thickened. Serve immediately.

# PRAWN PULLAO

## *Jhinga Pullao*

*INDIA*

Serves 6

Patna rice is ideal for this recipe, though you could use any other long-grain rice, as long as it isn't a quick-cook or instant variety. Fresh prawns are a delicious feature, but any firm-fleshed fish – such as cod or halibut – works well. You would need 350 g (12 oz) cod or halibut steaks, 1-2 cm (½-¾ inch) thick. Cut the fish into strips, 4-5 cm (1½-2 inches) long and about 2.5 cm (1 inch) wide.

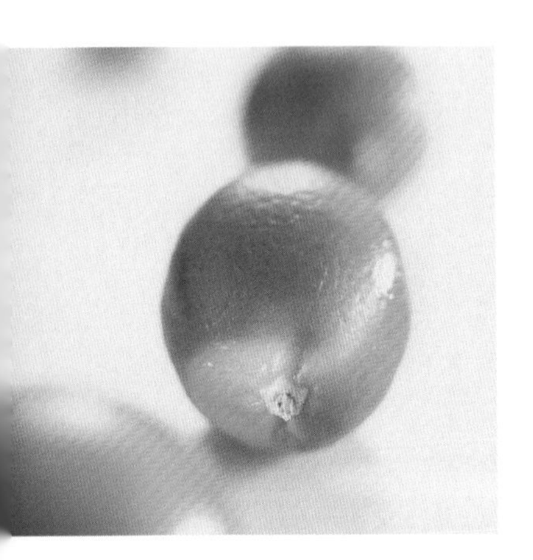

**350 g (12 oz) uncooked unpeeled prawns**
**3 tablespoons finely chopped fresh coriander leaves**
**1 teaspoon ground turmeric**
**1 teaspoon garam masala**
**1-1½ teaspoons salt**
**1 tablespoon lime or lemon juice**
**½-1 fresh hot green chilli (optional)**
**4 tablespoons vegetable oil**
**1 medium onion**
**350 g (12 oz) long-grain rice**

■ Peel and de-vein the prawns. Rinse well, then pat them dry.

■ In a small bowl, mix the chopped coriander, turmeric, garam masala, ½ teaspoon salt, and the lime or lemon juice together with 1 tablespoon warm water. Finely slice the chilli if using and add to the mixture.

■ Heat 2 tablespoons oil in a large frying pan over a medium-low heat. Pour in the coriander mixture and fry, stirring, for 2 to 3 minutes. Add the prawns and fry, stirring, for about 4 minutes.

■ With a slotted spoon, transfer the prawns to a dish, leaving the sauce in the pan. Cover and set aside.

■ Pour 275 ml (9 fl oz) warm water into the frying pan and scrape up all the spices stuck to the bottom and sides, increasing the heat if necessary. Remove from the heat.

■ Peel, halve and finely slice the onion. Heat the remaining 2 tablespoons oil in a large heavy-based cooking pot or flameproof casserole over a medium heat. Add the sliced onions and fry for 3-4 minutes until the edges are tinged brown. Add the rice, 450 ml (¾ pint) water, ½-1 teaspoon salt and the liquid from the frying pan. Stir and bring to the boil, then cover and turn the heat to very low. Cook for 25 minutes.

■ Add the prawns and fork them through the pullao. Re-cover and cook for a further 5 minutes. Serve with a vegetable side dish.

# PRAWNS WITH CRUSHED MUSTARD SEEDS

## *Chingri Jhai*

*INDIA*

Serves 3-4

This recipe originates from Bengal, where a paste made from ground black mustard seeds is often added to fish to give it a very special nose-tingling pungency.

- 450 g (1 lb) uncooked unpeeled prawns
- 1 teaspoon black mustard seeds
- ⅛ teaspoon ground turmeric
- 2 teaspoons tomato purée
- 4 tablespoons mustard oil, or other vegetable oil
- 2 cloves garlic, peeled
- 2 thin slices fresh root ginger, peeled
- 1 hot dried red chilli
- ¾ teaspoon salt
- large pinch of freshly ground black pepper
- 1 tablespoon lemon or lime juice

■ Peel and de-vein the prawns. Rinse well, then pat them dry.

■ Crush the mustard seeds, using a pestle and mortar or spice or coffee grinder. In a small bowl, mix the crushed mustard seeds, turmeric and tomato purée together with 3 tablespoons hot water. Set aside.

■ Heat the oil in a large frying pan over a medium high heat. Add the garlic cloves, ginger slices and dried chilli and fry, stirring, for a few seconds until the mixture begins to darken, then add the prawns. Fry, stirring, until the prawns turn opaque.

■ Stir in the mustard seed paste and turn the heat to medium-low. Add the salt, pepper and lemon or lime juice. Fry, stirring, for a further 2 minutes.

■ Transfer to a warm serving dish. Serve with a rice dish, one or two vegetable side dishes and a yogurt relish, such as Fresh Coriander and Yogurt Chutney (see page 224).

# PIQUANT PRAWNS

## *Gambas Picantes*

*PHILIPPINES*

Serves 4 as a main course, or 6 as a first course

This dish, Spanish in its origins as are many other Filipino dishes, is served in of some of Manila's most distinguished restaurants as an appetizer. I often serve it as a main course with rice and a simple vegetable. If you prefer a milder flavour, substitute 40 g (1½ oz) finely chopped green pepper for the chillies.

**450 g (1 lb) uncooked unpeeled prawns**
**1 teaspoon paprika**
**5 cloves garlic**
**1–2 fresh hot green chillies**
**4 tablespoons olive oil**
**½ teaspoon salt**
**freshly ground black pepper**

■ Peel and de-vein the prawns. Rinse them, pat dry and put them in a bowl. Add the paprika and toss to mix. Peel the garlic and chop it finely. Chop the chillies finely.

■ Put the oil in a wok or large frying pan and set it over a high heat. When the oil is hot, add the garlic and stir-fry for 30 seconds or until it turns golden.

■ Add the prawns and green chillies. Stir-fry over a high heat for 2-3 minutes or until the prawns turn opaque all the way through. Add the salt and pepper. Toss again and serve.

*The Spanish ruled the Philippines from 1521 until 1898. At that point the Americans took over, staying through the Second World War until 1946. The Spanish occupation not only gave the Philippines its name (the country is named after Philip II of Spain) and its major religion, Catholicism, but introduced a Mediterranean style of eating. Spanish food was mostly cooked in olive oil, with seasonings limited to garlic, onions, tomatoes, sweet peppers and vinegar. The Filipinos began to add Spanish ingredients to their own recipes and to cook the newcomers' fancy food as well. They thought it rather grand, however, to call most dishes by Spanish names, especially on menus.*

# SQUID WITH TOMATOES

## *Adobong Pusit*

*PHILIPPINES*

Serves 3-4

This easy dish, very Spanish in its heritage, is generally eaten with rice in the Philippines. I often serve it with pasta or enjoy it all by itself with a salad on the side when I want to eat lightly. It never ceases to amaze me that something as good should still be so cheap to make.

Flavourful fresh plum tomatoes at their peak of ripeness are ideal for this recipe. If you are unable to find any good fresh tomatoes, use 6 canned plum tomatoes, lightly drained instead.

**450 g (1 lb) squid, cleaned (see page 15)**
**4 cloves garlic**
**50 g (2 oz) onion**
**225 g (8 oz) flavourful ripe tomatoes**
**3 tablespoons olive oil**
**1 teaspoon vinegar**
**¾ teaspoon salt**

■ Wash the squid and pat it dry. Cut the tubular bodies crossways into 1 cm (½ inch) wide rings. Cut the tentacles into 2 or 3 pieces.

■ Peel and finely chop the garlic and onion. Immerse the tomatoes in boiling water for 15 seconds, then remove and peel away the skins. Chop the tomatoes coarsely.

■ Heat the oil in a medium pan over a medium-high heat. Add the garlic and stir once or twice, then add the onion. Lower the heat to medium and cook, stirring, for 1 minute. Add the tomatoes and cook, stirring, on a medium-high heat for 2-3 minutes or until you have a fairly thick sauce.

■ Increase the heat to high and put in the squid, vinegar and salt. Stir and cook for a few minutes – just until the squid turns opaque. Serve at once.

# SQUID IN BLACK BEAN SAUCE

## *Sotong Masak Kicap*

*MALAYSIA*

Serves 4

The ingredients used in this recipe are simple and humble, but the dish, a Nonya classic, is exquisite. The black sauce used here is thick, smooth, very slightly sweet and made with mashed fermented soya beans. I find bottled black bean sauce to be fairly similar. If you cannot obtain it, use 1½ tablespoons canned or dried fermented black beans, washed and mashed, mixed with 1 tablespoon oyster sauce.

**250-275 g (9-10 oz) onions**
**450 g (1 lb) squid, cleaned (see page 15)**
**4 tablespoons vegetable oil**
**2 tablespoons bottled black bean sauce**
**1 tablespoon Chinese light soy sauce**
**1-1½ teaspoons ground white pepper**

**TO GARNISH**
**1 spring onion, green part only, cut into rings**
**25 g (1 oz) fresh coriander leaves (optional)**
**few hot red chilli slices (optional)**

■ Peel the onions and cut them in half lengthways. Cut each half crossways into 3 mm (⅛ inch) thick slices.

■ Wash the squid and pat it dry. Cut the tubular bodies crossways into 2 cm (¾ inch) wide rings. The tentacles may be left clumped together or separated into 2-3 clumps.

■ Heat the oil in a frying pan over a medium-high heat. When the oil is hot, add the onions and fry, stirring, for about 4 minutes or until they are softened.

■ Add the squid, black bean sauce, soy sauce and white pepper. Stir and cook for about 3 minutes or until the squid is opaque. Transfer to a serving dish.

■ Garnish with the chopped spring onion and, if liked, coriander leaves and red chilli rings.

*The intermarriage between the Malay men and Chinese women in the Straits settlements of Penang and Malacca (as well as Singapore) has led to a new mixed culture – that of the 'Straits Chinese' – and to a style of cooking now favoured in restaurants. Named after the women in the community, this cuisine is known as the food of the Nonyas. The Straits Chinese gave up the use of chopsticks and took to their fingers. They began to perfume and enliven their pork, prawns and chicken with coconut milk, candlenuts and tamarind. They still enjoyed mild dishes and airy stuffed pancakes (Po piah) but ate many fiery ones too. Cooking skills were passed on from mother to daughter, a young girl's eligibility often depending on her ability to chop, cut and pound!*

*Sometimes a cuisine can best be gauged by its treatment of seafood. Many restaurants in and around Bangkok have large tanks of fresh fish. So first you go and pick it: 'I want those prawns, that crab, etc.' Then you seat yourself in some airy pavilion and wait. Soon the dishes begin to arrive. There are large prawns that have been grilled over wet straw (the smoke penetrates their flesh); you eat these with fish sauce, vinegar and a chilli dipping sauce. Small prawns float in a delicate broth with little creamy pieces of young coconut. Juicy crabs that have been stir-fried with green chillies, mint and lemon grass are also bought to the table. There is a phrase in Thailand which says, 'There is rice in the fields and fish in the water.' It means that all is well. Certainly in the culinary sense all seems to be very well in this marvellous country.*

# SQUID SALAD

## *Yam Pla Muk*

*THAILAND*

Serves 4-6 as a main course, or 8 as a first course

Squid is such an underused seafood. It is cheap and I happen to love it, so I cook it in as many different ways as I can. This is an easy salad that can be served as a main course in the summer, and as an appetizer in the winter.

- 1 kg (2 lb) squid, cleaned (see page 15)
- 75 g (3 oz) shallots or onions
- 4 tablespoons lime juice
- 3 tablespoons fish sauce, or salt to taste
- 1 teaspoon sugar
- ¼ teaspoon chilli powder
- 6-8 tablespoons fresh coriander leaves

TO SERVE

- 3-4 lettuce leaves
- 150 g (5 oz) cucumber
- 8-10 cherry or baby plum tomatoes
- lime wedges

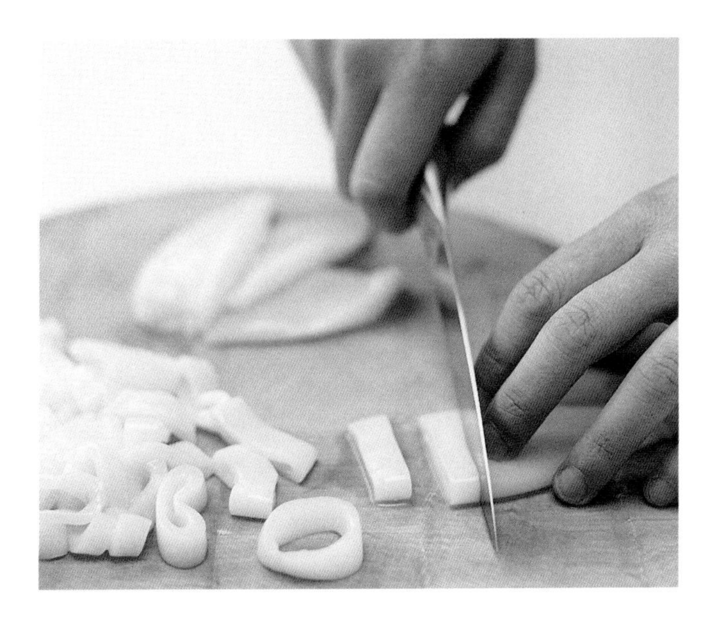

**1** Cut the tubular squid bodies crossways into 5 mm (¼ inch) wide rings. Wash these rings and the tentacles, then put them in a pan with 4 tablespoons water.

**2** Bring to the boil, cover and simmer for about 3 minutes or until the squid turns opaque. Drain them and place in a bowl.

**3** Peel and finely slice the shallots. Add these to the squid along with the lime juice, fish sauce, sugar, chilli powder and coriander leaves. Toss well. Check the seasoning.

**4** Just before serving, arrange the lettuce leaves on a serving plate. Peel the cucumber and slice it into thin rounds. Cut the tomatoes in half. Pile the squid salad on top of the lettuce leaves with the cucumber slices and tomato halves. Serve with lime wedges.

# poultry and eggs

*A yakitori bar in Japan is really a drinking establishment that offers specialised snacks, usually made of chicken and generally cooked on bamboo skewers over charcoal. As offices close in the evenings, men and women head towards these bars to drink and have a snack, and even to stay on for a full meal.*

# CHICKEN ON A SKEWER

## *Yakitori*

JAPAN

Serves 4 as a main course, or up to 8 with drinks

*Yakitori* at its simplest is a chicken shish kebab with a very Japanese flavour. Pieces of dark meat are served either by themselves, neatly speared on to the ends of small bamboo skewers (three makes a serving), or interspersed with bits of green pepper or spring onion. As the meat is grilled, it is dipped into a sweetened soy-based sauce. The servings are tantalisingly small, but you can have as many as you want. If you are hungry enough for a full meal, you can serve *yakitori* on a bowl of rice with tea and pickles on the side.

You may serve the simple *yakitori* described below either with drinks or as a meal. A note about the skewers: most oriental shops sell 15-20 cm (6-8 inch) bamboo skewers. They should be soaked in water for 30 minutes-1 hour before using to prevent scorching during grilling. All the meat should be placed at one end, which will be set over or under the heat source. In Japan the small *yakitori* sticks are a little like lollipops – you pull the meat off with your mouth.

You could use metal skewers instead – the best kind are somewhat flattened, like swords, because the meat does not roll around on them when it is turned. If long metal skewers are used, the meat is best pushed off on to a plate to serve. If you are serving the *yakitori* with drinks, push cocktail sticks into the pieces of meat so that they may be picked up easily.

The chicken can be skewered well ahead of time, covered and refrigerated. You may cook this dish outdoors over charcoal or indoors under your kitchen grill.

**4 medium chicken legs (thighs and drumsticks), boned (see page 14)**
**1 large green pepper**
**8 tablespoons Japanese soy sauce (*shoyu*)**
**4 tablespoons sake**
**3 tablespoons sugar**

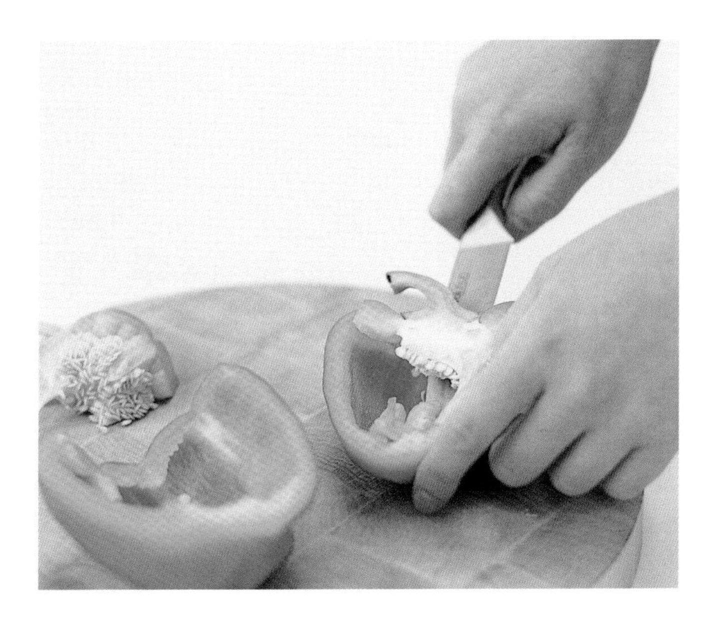

**1** Cut the boned chicken leg meat into 2.5 cm (1 inch) chunks. If some skin separates from the meat, discard it; leave any skin that clings naturally. Halve, core and deseed the green pepper, then cut it into 2.5 cm (1 inch) squares.

**2** Thread two pieces of meat on to a skewer followed by a piece of pepper. If you are preparing bamboo skewers, Japanese-style, push the meat to one end and keep alternating two pieces of meat with a piece of pepper until you have loaded about 7.5 cm (3 inches) of each skewer. If you are using long metal skewers, you can thread their entire length, leaving each end empty. Thread all the meat in this way, using as many skewers as required. Cover with cling film and refrigerate until needed.

**3** Meanwhile combine the soy sauce, sake and sugar in a small pan and bring to the boil. Lower the heat and heat gently until the sugar has dissolved.

**4** Preheat an indoor grill or outdoor charcoal grill. Position the skewers 10-13 cm (4-5 inches) from the heat source and grill for 4-5 minutes on each side or until the meat is three-quarters cooked. Brush with the sauce and grill briefly on both sides until the meat is almost done. Brush with the sauce a second time and grill for another 30 seconds on each side. Serve hot.

# SPICY CHICKEN KEBABS WITH PEANUT SAUCE

## *Satay Ayam*

*INDONESIA*

Serves 4

This recipe is one of my favourite Indonesian *satays*. The peanut sauce is exactly the same as the dressing for *gado-gado*. It needs to be heated, beaten lightly and then poured over the grilled kebabs. You may serve these kebabs as a first course, all by themselves, or as a main dish along with rice, a vegetable or salad, and perhaps some crisp Prawn Wafers (see page 40).

I prefer to use boned and skinned chicken legs for *satays* as the meat stays succulent, though you can use boned and skinned chicken breast if you wish. I generally find it easier to use flat metal skewers, but if you want to use the more traditional bamboo *satay* skewers, soak them in water for 30 minutes-1 hour before threading the meat on to them.

*It is believed that satays spread throughout much of East Asia from Java. Before they reached Java, their origins can surely be traced to the kebabs of India, and beyond India to the Middle East. Satays take different forms in different parts of this vast Indonesian archipelago. In Jogyakarta, for example, they tend to be rather sweet, eaten as they are with ritual dips in a thick, syrupy, sweet soy sauce known as kecap manis. Crushed peanuts or sliced shallots and an occasional hot chilli may be added to the kecap. As you travel west, the sweetness gives way to greater pungency and nuttiness.*

**4 medium chicken legs (thighs and drumsticks; see page 14), boned, or 450 g (1 lb) chicken breast, boned and skinned**
**1 clove garlic**
**2.5 cm (1 inch) cube fresh root ginger**
**10 g (¼ oz) shallot or onion**
**4 teaspoons Chinese light soy sauce**
**1 tablespoon lime or lemon juice**
**1 teaspoon ground coriander seeds**
**½ teaspoon sugar**
**¼ teaspoon chilli powder**

**FOR THE PEANUT DRESSING**
**100 g (4 oz) Roasted Peanuts (see page 223)**
**2 cloves garlic**
**25 g (1 oz) shallots or onion**
**2 tablespoons vegetable oil**
**½ teaspoon chilli powder**
**½ teaspoon salt**
**2 teaspoons dark brown soft sugar**
**freshly ground black pepper**
**4-5 teaspoons lime or lemon juice**

■ First make the peanut dressing. Grind the peanuts in a clean coffee grinder or blender, as finely as possible. Peel and finely chop the garlic and shallots. Heat the oil in a small pan over a medium heat. When hot, add the garlic and shallots, and fry, stirring, for about 1 minute or until they are golden brown.

■ Pour in 450 ml (¾ pint) water, and stir in the chilli powder, salt, sugar and ground peanuts. Bring to the boil, turn the heat to medium-low and simmer for 15-20 minutes, stirring occasionally, until the sauce has thickened. It should be no thicker than a creamy salad dressing. Allow to cool slightly, then add the black pepper and beat in the lime juice. Check the seasoning.

■ Preheat an indoor grill or an outdoor charcoal grill. If using bamboo skewers, thread about 7.5 cm (3 inches) of chicken pieces on to one end of each skewer, using as many skewers as needed. If you are using long metal skewers, divide the meat evenly between 4 skewers.

■ If you are grilling indoors, balance the skewer ends on the raised edges of a grill rack and position 10 cm (4 inches) from the heat source. If grilling over charcoal, place the skewers about 10 cm (4 inches) from the heat source. Grill for about 5 minutes on each side until the meat is browned.

■ Reheat the peanut dressing, if necessary, and beat it lightly. Place the bamboo skewers (if using) directly on individual plates. Pour a few tablespoons of the dressing over each portion and serve. If you are using metal skewers, remove the meat with the help of a fork and divide it among 4 plates. Spoon a few tablespoons of dressing over each serving.

# CHICKEN WITH A SWEET SAKE GLAZE

## *Toriniku No Teriyaki*

*JAPAN*

Serves 4

Under the guidance of Mr Saito, I learned much at Professor Tsuji's cookery school in Osaka. To turn out simple dishes – like this *teriyaki* – trusted techniques are used with precision, and simple logical steps are followed methodically. For example, only chicken thighs are used in this recipe. Thigh meat is juicy and moist, much more so than breast meat. The thigh is boned, which allows the meat to be cooked evenly and quickly. It also allows the meat to be sliced after it is cooked so that it can be picked up easily with chopsticks. The chicken is marinated for an hour so that the flavours of the sauce can penetrate the meat. Even though chicken *teriyaki* is generally cooked on a grill, Mr Saito favours another method. He browns the chicken first in a frying pan and then lets it cook very briefly in a moderately hot oven. The chicken is marvellous; it is moist, slightly sweet, slightly salty, crisp on the outside and meltingly tender inside. Once you have tried this technique, I am sure you will want to use it to cook chicken thighs with other seasonings of your choice.

The Japanese tend to eat small portions of meat. One thigh would be just enough for a single serving at a fine restaurant. It would sit alone on a plate in glorious splendour, garnished perhaps with a few young bamboo shoots leaning against it, a few lime wedges and a few boiled pods of freshly plucked green soya beans. You may substitute green beans or carrots (see page 229), for the soya beans. There should be Plain Japanese Rice (page 191) on the side. Keeping Western appetites in mind, I've allowed two thighs per person.

Make sure that you do not pierce the skin when boning the chicken thighs. You will need to cook them in a large frying pan, or in two batches.

**Sweet Glazing Sauce (see page 222)**

**8 chicken thighs, weighing 1 kg (2 lb), boned (see page 14), with skin intact**

**about 2 tablespoons vegetable oil**

TO GARNISH

**bamboo shoots, green beans and carrots (see page 229)**

**lime wedges**

■ First make the Sweet Glazing Sauce. Pour it into a medium bowl and allow to cool.

■ Add the boned chicken thighs to the bowl of glazing sauce. Toss to mix, cover and leave to marinate in a cool place for 1 hour, turning the thighs occasionally, so that they absorb the flavours and colour evenly. Set a shelf in the top third of the oven. Preheat the oven to 200°C (400°F) gas mark 6.

■ About 15 minutes before you wish to eat, put the oil in a very large non-stick frying pan and set it over a medium-high heat. Lift the chicken pieces out of the sauce, reserving the sauce, and place them in a single layer, skin-side down, in the frying pan. Cook for 5-6 minutes or until the skin is browned. Turn the chicken pieces over and cook for 30 seconds only to seal the other side.

■ Lift the chicken pieces out with a slotted spoon and lay them, skin-side up, on a rack set over a roasting tin. Bake on the positioned shelf in the oven for 8 minutes, basting the skin three times during this time with the reserved sauce.

■ Put the chicken pieces on a chopping board and cut each lengthways into 3 segments. Re-assemble each thigh into its original form and place 2 thighs in the centre of each serving plate. Garnish with bamboo shoots, green beans and carrots. Serve with lime wedges.

# TANDOORI CHICKEN

## *Tandoori Murghi*

*INDIA*

Serves 6-8

In a traditional *tandoor* clay oven – heated with charcoal or wood – food cooks very quickly in the intense heat which builds up inside. The chickens used for the *tandoor* in India are usually spring chickens, weighing 900 g-1.25 kg (2-2½ lb) each. They are cooked whole, with only wings and neck removed, on all sides at once.

I find it more convenient to marinate and cook chicken cut into pieces – it is also easier to serve and to eat it this way. I buy legs and breasts for tandoori chicken. Assuming that most people like both dark and light meat, I am generously allocating one whole leg and half a breast for each of 6 people.

The chicken in this recipe should be marinated for about 24 hours. If you want to obtain a characteristic red tandoori colour, you will need to add food colouring to the marinade (the chicken illustrated opposite is not coloured). If required, use the Spanish bijol, or Indian powdered food colouring, or Bush's orange-red powder.

Tandoori chicken is considered a delicacy in India and may be served at a banquet with basmati rice, naans, a few vegetable dishes, and onions pickled in vinegar.

**6 chicken legs, halved**
**3 chicken breasts, halved**

**FOR THE MARINADE**
**1 medium onion**
**6 cloves garlic**
**4 cm (1½ inch) cube fresh root ginger**
**3 tablespoons lemon juice**
**225 g (8 oz) yogurt**
**1 tablespoon ground coriander**
**1 teaspoon ground cumin**
**1 teaspoon ground turmeric**
**1 teaspoon garam masala**
**¼ teaspoon ground mace**
**¼ teaspoon ground nutmeg**
**¼ teaspoon ground cloves**
**¼ teaspoon ground cinnamon**
**¼-½ teaspoon cayenne pepper (optional, or to taste)**
**2 teaspoons salt**
**¼ teaspoon freshly ground black pepper**
**4 tablespoons olive or vegetable oil**
**½-1 teaspoon orange food colouring (optional, see left)**

**TO SERVE**
**1 medium onion**
**fresh coriander sprigs**
**lemon wedges**

■ First prepare the marinade. Peel and coarsely chop the onion, garlic and ginger. Put them in a blender with the lemon juice and blend to a smooth paste. Transfer to a bowl (large enough to accommodate the chicken). Add the yogurt, spices, salt, black pepper, oil, and food colouring if using. Mix thoroughly.

■ Skin the chicken legs and breasts. With a sharp knife, make 3 diagonal slashes on each breast section, going halfway down to the bone. Make 2 diagonal slashes on each thigh, also going halfway down to the bone. With the point of a sharp knife, make 4 or 5 slits in each drumstick.

■ Add the chicken to the marinade and rub the marinade into the slashes with your fingertips. Cover and leave to marinate in the refrigerator for 24 hours, turning the chicken 4 or 5 times while it is marinating.

■ If barbecuing, light your charcoal about 1½ hours before serving; it should take 20-30 minutes to get red hot. Place the barbecue grid on its lowest setting. (Alternatively, preheat the oven to its highest setting.)

■ Peel the onion for the garnish and cut into paper-thin slices. Separate the rings and set in a small bowl of iced water; cover and refrigerate.

■ Lift the chicken pieces out of the marinade and place on the barbecue rack (or in a single layer in a large shallow baking tin). Cook for about 6-8 minutes on each side, then position the rack further from the heat source. Cook the chicken more slowly for a further 15-20 minutes, turning occasionally and basting with the marinade from time to time. (Alternatively bake in the oven for 20-25 minutes until just cooked through).

■ Drain the onion rings and pat dry. Arrange the chicken on a warm large platter and garnish with the onion rings and coriander sprigs. Serve with lemon wedges, rice and/or naan bread, and vegetable side dishes or a salad.

# FRIED CHICKEN WITH SPRING ONION SAUCE

## *Youpi Ziji*

*HONG KONG*

Serves 4

I first tasted this dish at the Shanghai Club in Hong Kong. A whole chicken was opened up at the breast bone, marinated with (among other things) Sichuan peppercorns, then deep-fried, beak, feet and all. The crisply fried bird was then cut up, re-assembled to look like itself, head chirpily upright, and smothered with an unusual sauce, chock-full of fresh herbs and seasonings. The dish is uncommonly good.

I have simplified it somewhat here. I am assuming that – like me – you would have difficulty in obtaining a chicken with head and feet and even if you did, your heart might yearn for the safer look you know and understand! I have used chicken pieces as they are easier to fry in hot oil. If you prefer, you can grill them and then smother them with the sauce.

If you can find Chinese celery at a Chinese food store, do buy it. Only the stems are used here. If you cannot obtain it, ordinary celery – especially the thin uppermost stems – makes a good substitute. This recipe uses stalks and stems of herbs, that are normally thrown away.

**1.5 kg (3 lb) chicken pieces (preferably thighs and drumsticks)**

FOR THE MARINADE

**2.5 cm (1 inch) cube fresh root ginger**

**1 spring onion**

**2 teaspoons roasted and ground Sichuan peppercorns (see page 264)**

**2 tablespoons Chinese light soy sauce**

**½ teaspoon sugar**

FOR THE SAUCE

**3 cloves garlic**

**2.5 cm (1 inch) cube fresh root ginger**

**2 spring onions**

**few sticks Chinese celery, or top part of ordinary celery sticks**

**few fresh coriander or parsley stems**

**2 tablespoons Chinese light soy sauce**

**2 teaspoons distilled white vinegar**

**4 tablespoons chicken stock**

**1 tablespoon tomato ketchup**

**½ teaspoon sugar**

**2 tablespoons sesame oil**

YOU ALSO NEED

**about 3 tablespoons cornflour**

**oil for deep-frying**

■ For the marinade, peel and finely grate the ginger. Slice the spring onion into fine rounds.

■ Divide the chicken legs into thighs and drumsticks. If using chicken breasts, cut each one in half. Put the chicken in a bowl and prod the areas without skin with the point of a sharp knife. Sprinkle the ground Sichuan pepper, ginger, spring onion, soy sauce and sugar over the chicken.

■ Rub the marinade well into the chicken with your hands. Cover and leave to marinate for 2-4 hours, refrigerating if necessary.

■ Meanwhile, prepare the sauce. Peel and chop the garlic as finely as possible. Peel the ginger, cut into paper-thin slices, then into minute dice. Cut the spring onions and Chinese celery stems into very fine rounds. (If using ordinary celery, cut into minute dice – you need about 3 tablespoons.) Cut several stems of coriander together into minute pieces – you need about 1 tablespoon. Combine the garlic, ginger, spring onions, celery and coriander in a small bowl. Cover and set aside.

■ In another bowl combine the soy sauce, vinegar, stock, tomato ketchup, sugar and sesame oil. Stir well to mix and set aside.

■ Lay the chicken pieces out on a board in a single layer and dust both sides with cornflour, patting to coat well, then set aside for 20 minutes.

■ Heat the oil for deep-frying in a large wok over a medium heat, or in a deep-fat fryer. When it is hot, add the chicken pieces and fry for approximately 15-20 minutes or until they are nicely browned on the outside and cooked all the way through, turning the pieces as necessary. Remove and drain on kitchen paper.

■ Transfer the chicken to a serving dish. Mix together the two bowls of sauce ingredients and pour over the chicken. Serve at once.

# SPICY STIR-FRIED CHICKEN WITH LEMON GRASS

## *Ga Xao Xa Ot*

*VIETNAM*

Serves 4

This was one of the quick, very flavourful, stir-fried dishes served to me in a floating restaurant on Saigon River. Even though the chicken cooks quickly, it is a good idea to let it sit in its marinade for at least an hour. It is important that the chicken (while still on the bone) be cut into fairly small, bite-sized pieces. As chicken bones, especially those in the leg, have a tendency to splinter, it is best to let the butcher cut up the chicken for you.

**1 kg (2 lb) chicken pieces, cut into small pieces**

FOR THE MARINADE

**1 stick fresh lemon grass**
**1 large clove garlic**
**1 cm (½ inch) cube fresh root ginger**
**1 tablespoon sugar**
**1½ teaspoons tomato paste**
**½ teaspoon salt**
**¼ teaspoon chilli powder**
**¼ teaspoon ground turmeric**

YOU ALSO NEED

**5-6 cloves garlic**
**3 tablespoons vegetable oil**
**1 tablespoon fish sauce, or salt to taste**
**120 ml (4 fl oz) chicken stock**
**90 g (3½ oz) onions**

■ First prepare the marinade. Cut the lemon grass crossways into very thin slices, starting at the bulbous base and slicing up to about 15 cm (6 inches); discard the straw-like top. Peel and crush the garlic. Peel and finely grate the ginger.

■ Put the chicken pieces in a bowl. Add the lemon grass, garlic, ginger, sugar, tomato paste, salt, chilli powder and turmeric to the chicken. Mix thoroughly. Cover and set aside for 1-24 hours, refrigerating if necessary.

■ Peel and finely chop the 5-6 garlic cloves. Heat the oil in a wok or large, lidded frying pan over a high heat. When hot, add the garlic and fry, stirring, for 30 seconds or until golden. Add the chicken with its marinade. Stir and fry for 5-6 minutes or until the chicken browns a little.

■ Add the fish sauce and 4 tablespoons chicken stock, stir once, then cover and cook on a high heat for 5 minutes. Add the remaining 4 tablespoons stock, re-cover, turn the heat to low and cook for a further 5 minutes.

■ In the meantime, peel the onion and cut into 2 cm (¾ inch) dice; separate the onion layers.

■ Remove the lid from the wok and turn the heat to high. Add the onion and fry, stirring, for 1 minute. Skim off any excess oil from the chicken and serve.

*Aromatic herbs grow abundantly in tropical Thailand and are used generously. They include enormous families of mints and basils, coriander (leaves and roots are used), kaffir lime leaves, the highly scented pandanus leaves and lemon grass. 'Indian' spices, such as cumin, coriander, turmeric, cinnamon, cardamom and cloves, are used in Thai cooking, but only for curries and in such small quantities as to leave more of a herby flavour than a spicy one. Gingers are used, particularly galangal, as well as various limes and tamarind for souring. Fish sauce (nam pla) and shrimp paste provide saltiness and added flavouring.*

# MINCED CHICKEN STIR-FRIED WITH BASIL

## *Kai Pad Bai Kaprow*

*THAILAND*

Serves 4

Here is an exquisite, quick-cooking dish that is made with fresh holy basil (*bai kaprow*). I cannot always obtain this Thai basil, but I find ordinary basil makes a good substitute. The green herb is used in two ways: it is stir-fried with the chicken and it is also shallow-fried until crisp and used as a generous topping. The result is uncommonly good. (If red chillies are unavailable, increase the number of green chillies accordingly.)

**100 g (4 oz) fresh holy basil leaves, or ordinary basil (weight after removing stems)**
**vegetable oil for shallow-frying**
**5 cloves garlic**
**75 g (3 oz) shallots or onions**
**2.5 cm (1 inch) cube fresh root ginger**
**2 fresh hot green chillies, or to taste**
**2 fresh hot red chillies, or to taste**
**450 g (1 lb) minced chicken (from boned, skinned breast and/or legs)**
**5 teaspoons fish sauce, or salt to taste**
**1½ teaspoons dark brown sugar**

■ Wash the basil leaves and pat them dry. Set aside half of the whole leaves; chop the rest very coarsely and set aside.

■ Heat a 1 cm (½ inch) depth of oil in a medium frying pan over a medium-high heat. Put a plate lined with kitchen paper near the hob. If available, have ready a splatter screen or an upturned sieve to cover the pan to prevent the oil splattering.

■ When the oil is hot, add a small handful of whole basil leaves. Cover immediately with the screen or sieve (if using). Remove the cover as soon as the intense sizzling has died down – after a matter of seconds – and stir the leaves once or twice. They will turn crisp very quickly. Remove with a slotted spoon and spread out on the kitchen paper to drain. Fry the rest of the whole basil leaves in the same way. (Replace the kitchen paper under the basil leaves several times to prevent the crisp leaves from becoming soggy.) Once the oil has cooled sufficiently, strain and reserve it.

■ Peel and finely chop the garlic. Peel and finely slice the shallots. Peel and finely grate the ginger. Cut the green and red chillies into fine rounds.

■ Just before serving, heat 4 tablespoons of the reserved oil in a large frying pan or wok over a medium-high heat. Add the garlic and shallots, and fry, stirring, for about 2 minutes or until the shallots are golden brown. Add the chillies and ginger and give a few vigorous stirs.

■ Increase the heat to high and stir in the chopped basil. Add the minced chicken and fry for about 3 minutes, stirring to break up the lumps as you do so. The chicken should turn white all the way through. Stir in the fish sauce and sugar.

■ Transfer to a serving dish, top with the crisp-fried basil leaves and serve.

# CHICKEN STIR-FRIED WITH CELERY

## *Jiancai Jiding*

*HONG KONG*

Serves 2-4

Some of the best food that I have eaten in Hong Kong has been at a restaurant that calls itself, strangely enough, the American Restaurant. It specialises in northern food, although not all the chefs in the kitchen are from the north. After feeding the clients superlative Beijing-style food, the chefs settle down to a meal of their own which is often a mixture of northern and their own Cantonese food. Here is a Cantonese dish that I caught the staff eating one day.

**275 g (10 oz) boned, skinned chicken breast**
**1 egg white**
**3 teaspoons cornflour**
**¼ teaspoon salt**
**6 tablespoons chicken stock**
**½ dried hot red chilli**
**1 tablespoon Chinese light soy sauce**
**2 teaspoons Chinese rice wine or dry sherry**
**2 teaspoons lemon juice**
**1 clove garlic**
**4 sticks celery (preferably from the middle of the bunch)**
**2 tablespoons vegetable oil**

■ Spread the chicken breast out and beat with a meat mallet to flatten it until approximately 5 mm (¼ inch) thick. Cut into 2.5 cm (1 inch) squares.

■ Combine the egg white, 2 teaspoons of the cornflour and the salt in a small bowl. Beat lightly to mix. Toss the chicken in the egg mixture until it is well coated. Cover and set aside for 2 hours or longer.

■ Meanwhile, make the sauce. Put the remaining 1 teaspoon of cornflour in a cup. Slowly add 5 tablespoons of the chicken stock, mixing well between each addition. Crumble in the red chilli. Add the light soy sauce, rice wine and lemon juice. Mix well and set aside.

■ Peel and finely chop the garlic. Cut the celery sticks crossways into 2.5 cm (1 inch) pieces.

■ When the chicken is ready, pour a 4 cm (1½ inch) depth of water into a medium frying pan or a wide shallow saucepan and bring to the boil over a high heat. When it starts bubbling, add the chicken, separating the pieces with a spoon. Return to the boil: this should take about 30 seconds, by which time the chicken should have turned white. (If the water returns to the boil more quickly, turn the heat to low.) Drain the chicken and set aside; do not refrigerate.

■ Just before serving, set a wok over a high heat and add 1 tablespoon of the oil. When the oil is hot, add half of the chopped garlic, stir once or twice, then add the chicken. Cook, stirring, for about 1 minute. Remove the chicken and set aside in a bowl.

■ Clean and dry the wok, then return to a high heat. Add the remaining 1 tablespoon of oil. When the oil is hot, add the remaining chopped garlic, stir once or twice, then add the chopped celery and stir-fry for 30-40 seconds.

■ Add the remaining 1 tablespoon of chicken stock and cover. Turn the heat to low and cook for about 3 minutes or until the celery is just tender. Take the wok off the heat.

■ Give the sauce a stir and add to the wok. Place over a low heat, add the chicken and cook, stirring, until the sauce has thickened. Serve immediately.

# CHICKEN WITH GARLIC AND BLACK PEPPER

## *Kai Tod Kratium Priktai*

*THAILAND*

Serves 2-4

For a simple Thai family meal, this quick-cooking dish is usually served with plain rice and a soupy dish or a curry. I find that a green salad – with lots of fresh basil, mint and green coriander thrown in – also goes very well with it.

Make sure that you do not pierce the skin when boning the chicken thighs. The chicken takes about 9 minutes to cook and is best prepared just before eating. The accompanying dipping sauce can be made several hours in advance.

**4 chicken thighs, about 450 g (1 lb), boned** (**see page 14**)

**1½-2 teaspoons coarsely ground black pepper**

**4 large cloves garlic**

**about ½ packed teacup fresh coriander leaves**

**1½ tablespoons fish sauce**

**1 teaspoon sugar**

**¼ teaspoon chilli powder (optional)**

**2 tablespoons vegetable oil**

TO SERVE

**fresh mint, coriander and basil sprigs, to garnish (optional)**

**Fish Sauce with Lime Juice and Chilli** (**see page 216**)

■ Rub the chicken on both sides with the black pepper and set aside.

■ Peel and crush the garlic. Finely chop the coriander leaves. Combine the garlic, coriander leaves, fish sauce, sugar and chilli powder in a bowl and mix well. Rub this mixture over the chicken and leave to marinate for 1 hour.

■ Heat the oil in a non-stick frying pan over a medium-high heat. When hot, add the chicken pieces, skin-side down, and cook for about 5 minutes, or until the skin is brown and crisp.

■ Turn the chicken over, reduce the heat to medium-low and cook for a further 3½-4 minutes, or until the chicken is just cooked through.

■ Lift out the pieces with a slotted spoon and place on a chopping board, skin-side up. Using a sharp knife, cut each thigh into 3 strips, re-form it into its original shape and arrange on a serving plate. Garnish liberally with fresh herbs if desired, and serve with the seasoned fish sauce.

# CHICKEN WITH BAMBOO SHOOTS AND MUSHROOMS IN BLACK BEAN SAUCE

## *Ayam Pongtay*

*MALAYSIA*

Serves 4

The food of the Straits Chinese – the Chinese who migrated to the Straits settlements of Penang, Malacca and Singapore and married local Malay women – has become very popular in this region of South-east Asia. Known as the cooking of the Nonyas (the Straits Chinese women), it can now be found in elegant trendy restaurants, especially in Kuala Lumpur.

*Ayam pongtay* is a Nonya classic. Do not be fooled by its simple ingredients. Subtle, gentle, full of rich flavour and absolutely addictive, it is, to my mind, one of South-east Asia's finest dishes.

Ingredients are, of course, important. You need chunky tender bamboo shoots, which are available in cans. Soft, rounded, cone-shaped 'tips', usually about 4-5 cm (1½-2 inches) long, are ideal if you can find them. The best mushrooms to use are dried Chinese mushrooms – the thicker the caps, the better the quality. If you cannot find these, you could – at a pinch – use fresh button mushroom caps, which do not, of course, need to be soaked. Sauté them lightly in oil and add to the pan 10 minutes before the end of the cooking time. Instead of the mushroom-soaking liquid, use 600 ml (1 pint) light chicken stock for cooking. As a substitute for black bean sauce you could use 2½ tablespoons canned or dried fermented black beans, washed and mashed with 1 tablespoon oyster sauce.

**10-12 large dried Chinese mushrooms**
**100 g (4 oz) shallots or onions**
**6 cloves garlic**
**3 tablespoons black bean sauce**
**1 kg (2 lb) chicken pieces (preferably legs)**
**3 tablespoons vegetable oil**
**10-12 chunky pieces good-quality canned bamboo shoots**
**1½ teaspoons dark soy sauce**
**1½ teaspoons molasses**
**few fresh mint leaves, to garnish (optional)**

**1** Quickly rinse the dried mushrooms in cold water, then place in a bowl. Pour on 600 ml (1 pint) hot water and leave to soak for 30 minutes or until the caps are soft. Lift out the mushrooms and reserve the soaking liquid. Cut off and discard the hard stems. Strain the soaking liquid through a muslin-lined sieve.

**2** Peel the shallots and garlic and chop them coarsely. Put them in an electric blender with 3 tablespoons water and the black bean sauce. Blend to a paste.

**3** Skin the chicken pieces. If using whole legs, divide into thighs and drumsticks, then cut each thigh and drumstick in half using a cleaver or heavy knife to cut through the bone. (Or ask your butcher to do this for you.) If using chicken breasts, cut each one in half.

**4** Heat the oil in a wide, heavy, lidded frying pan on a medium-high heat. Add the paste from the blender and fry, stirring, for 2-3 minutes until slightly reduced and coloured. Stir in the chicken, bamboo shoots, mushroom caps and strained liquor. Bring to the boil, cover and cook on a medium heat for 15 minutes. Uncover, increase the heat and cook for a further 6 minutes or until the sauce is reduced and thick. Mix the soy sauce with the molasses and add to the pan; stir well. Serve garnished with torn mint leaves if you wish.

*A visit to any Korean home reveals tall ceramic jars standing like silent sentinels on balconies, roofs and yards. These hold the pastes and pickles that give Korean meats their special character. The pastes, such as toen chang and kochu chang, are made of fermented soya beans and grains. The former, like Japanese miso, is mild; the latter, filled with chillies, a virtual firebird. Both may be added to stews to thicken and flavour them, and to boost their nutritional content.*

# SPICY CHICKEN STEW WITH CARROTS AND POTATOES

## *Tak Tori Tang*

*KOREA*

Serves 4-6

This lightly spiced, hearty and warming stew gets its flavours from Hot Fermented Bean Paste (see page 218), an inspired mixture of fermented beans and red chillies, as well as from soy sauce and sesame seeds. It has a thinnish sauce and is best eaten with plain rice. The Koreans tend to leave the skin on the chicken pieces, but I prefer to remove it before I stew them. Do whichever you prefer.

**1.6 kg (3½ lb) chicken pieces (preferably thighs and drumsticks)**
**4 tablespoons Japanese soy sauce (*shoyu*)**
**2 tablespoons sugar**
**2½ tablespoons Hot Fermented Bean Paste (see page 218), or to taste**
**450 g (1 lb) potatoes**
**350 g (12 oz) carrots**
**4 spring onions**
**50 g (2 oz) red pepper**
**50 g (2 oz) green pepper**
**salt (optional)**
**1 tablespoon roasted sesame seeds (see page 263)**
**freshly ground black pepper**

■ Combine the chicken, soy sauce and sugar in a large wide pan.

■ Put the fermented bean paste in a bowl and slowly mix in 450 ml (¾ pint) water. Add this combination to the chicken and bring to the boil. Cover, turn the heat to medium-low and simmer for 10 minutes.

■ Meanwhile, peel the potatoes and cut them into 4 cm (1½ inch) cubes. Peel the carrots and cut into 5 cm (2 inch) lengths. Cut the spring onions into 5 cm (2 inch) lengths. Deseed the red and green peppers and cut into 1 cm (½ inch) squares.

■ Add the potatoes, carrots and spring onions to the chicken, stir gently and bring to the boil. Cover, turn the heat to medium-low and simmer for 15-20 minutes or until the chicken and potatoes are tender, stirring occasionally. Taste and add salt if needed.

■ Add the red and green peppers to the pan. Cook, stirring, for 1-2 minutes. Using a slotted spoon, transfer the chicken and vegetables to a serving bowl.

■ Boil the sauce for few minutes to reduce it slightly, then pour over the chicken. Top with the roasted sesame seeds and freshly ground pepper to serve.

# HEARTY CHICKEN CURRY WITH POTATOES

## *Lauk Ayam*

*MALAYSIA*

Serves 6

Malaysian curries are among the best in East Asia and this one is extra rich and spicy – and delicious. I first tasted it in Kuala Lumpar where it is often served for a casual lunch with local bread. It could be eaten with almost any bread, from crusty French or Italian loaves to pitta breads and Indian chapattis. It may also be served with rice. This curry seems to improve with time, so it can easily be made a day in advance and refrigerated. Use less than the recommended quantity of chilli powder if you prefer a mild curry.

**6-8 whole cardamom pods**
**6 whole cloves**
**2 whole star anise**
**two 2 inch (5 cm) sticks cinnamon**
**2 tablespoons fennel seeds**
**1½ tablespoons cumin seeds**
**4 tablespoons ground coriander seeds**
**1½-2 teaspoons chilli powder, or to taste**
**1 tablespoon paprika**
**4 medium onions**
**four 2.5 cm (1 inch) cubes fresh root ginger**
**3 large cloves garlic**
**1.75 kg (4 lb) chicken pieces (preferably legs)**
**450 g (1 lb) potatoes**
**175 ml (6 fl oz) vegetable oil**
**2 teaspoons salt, or to taste**
**200 ml (7 fl oz) coconut milk (see page 258)**
**good handful fresh mint leaves**

■ Put the cardamom pods, cloves, star anise, cinnamon, fennel and cumin in a clean coffee grinder or spice grinder and grind as finely as possible. Turn into a bowl, add the coriander, chilli powder, paprika and 8 tablespoons water. Mix to a thick paste.

■ Peel and finely slice one of the onions; set aside.

■ Peel and coarsely chop the ginger, garlic and remaining 3 onions. Put these ingredients in an electric blender with about 4 tablespoons water and blend to a smooth paste.

■ Skin the chicken and cut into smaller serving pieces. (Cut whole legs into thighs and drumsticks; halve breasts.)

■ Peel the potatoes and cut them into 2.5 cm (1 inch) cubes, dropping them into a bowl of water.

■ Heat the oil in a large wide pan over a medium-high heat. Add the sliced onion and fry, stirring, until golden brown. Add the paste from the blender, and the spice paste from the bowl. Stir and fry for 10-12 minutes until the mixture is well fried and dark in colour.

■ Pour in 750 ml (1¼ pints) water. Drain the potatoes and add them to the pan with the chicken and salt. Stir and bring to a simmer. Cover, lower the heat and simmer gently for 30 minutes or until the chicken is tender. Stir the coconut milk and pour it in. Cook, stirring, for 1 minute. Coarsely chop the mint leaves and stir them in. The oil floating on the top of the curry may be removed before serving.

# RED CHICKEN CURRY

## *Kaeng Pet Kai*

*THAILAND*

Serves 4

This dish is absolutely the best of Thai curries. You may use the recipe to cook chunks of fish or prawns as well as chicken – simply adjust the cooking time so that the fish does not fall apart or turn rubbery.

Most Thai curries are made with a basic paste of ground spices. Jars of Thai curry pastes are available from most larger supermarkets and Asian grocers but – for optimum flavour – it is best to make your own (see recipe on page 220).

For curries I prefer the darker leg meat to chicken breast as it stays moist. The meat needs to be boned and skinned. Ask your butcher to do this for you, or buy boned, skinless chicken thighs from a supermarket. Alternatively, prepare the chicken yourself, following the directions on page 14. If you wish to use boned, skinless breast meat, buy 500 g (1¼ lb), dice it and poach it in the coconut milk on low heat for just 5 minutes. This way it will remain soft and tender.

**400 ml (14 fl oz) coconut milk (see page 258)**
**4 chicken legs (thighs and drumsticks), boned (see page 14)**
**½ teaspoon salt**
**4 tablespoons vegetable oil**
**4 tablespoons Red Curry Paste (see page 220)**
**1-1½ tablespoons fish sauce, or salt to taste**
**1 teaspoon dark brown sugar**
**4 fresh kaffir lime leaves**
**15-20 fresh sweet basil leaves (*bai horapha*), or ordinary basil leaves, stems removed**

■ Whether using fresh or canned coconut milk, let stand until the cream rises to the top, then skim off 4 tablespoons of the thick cream and set it aside. Stir the rest of the milk to mix.

■ Skin the boned chicken legs and cut the flesh into 2.5 cm (1 inch) cubes.

■ Pour the thin coconut milk into a medium frying pan. Sprinkle in the salt. Now put in the chicken pieces and bring the milk to the boil. Simmer on a medium-high heat, stirring frequently, for about 20 minutes until the chicken is just cooked. Remove from the heat and set aside.

■ Heat the oil and reserved coconut cream in a heavy wok or wide heavy pan until bubbling. Add the curry paste and stir-fry on a medium-high heat until the oil separates and the paste is lightly browned. Lower the heat and stir in the fish sauce and sugar.

■ Add the chicken, together with its cooking liquor. Bring to the boil and simmer over a low heat for 1 minute. (The curry can be prepared to this stage several hours ahead of time.)

■ When you are ready to serve, remove the central vein from the kaffir lime leaves, then cut the leaves crossways into very fine strips. Reheat the curry if necessary.

■ Put the hot curry into a serving dish. Scatter the basil leaves over the chicken and, with the back of the spoon, submerge them slightly in the sauce. Scatter the kaffir lime leaves over the top.

NOTE If fresh kaffir lime leaves are not available, use dried ones, pre-soaking them in a little water for 30 minutes. Alternatively, you could use 2 teaspoons finely shredded lime or lemon rind.

# MARINATED GRILLED CHICKEN

## *Murgh Lajavaab*

*INDIA*

Serves 4-6

For this simple recipe, the chicken is marinated in a mixture of onions, ginger, garlic, cumin, coriander, vinegar and oil, then grilled. It could also be barbecued over charcoal.

**1.4-1.6 kg (3-3½ lb) chicken (preferably legs, thighs and breasts) or a whole chicken, cut into serving pieces**

**FOR THE MARINADE**

**2 medium onions**

**4 cloves garlic**

**2.5 cm (1 inch) cube fresh root ginger**

**2-3 fresh hot green chillies, or ¼-½ teaspoon cayenne pepper (optional)**

**1 teaspoon cumin seeds**

**1 tablespoon ground coriander**

**150 ml (¼ pint) wine vinegar**

**150 ml (¼ pint) olive or vegetable oil**

**2 teaspoons salt**

**pinch of freshly ground pepper**

**TO GARNISH**

**chopped fresh coriander leaves**

■ First prepare the marinade. Peel and coarsely chop the onions, garlic and ginger. Place in a blender with the remaining marinade ingredients and blend to a smooth paste.

■ Remove and discard the skin from the chicken pieces, then prick them all over with a fork and place in a bowl. Pour the marinade over the chicken. Cover and leave to marinate in the refrigerator for at least 2-3 hours, preferably 24 hours. Return to room temperature before cooking.

■ Preheat the grill to medium-high. Lift the chicken pieces from the bowl, with as much marinade clinging to them as possible, and place on a foil-lined baking sheet. Grill for about 15 minutes on each side until the chicken is well browned and cooked through, adjusting the distance from the heat source as necessary so it does not brown too fast.

■ Transfer the chicken to a warm serving platter and sprinkle generously with coriander. Serve accompanied by a rice dish, a green vegetable, and dal if you like.

# CHICKEN MOGHLAI

## *Murgh Moghlai* *INDIA*

Serves 6

The exquisite taste and appearance of this rich, elaborate saffron-flavoured dish justifies the time taken in preparing it. It has a burnt-red colour and an aroma of cardamom, cloves and cinnamon. It tastes even better if you cook it a day ahead, thus allowing the sauce to act as a marinade for the chicken.

I use legs, thighs and breasts of chicken for this recipe. However, you could buy a whole 1.25-1.4 kg (2½-3 lb) chicken and have it cut into smallish serving portions; this will then feed 4-6 depending on size. You could also use 6 whole quail, skinned, or 6 whole partridges, skinned.

**1.25-1.4 kg (2½-3 lb) chicken legs, thighs and breasts**
**1 medium tomato**
**4 cm (1½ inch) piece fresh root ginger, 2.5 cm (1 inch) wide**
**8 cloves garlic**
**4 medium onions**
**150 ml (¼ pint) vegetable oil**
**2 cinnamon sticks, 6-7.5 cm (2½-3 inches) long**
**2 bay leaves**
**10 whole cardamom pods, slightly crushed**
**10 whole cloves**
**1 teaspoon cumin seeds**
**1½ tablespoons ground coriander**
**1½ teaspoons ground cumin**
**½ teaspoon ground turmeric**
**¼-½ teaspoon cayenne pepper**
**3 tablespoons yogurt**
**1 teaspoon salt**
**1 teaspoon (well-packed) saffron threads**
**1 tablespoon warm milk**

■ Skin the chicken pieces. Quarter the breasts and divide each leg into drumstick and thigh. Pat the chicken pieces dry and set aside. Peel and chop the tomato and set aside.

■ Peel and roughly chop the ginger, garlic and half of the onions. Place in a blender with 4 tablespoons of water and blend to a smooth paste.

■ Halve the other 2 onions lengthwise and slice thinly. Heat 7 tablespoons of the oil in a 25 cm (10 inch) heavy-based cooking pot or flameproof casserole. Add the sliced onions and fry, stirring, over a medium-high heat for 10-12 minutes or until dark brown and crisp, but not burned. Remove with a slotted spoon and set aside on a plate.

■ Increase the heat to high and brown the chicken pieces briefly in the hot oil, a few at a time. Transfer to a large plate.

■ Turn the heat down to medium-high. Add the remaining 2 tablespoons of oil to the cooking pot, then put in the cinnamon sticks, bay leaves, cardamom pods, cloves and cumin seeds. Stir and turn the spices once. Add the paste from the blender and fry, stirring, for 10 minutes.

■ Meanwhile, preheat a small, cast-iron frying pan over a medium heat, then add the coriander and cumin powder and dry-roast until they begin to release their aroma, shaking the pan constantly. Take off the heat.

■ Turn the heat down under the cooking pot to medium and add the dry-roasted spices, the turmeric, and cayenne pepper. Cook, stirring, for 1 minute.

■ Add the yogurt, a spoonful at a time, stirring constantly, then add the tomato and cook, stirring, for 1 minute. Return the chicken pieces to the pot and season with the salt. Cook for 2 minutes, then add 150 ml (¼ pint) water. Stir well.

■ Bring to the boil, cover, lower the heat and simmer gently for 30 minutes, turning the chicken pieces 3 or 4 times.

■ Meanwhile dry-roast the saffron in the cast-iron frying pan, cool slightly, then crumble into the warm milk and leave to soak for 20 minutes.

■ When the chicken is just cooked, add the browned onions and saffron with the infused liquid. Mix well, cover and simmer gently for another 5 minutes.

■ Serve simply with naan and a relish, or as part of a more elaborate meal with rice and other dishes of your choice.

*When I was a child there were only two ways one could buy poultry in India. Either you went to the poultry market where you selected a live bird from a coop, or you would wait for the poultry man to come around, hawking his wares. He might arrive on a bicycle, but more often than not came by foot, carrying a bamboo across his shoulders, bent by the weight of the large wicker baskets hanging at each end. The occupants of these swaying baskets – usually chicken and ducks – could hardly be seen, but could be heard from a distance, squawking, quacking and cackling. One had to know how to pick a bird by feeling its flesh. Experts like my father could even tell the age of a bird by prodding and squeezing in the right places.*

# CHICKEN BIRYANI

## *Biryani* — *INDIA*

Serves 6-8

Biryani is one of our most elaborate rice dishes and is served at Indian weddings and important dinners. It is definitely not an everyday dish. I find it an excellent choice for a late supper party.

Of Moghul origin, biryani is cooked with lamb or chicken, flavoured with aromatic spices – including saffron – and garnished with raisins and nuts. The chicken is first marinated for at least 2 hours in a delicious paste of ginger, garlic, onions, yogurt, lemon juice and spices. It is then cooked briefly. Partially cooked rice is placed over it, and the chicken and rice are allowed to steam for about an hour. As you lift the cover off your casserole dish, you will see the white rice is beautifully streaked with saffron.

There are several garnishes that can be used for biryani; the fried onions are a must; the others are up to you. If you include raisins, fry them in a tablespoon of the reserved oil (see recipe). If you wish to serve a vegetable dish, Cauliflower with Ginger and Coriander (see page 170) would be ideal.

**900 g (2 lb) chicken pieces (legs and breasts)**
**4 cloves garlic**
**5 cm (2 inch) piece fresh root ginger, 2.5 cm (1 inch) wide**
**6 medium onions**
**10 cloves**
**20 black peppercorns**
**seeds from 8 cardamom pods**
**¼ teaspoon ground cinnamon**
**1 teaspoon ground coriander**
**1 teaspoon ground cumin**
**1 teaspoon poppy seeds**
**¼ teaspoon ground mace**
**salt**
**3 tablespoons lemon juice**
**275 g (10 oz) yogurt**
**8 tablespoons vegetable oil**
**2 bay leaves**
**4 large whole black cardamom pods**
**2 teaspoons saffron threads, dry-roasted (see page 17)**
**2 tablespoons milk**
**350 g (12 oz) long-grain rice**

OPTIONAL GARNISHES

**2 tablespoons golden raisins**
**2 tablespoons blanched almonds**
**2 hard-boiled eggs**

■ Remove and discard the skin from the chicken legs and breasts. Cut each leg into drumstick and thigh, and quarter the breasts.

■ To prepare the marinade paste, peel and coarsely chop the garlic, ginger and 3 onions. Place in an electric blender with the cloves, peppercorns, cardamom seeds, cinnamon, coriander, cumin, poppy seeds, mace, 1 teaspoon salt and the lemon juice. Blend to a smooth paste. Turn into a large bowl, add the yogurt and mix well.

■ Peel the 3 remaining onions, halve lengthwise and slice finely. Heat the oil in a large heavy-based frying pan over a medium heat. When hot, add the bay leaves and cardamom pods. Fry for 10-15 seconds. Add the sliced onions and fry, stirring, for about 10 minutes or until brown and crisp, but not burned. Remove with a slotted spoon, squeezing out as much oil as possible. Reserve the oil, cardamoms and bay leaves. Add two thirds of the fried onions to the marinade paste and mix well. Drain the rest on kitchen paper and set aside for garnishing.

■ Pierce the chicken pieces with a fork and add to the bowl of marinade paste; mix well. Cover the bowl and refrigerate for at least 2 hours, preferably overnight, turning the chicken occasionally.

■ Transfer the chicken and marinade to a large heavy-based cooking pot or pan. Bring slowly to the boil, cover, lower the heat and simmer for 15 minutes. Lift out the chicken pieces with a slotted spoon and place them in a 5.7 litre (10 pint) casserole dish; cover and set aside.

■ Preheat the oven to 150°C (300°F) gas mark 2. Crumble the saffron into the warm milk and set aside to soak.

■ Boil the marinade paste, stirring, over a medium heat, until reduced to about 9-10 tablespoons. Spoon the paste over the chicken. Cover again.

■ Pour about 2.8 litres (5 pints) water into a large cooking pot or flameproof casserole. Add 3 teaspoons of salt and bring to the boil. Add the rice, bring back to the boil, then simmer for precisely 5 minutes. Drain the rice in a colander, then place it on top of the chicken in the casserole.

■ Pour the saffron-infused milk over the rice, streaking it with orange lines. Sprinkle the reserved cardamom, bay leaves and oil over the rice (retaining 1 tablespoon oil for frying the raisins if using). Cover the casserole dish with foil, cut 5 cm (2 inches) wider than the rim of the dish. Now put the lid on and use the protruding foil edges to seal the dish as best you can by crinkling it and pushing it against the sides. Bake in the oven for 1 hour.

■ To prepare the garnishes, if including raisins fry them briefly in the reserved oil. Lightly toast the almonds if you wish. Quarter the hard-boiled eggs lengthwise, or cut into slices.

■ Spoon the rice and chicken on to a large warm platter. Sprinkle with the fried onions, raisins, almonds and hard-boiled eggs. Serve hot.

# CHICKEN PATTIES WITH GINGER AND SESAME SEEDS

## *Tak Kogi Sopsanjok* 

*KOREA*

Makes 6 patties

These delightfully seasoned chicken hamburgers are easy to prepare for light informal meals and picnics. While they may be grilled indoors under the kitchen grill or outdoors over charcoal, here I have cooked them in a frying pan.

Boned and skinned minced chicken is required for this dish. I get my butcher to mince a half-and-half combination of light and dark meat for me as that gives the best texture. These patties are normally served with Korean Dipping Sauce and rice. You could, if you like, spoon a generous amount of the sauce over them, then slap them inside a hamburger bun.

- 1 spring onion
- 1 large clove garlic
- 2.5 cm (1 inch) cube fresh root ginger
- 450 g (1 lb) minced chicken
- 1 tablespoon roasted sesame seeds (see page 263)
- 1 tablespoon sesame oil
- 1 tablespoon soy sauce (preferably Japanese *shoyu*)
- freshly ground black pepper
- ¼-½ teaspoon chilli powder
- Korean Dipping Sauce (see page 219)
- 1-2 tablespoons vegetable oil
- fresh coriander sprigs, to garnish (optional)

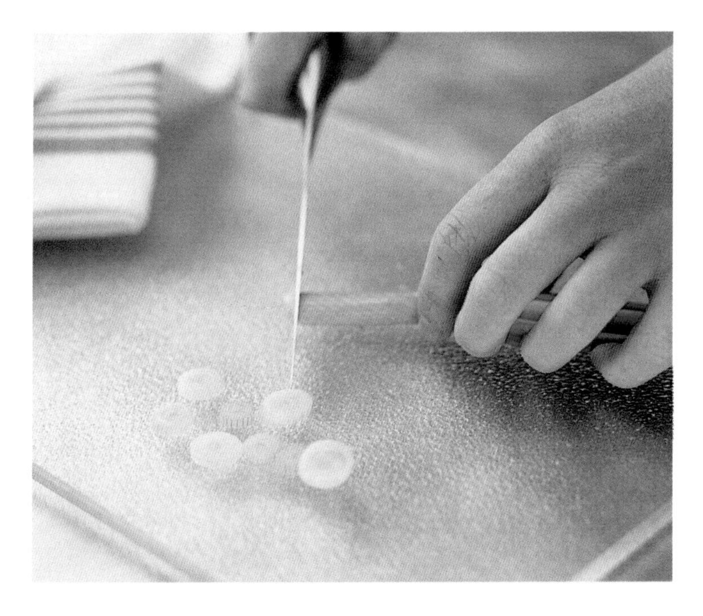

**1** Cut the spring onion crossways into very fine rounds along its entire length, including the green section. Peel and crush the garlic. Peel and finely grate the ginger.

**2** Put the chicken in a bowl. Add the spring onion, garlic, ginger, roasted sesame seeds, sesame oil, soy sauce, black pepper and chilli powder. Mix thoroughly.

**3** Shape the mixture into 6 patties, each about 9 cm (3½ inches) in diameter. Put them in a single layer on a plate and cover with cling film. Set the patties aside until you are ready to eat. Prepare the Korean Dipping Sauce.

**4** Lightly grease a large non-stick frying pan with the oil and set over a medium-high heat. When hot, add the patties and cook for 1-1½ minutes or until golden brown underneath. Turn the patties over and cook the other side for the same time. Turn the heat to medium and cook the patties for a further 1 minute or longer on each side, until browned and cooked through. To test, pierce the centre with the point of a sharp knife – if it is no longer pink inside, the patty is cooked. Serve hot, garnished with sprigs of coriander if you like.

# BON BON CHICKEN

## *Malaji*

*HONG KONG*

Serves 4-6

This spicy dish from the Sichuan province of China takes its name from the sound of the pounding once required to shred the chicken. It tastes superb. It is often served as a first course, though I like to serve it for lunch with a leafy salad.

It is the Sichuan peppercorns that give this dish its special character. You can buy these from Chinese grocers, selected supermarkets, or else send for them by mail order. Even though you could, at a pinch, substitute black peppercorns, Sichuan peppercorns are worth having in your storecupboard. You will find yourself using them crushed in salads, over eggs, over oily fish (such as mackerel) and in hearty meat stews.

The sesame paste – tahini – is sold in larger supermarkets, Asian, Chinese and Greek grocers, as well healthfood shops.

In Hong Kong a whole chicken is steamed, plunged into cold water and then shredded. I simply poach boned and skinned chicken breasts in order to make this dish easy to prepare. Serve Bon Bon Chicken at room temperature, not cold from the refrigerator.

**450 g (1 lb) chicken breasts, boned and skinned**

FOR THE SAUCE

**2.5 cm (1 inch) cube fresh root ginger**

**1 clove garlic**

**2 tablespoons sesame paste (tahini)**

**1 tablespoon sesame oil**

**1 teaspoon sugar**

**2½ teaspoons Chilli Oil (see page 216)**

**4 teaspoons Chinese light soy sauce**

**½ teaspoon roasted and ground Sichuan peppercorns (see page 264)**

YOU ALSO NEED

**1 spring onion**

**3 mm (⅛ inch) slice fresh root ginger**

**salt**

**1 stick celery**

**40 g (1½ oz) fresh coriander (stalks and leaves)**

■ First make the sauce. Peel and finely grate the ginger. Peel and crush the garlic. Combine the ginger, garlic, sesame paste, sesame oil, sugar, chilli oil, soy sauce and roasted and ground Sichuan peppercorns. Mix well.

■ Cut the chicken breasts lengthways into 1 cm (½ inch) wide strips. Put the strips into a medium frying pan. Pour in just enough water to cover them by 5 mm (¼ inch). Add the spring onion, slice of ginger and a generous pinch of salt. Bring to the boil, then immediately turn the heat to low. Simmer very gently and briefly, turning the pieces, until the meat turns white all the way through – this happens very quickly, so keep watching it. Remove the chicken with a slotted spoon and briefly rinse under cold running water; reserve 3 tablespoons poaching liquid. Using both hands, pull the chicken into long shreds; they do not have to be very fine.

■ Finely dice the celery. Wash the coriander and pat dry. Cut the coriander stalks crossways into very fine pieces. Coarsely chop the coriander leaves, cover with cling film and set aside. Add the reserved poaching liquid to the sesame sauce; stir to mix.

■ To serve, combine the chicken, celery, diced coriander stalks and sesame sauce and mix well. Transfer to a serving dish and sprinkle the chopped coriander leaves over the top.

# ROAST CHICKEN WITH FIVE-SPICE POWDER

## *Ga Xoi Mo*

*VIETNAM*

Serves 4

In South Vietnam, this popular dish is traditionally made by first roasting a whole marinated chicken over charcoal to dry it out, and then deep-frying it. Vietnamese friends with Western kitchens take the easy way out and simply roast the whole bird in the oven. That is what I have chosen to do.

Five-spice is a Chinese spice mixture, comprising star anise, fennel, cloves, cinnamon and Sichuan peppercorns. It is sold by Chinese grocers and selected supermarkets in powdered form. For instructions on how to make your own five-spice powder, see page 259.

1.6 kg (3½ lb) whole chicken
2 cloves garlic
25 g (1 oz) onion
2 tablespoons Chinese rice wine or dry sherry
2 tablespoons Chinese light soy sauce
2 tablespoons Chinese dark soy sauce
2 teaspoons sugar
1¼ teaspoons five-spice powder
2 tablespoons sesame oil

TO SERVE
soft lettuce leaves
fresh mint sprigs
Fish Sauce Seasoned with Lime Juice (see page 216)

■ Wash the chicken and pat it dry. Peel the garlic and onion and chop them finely. Combine the garlic, onion, rice wine, the two soy sauces, sugar and five-spice powder in a small bowl. Stir until the sugar has dissolved.

■ Put the chicken in a bowl and rub the marinade generously both inside and all over the outside of the bird. Pour any remaining mixture over the chicken and leave to marinate in a cool place for 2-3 hours. Turn the chicken every 20 minutes or so, to ensure that it absorbs the flavours and colour of the marinade evenly.

■ Preheat the oven to 220°C (425°F) gas mark 7. Lift the chicken out of its marinade and lay it, breast-side down, on a rack set in a roasting tin. Roast for 10 minutes. Brush the back with the marinade and turn the chicken over so that the breast is now facing upwards. Brush the breast with the marinade and roast it for 15 minutes.

■ Brush the chicken with the marinade again, turn the heat down to 180°C (350°F) gas mark 4 and cook for a further 45 minutes, brushing with the marinade every 15-20 minutes.

■ Finally, brush the chicken generously with the sesame oil and cook it for another 2-5 minutes or until the juices run clear when you pierce the thickest part of a thigh with a fork or skewer. Let the chicken rest in a warm place for 10 minutes before carving.

■ Transfer the roast chicken to a serving platter and pour over a little of the seasoned fish sauce. Serve accompanied by the lettuce leaves, mint sprigs and the rest of the sauce. Diners can either use the lettuce leaves to make mint and chicken parcels, Vietnamese style, or simply nibble at them.

# STUFFED WHOLE CHICKEN IN A PARCEL

## *Betutu Ayam*

*INDONESIA*

Serves 4

The Balinese specialize in cooking a whole duck or chicken by smothering it with a spice paste of chillies, shallots and turmeric, wrapping up the bird in banana leaves and baking it slowly over charcoal. It is moist, spicy and very good. My version is cooked in the oven. If I cannot obtain fresh banana leaves, I simply use foil instead – the chicken still tastes delicious. If you are unable to find lemon grass, substitute 1½ tablespoons grated lemon rind, adding it to the blender when mixing the ingredients.

**4½ tablespoons lime or lemon juice**
**1 tablespoon, plus 1 teaspoon dark brown sugar**
**salt**
**½ teaspoon ground turmeric**
**¼ teaspoon chilli powder**
**1.6 kg (3½ lb) whole chicken**
**4 dried hot red chillies**
**1 stick fresh lemon grass**
**225 g (8 oz) red pepper**
**75 g (3 oz) shallots or onions**
**4 cm (1½ inch) cube fresh root ginger**
**8 cloves garlic**
**25 g (1 oz) candlenuts or cashew nuts**
**1½ teaspoons coarsely ground black pepper**
**5 tablespoons vegetable oil**

■ To make the marinade, combine 3 tablespoons of the lime juice, 1 tablespoon sugar, 1 teaspoon salt, the turmeric and chilli powder in a small bowl; mix well.

■ Put the chicken, breast-side down, in a large bowl or deep dish. Cut 4 deep diagonal slits on the back, 2 on each side. Rub some of the lime juice mixture into the slits and all over the back. Turn the chicken over and cut 2 diagonal slits on each side of the breast, 2 slits on the wings, 2 slits on each side of both thighs and 2 slits on each side of both drumsticks.

■ Rub the remaining marinade over the rest of the chicken, working it deeply into all the slits. Set aside to marinate for 40 minutes to 1 hour.

■ Crumble the dried red chillies into a small bowl, add 5 tablespoons water and set aside for 30 minutes.

■ Cut the lemon grass into the thinnest possible slices, starting at the root end and discarding the straw-like top. Deseed and coarsely chop the red pepper. Peel and coarsely chop the shallots, ginger and garlic. Coarsely chop the nuts.

■ Put the red pepper, shallots, ginger, garlic, nuts and remaining 1½ tablespoons lime juice into a blender and blend until smooth. Add 1 teaspoon salt, 1 teaspoon sugar, the black pepper, lemon grass, and red chillies with their soaking liquid. Blend again.

■ Heat the oil in a non-stick frying pan over a medium-high heat. When hot, add the paste from the blender and fry, stirring, for about 15 minutes or until the oil separates from the spices and the paste is a dark reddish-brown.

■ Preheat the oven to 180°C (350°F) gas mark 4. Spread out a few banana leaves on a work surface, overlapping them slightly to form a sheet, or use a large piece of heavy-duty foil about 75 cm (30 inches) long.

■ Put the chicken, breast down, in the centre. Rub about a quarter of the fried spice mixture on to the back of the chicken. Turn the bird over and rub another quarter of the spice mixture over the breast. Stuff the remaining spice mixture inside the chicken. Now wrap the banana leaves around the chicken to enclose, or fold the foil over the bird, crimping the edges together to seal. Put the chicken parcel on a baking tray and bake in the oven for 1¾ hours.

■ Open the parcel carefully and pour out the collected liquid into a small pan; spoon off the fat. Take the stuffing out of the bird and add it to the liquid. Stir to mix, heating it if necessary. Put the chicken in a dish and pour on the hot sauce to serve.

*Many years ago a large banana-leaf package was unwrapped before me on the beach in Bali to reveal a whole cooked chicken, beautifully red and aromatic from all the spices still clinging to it. The chicken was a Balinese speciality and tasted heavenly. There are more than 13,000 islands in Indonesia and each has a different culinary slant. Bali, for example, never turned to Islam as the rest of the nation did, so its inhabitants eat pork and turtle with great enthusiasm.*

# ROAST DUCK STUFFED WITH NUTS AND SPICES

## *Battack Mussallam*

*INDIA*

Serves 2

This duck is stuffed with rice, spices, raisins and nuts to make a superbly festive meal. I find that a 1.75-2 kg (4-4½ lb) duck only really serves 2 adequately.

- 1.8-2 kg (4-4½ lb) whole duck, including liver, gizzard and heart
- 1 medium onion
- 2.5 cm (1 inch) cube fresh root ginger
- 1 hot green chilli, or ⅛-¼ teaspoon cayenne pepper (optional)
- 2 tablespoons vegetable oil
- ½ teaspoon cumin seeds
- ½ teaspoon fennel seeds
- 15 fenugreek seeds
- 1 tablespoon tomato purée
- 3 tablespoons minced or finely chopped fresh coriander leaves
- 2 teacups cooked rice
- 2 tablespoons golden raisins
- 1 tablespoon dried apricots, chopped
- 3 tablespoons pine nuts, or slivered blanched almonds
- salt
- freshly ground black pepper
- 1½ teaspoons lemon juice
- 1½ teaspoons sugar

■ Pick the skin of the duck all over with a fork to allow the fat to be released on cooking. Mince the liver, gizzard and heart.

■ Preheat the oven to 230°C (450°F) gas mark 8.

■ Peel and finely chop the onion. Peel and grate the ginger. Finely slice the green chilli into rings, if using.

■ Heat the oil in a large frying pan over a medium-high heat. Add the cumin, fennel and fenugreek seeds. Stir-fry for 10-20 seconds until the cumin seeds begin to darken, then add the onions, ginger and green chilli if using. Fry, stirring, for about 2 minutes or until the onions are golden brown.

■ Add the minced liver, gizzard and heart. Stir and fry for 1-2 minutes, then add the tomato purée mixed with 2 tablespoons water, and the fresh coriander. Cook, stirring, for 2 minutes, then turn the heat to low and add the cooked rice. Finally mix in the raisins, apricots and pine nuts or almonds. Stir and fry for another 5 minutes. Season with salt, cayenne pepper if using, black pepper, lemon juice and sugar.

■ Stuff the duck loosely with the mixture, then truss and place in a roasting tin, breast up. Roast in the preheated oven for 20-25 minutes until brown; there is no need to baste the duck. Remove the fat with a bulb baster as it accumulates in the roasting tin.

■ Turn the heat to 180°C (350°F) gas mark 4 and cook for a further 1½ hours, or until the juices run a clear yellow when the duck is pricked.

■ Lift the duck on to a warm serving platter. Sprinkle with a little salt and freshly ground pepper. Serve accompanied by green beans or peas, or a leafy salad if you prefer.

# DUCK BRAISED IN WINE

## *Teo Chew-Style Duck*

*MALAYSIA*

Serves 4

Duck is good cooked in most ways but I find that braising – an underused technique for this bird – is the best way to bring out its flavour. All of the meat remains moist; even the bones become tempting to chew. You may make this dish ahead of time and then reheat it. In fact I prefer to do this as it is much easier to de-grease the sauce once it has been chilled. The duck is normally cooked whole in Malaysia. I quarter it only to make it easier to handle – you could ask the butcher to do this for you.

Served with an elegant rice dish and stir-fried greens, such as spinach, this duck becomes decidedly festive.

**1.75 kg (4 lb) duck, quartered**
**¼ teaspoon five-spice powder (optional)**
**2 tablespoons vegetable oil**
**3 cloves garlic**
**6 spring onions**
**450 ml (¾ pint) Chinese rice wine or dry sherry**
**4 tablespoons Chinese dark soy sauce**
**1 tablespoon Chinese light soy sauce**
**3½ tablespoons sugar**
**7.5 cm (3 inch) stick cinnamon**
**½ teaspoon Sichuan peppercorns**
**3 whole star anise**
**8-10 slices fresh or dried galangal, or fresh root ginger**

■ Cut off any parts of the duck that appear to be nothing but skin or fat. Wash the duck and pat it as dry as you can. Dust on both sides with the five-spice powder.

■ Heat the oil in a large frying pan over a high heat. When the oil is hot, put in as many duck pieces as the pan will hold easily, skin-side down. Fry quickly, turning the pieces, so the skin is seared on all sides, then remove with a slotted spoon. Brown all the duck pieces in this way.

■ Peel the garlic cloves and mash them lightly; set aside. Lay the spring onions over the base of a wide pan large enough to hold the duck easily, preferably in one layer. Put the duck pieces on top, skin-side down. Pour the wine and 600 ml (1 pint) water over the duck. Add the garlic and all the remaining ingredients, and bring to a simmer. Cover and simmer for 45 minutes.

■ Turn the duck pieces over and simmer, covered, for a further 45 minutes. Remove the cover and turn the heat up to medium. Turn the duck over again and cook for 6-7 minutes. Turn the duck pieces over a third time and cook for another 6-7 minutes. Using a slotted spoon, carefully lift out the duck pieces and transfer to a plate to cool.

■ Strain the duck broth; you should have about 600 ml (1 pint.) Skim off the fat from the surface if you are serving immediately. If you are preparing a day ahead, cover the duck pieces well once they have cooled and refrigerate. Cool the broth and refrigerate in a covered container.

■ To serve, remove the fat from the surface of the broth, then pour it into a large pan. Add the duck pieces, cover the pan and heat through. Lift the duck pieces out.

■ Arrange the duck pieces on a plate and pour on a little of the broth. Hand the rest of the broth round separately in a sauce boat.

# SAVOURY EGG CUSTARD WITH PRAWNS AND MUSHROOMS

## *Keran Chim*

*KOREA*

Serves 4-5

Savoury egg custards, quivering, soft and soothing, are eaten in many areas of China, Japan and Korea. They can be very delicately flavoured or quite robust in their seasonings. In Japan, where they are called *chawanmushi*, they are steamed in individual cups and served almost as a soup course. In Korea, where most dishes at a meal (except rice) tend to be communal, a large bowl is generally put in the centre of the table and then everyone reaches out with soup spoons. You may serve this custard in any way you like; though, with Western table settings, individual servings are much easier to handle. Incidentally, egg coddlers are ideal for cooking single portions.

To steam *keran chim* properly, the dish containing the custard should never be set on the bottom of your steaming pan. It should be placed on a rack or trivet. Water should come three quarters of the way up its sides and should simmer gently in order to prevent bubbles from forming in the custard. Do not overcook it or the custard might separate. The custard should be cooked just before it is eaten. All the ingredients can, however, be prepared ahead of time but not mixed. The cooking time is 13-25 minutes, depending on the size of dish you use. Koreans, of course, use fresh oyster mushrooms.

**1 clove garlic**
**3 spring onions**
**5 oyster mushrooms, or 6-8 medium ordinary mushrooms**
**100 g (4 oz) uncooked unpeeled prawns**
**5 large eggs**
**600 ml (1 pint) unsalted chicken stock or water**
**1 tablespoon sesame oil**
**¾ teaspoon salt**
**4 teaspoons Japanese soy sauce (*shoyu*)**
**1 tablespoon roasted sesame seeds (see page 263)**

■ Peel and crush the garlic. Cut the spring onions into very fine rounds along their entire length, including the green part. Slice the mushrooms finely.

■ Peel and de-vein the prawns, wash and pat them dry. Cut the prawns crossways into 1 cm (½ inch) sections.

■ Beat the eggs lightly in a bowl. Add the chicken stock or water, the sesame oil, salt and soy sauce. Mix well, then strain through a fine sieve into another bowl.

■ Set some water to heat in a wok, large saucepan or steamer wide enough to hold a custard bowl or individual egg coddlers easily. (Remember that the bowl in which you cook will also be your serving bowl.) Bring the water to a simmer. Set a rack or trivet on the bottom of your steaming pan.

■ Stir the egg mixture again and add the garlic, spring onions, mushrooms and prawns to it. Pour the mixture into the custard bowl or spoon evenly into the coddlers. Sprinkle the roasted sesame seeds over the surface.

■ Cover (with a plate if using a bowl, or foil for individual containers), then stand on the rack. The simmering water should come three quarters of the way up the sides of the container(s), so top it up if necessary. Cover the steaming pan and simmer gently for 13-25 minutes. To test whether the custard is set, insert a knife in the centre – it should come out clean. If it does not, cook for another minute or so. Carefully remove the custard dish(es) from the water and serve.

# EGG CURRY

## *Gulai Telor*

*MALAYSIA*

Serves 6-8

Here is one of my favourite egg curries. It is hot and spicy, and quite typical of Malaysian food. Served with plain rice and a salad, it is perfect for a Sunday lunch. I have even been known to serve it with crusty bread or with thick toast. In Malaysia the spices are pounded very finely on stone. Since I can never quite manage to get the same effect in a blender, I strain the coarse particles out of the curry sauce before putting the eggs into it.

A note about the hotness of this dish: in Malaysia, it is prepared with 20-30 dried red chillies, and is certainly hot. I tone it down by using 10-15 chillies and I would describe my dish as fairly hot. You may use as few as 2 chillies, if you want it very mild. The fresh red and green chillies added at the end are more of a garnish than anything else. They give the dish a Malaysian look. If fresh red chillies are unavailable, simply use twice as many green ones. You may use slivers cut from fresh red and green peppers, if you prefer. If you cannot get lemon grass, use 1 tablespoon of grated lemon rind, adding it to the curry at the same time as the tomato. This curry may be made a day in advance, refrigerated and then reheated.

**2-15 dried hot red chillies, to taste**
**½ teaspoon black peppercorns**
**2 tablespoons coriander seeds**
**1 stick fresh lemon grass**
**4 cm (1½ inch) cube fresh root ginger**
**4 cm (1½ inch) cube fresh galangal (optional)**
**¾ teaspoon ground turmeric**
**18 eggs**
**90 g (3½ oz) shallots or onions**
**5 cloves garlic**
**9 tablespoons vegetable oil**
**1 litre (1¾ pints) coconut milk (see page 258)**
**3 tablespoons tamarind paste (see page 264), or 2 tablespoons lime juice**
**2½ teaspoons salt**
**1 teaspoon sugar**

**TO SERVE**
**275 g (10 oz) tomatoes**
**4 fresh hot green chillies**
**4 fresh hot red chillies**
**fresh mint leaves, to garnish**

■ Crumble the dried red chillies into a bowl. Add the peppercorns, coriander seeds and about 350 ml (12 fl oz) water. Leave to soak for at least 1 hour.

■ Slice the lemon grass crossways very finely, starting at the bulbous end and going up about 6 inches (15 cm). Discard the straw-like top. Peel and coarsely chop the ginger and galangal if using.

■ Put the soaked ingredients and soaking liquor in a blender with the lemon grass, ginger, galangal if using, and the turmeric. Blend thoroughly, adding a few tablespoons of water if needed to give a paste-like consistency.

■ Put all the eggs in a large pan. Add water to cover well and bring to the boil. Turn the heat to very low and simmer for 10-12 minutes until the eggs are hard-boiled. Shell them under cold running water.

■ Peel and finely slice the shallots and garlic. Heat the oil in a large, wide, preferably non-stick pan over a medium-high heat. Add the shallots and garlic, and fry, stirring, until golden.

■ Add the paste from the blender. Stir and fry for about 10 minutes or until the oil separates and the paste darkens. Stir the coconut milk and pour it in. Add the tamarind paste (or lime juice), salt and sugar. Mix well and adjust the seasoning if necessary. Bring to a simmer, stirring, then immediately turn off the heat.

■ Strain the sauce through a sieve, pushing out as much liquid as possible. Return the sauce to the pan and add the hard-boiled eggs. (The dish can be prepared to this stage a day ahead and refrigerated.)

■ Cut the tomatoes into small wedges or chop them. Just before serving, bring the egg curry to a simmer. Stir in the tomatoes and bring back to a simmer. Transfer the curry to a serving bowl and garnish with fresh chillies and mint leaves.

# meat

# SPICY BEEF SALAD

## *Laab*

*THAILAND*

Serves 4

*Laab* is an exquisite Thai salad that comes from the north-east part of the country, an area that borders Laos. The beef is sometimes left raw or it may be quickly stirred in a very hot wok so it is 'rare' – as I have cooked it here. It is then magically seasoned with sliced shallots, lime juice and mint. There is a secret ingredient that binds the salad and gives it a nutty aroma. It is rice – rice that has been roasted and ground!

A plate of *laab* usually has the seasoned meat on one side and a whole forest of fresh herbs and raw vegetables on the other. The two are then eaten together, the spicy meat nicely balanced by the crisp vegetables. Incidentally, you may also make this salad with leftover roast beef. Cut it into very thin slices and then cut the slices into 2.5 x 5 cm (1 x 2 inch) strips. You do not, of course, need to cook them.

**FOR THE SPICED BEEF**

**3 tablespoons long-grain rice**

**450 g (1 lb) good-quality tender beef steak**

**65 g (2½ oz) shallots or onions (preferably red)**

**2 cloves garlic**

**2 tablespoons vegetable oil**

**4 tablespoons lime or lemon juice**

**4 tablespoons fish sauce, or salt to taste**

**1 tablespoon sugar**

**¼ teaspoon chilli powder**

**25 g (1 oz) fresh mint leaves**

**1 fresh hot red or green chilli**

**FOR THE SALAD**

**about 12 crisp inner leaves of iceberg, cos, or other crisp lettuce**

**4-8 fresh mint sprigs**

**225 g (8 oz) fresh bean sprouts**

**12 tender green beans, or about 8 long beans**

**7 fresh hot red chillies, or 1 red pepper**

■ First prepare the salad. Wash the lettuce and pat dry. Remove any large coarse stems from the mint; otherwise leave in sprigs. Wash these and pat dry. Refrigerate the lettuce and mint in separate polythene bags.

■ Top and tail the bean sprouts (see page 256) if you prefer. Wash, then immerse in a bowl of cold water and set aside.

■ Wash and trim the beans; cut long ones into thirds. Blanch the beans in boiling water for about 1 minute to soften slightly; they should still be crisp and bright green. Immediately refresh in cold water, then drain, cover and refrigerate. Deseed the red chillies or pepper and cut into long strips. Cover and refrigerate.

■ Set a small cast-iron frying pan over a medium-high heat. When it is hot, add the rice and cook, stirring, for 2-3 minutes until the grains turn golden; some might even pop. Remove from the pan, cool slightly, then put the rice into a clean coffee-grinder or mortar and pulverise it.

■ Mince the steak or cut it into small dice. Peel the shallots and cut into very fine, long slivers. Peel the garlic and chop it finely.

■ Just before eating, place a wok on a high heat. When hot, swirl in the oil. When the oil is hot, add the meat and stir-fry for about 30 seconds; it should still be rare. Lift out with a slotted spoon and put it into a bowl. Add the rice, shallots, garlic, lime juice, fish sauce, sugar and chilli powder. Chop the mint leaves coarsely, finely slice the chilli, then add both to the mixture. Mix well and check the seasoning.

■ Put the beef mixture in a bowl on one side of a large serving plate. Drain the bean sprouts thoroughly. Arrange the salad attractively on the other side of the plate.

# MARINATED AND GRILLED BEEF STRIPS

## *Bulgogi*

*KOREA*

Serves 4

In Korea, this popular dish is typically cooked in a special *bulgogi* grill, over gas or charcoal, either at the table or outdoors. The grill itself is usually portable and varies from a ridged, heavy, metal plate that is raised in the centre, to a more conventional cross-hatched surface. Since I do not have a *bulgogi* grill, I use a large, well-heated, cast-iron frying pan. I happen to have a 35 cm (14 inch) pan that is perfect for the job but a smaller one will do. You could also cook the meat, spread out, under a very hot grill.

In Korea thin slices of meat, marinated in a mixture of soy sauce, sugar, spring onions, ginger and garlic, are flung over the fire. Diners cook the meat themselves, turning it over with their chopsticks until it is cooked to their liking. Other ingredients can be added to the marinade as well, such as roasted sesame seeds and pear. This is the hard, round and very crisp 'pear-apple' that is found in Korea and China. It has a mellowing, softening effect on a mixture of somewhat sharper flavours. I use any hard pear that is available and find that it works well as a substitute.

This beef is usually eaten with rice, Cabbage Pickle (see page 226) and vegetables such as Seasoned Spinach (see page 179) or Stir-Fried Courgettes with Sesame Seeds (see page 167). Sometimes soft lettuce leaves are served on the side for diners to make small packages of the meat, rice and vegetables. A package is usually dipped in soy sauce before it is eaten.

**500 g (1¼ lb) lean tender beef steak**
**½ very firm pear**
**4-5 cloves garlic**
**5 cm (2 inch) cube fresh root ginger**
**4 tablespoons Japanese soy sauce (*shoyu*)**
**5 medium mushrooms**
**120 g (4½ oz) onions**
**3 spring onions**
**1 medium carrot**
**2 tablespoons sesame oil**
**1 tablespoon roasted sesame seeds (see page 263)**
**2½ tablespoons sugar**

■ Cut the meat against the grain into 7.5 x 5 cm (3 x 2 inch) rectangles that are about 3 mm (⅛ inch) thick.

■ Peel, core and coarsely chop the pear half. Peel the garlic and ginger and chop them coarsely. Put the pear, garlic, ginger and soy sauce into an electric blender and blend until smooth.

■ Thinly slice the mushrooms. Peel and thickly slice the onions. Cut the spring onions into 6 cm (2½ inch) lengths. Peel the carrot and cut into 6 cm (2½ inch) lengths, then cut these lengthways into 3 mm (⅛ inch) slices.

■ Put the meat in a bowl. Add the paste from the blender, the mushrooms, onions, spring onions, carrot, sesame oil, sesame seeds and sugar. Mix well. Cover and set aside to marinate for at least 1 hour, or up to 24 hours if possible, refrigerating as necessary.

■ Set a large cast-iron frying pan on a high heat. When it is very hot, add as many of the meat slices as will fit in one layer and cook briefly, turning them over as soon as they brown slightly. Once the meat is cooked 'rare', or according to taste, transfer to a warm plate; keep warm. Cook all of the meat in this way.

■ Then put the vegetables and marinade into the pan and cook, stirring, over a high heat for 1-2 minutes. Spoon over or beside the meat and serve immediately.

*Koreans have a great fondness for beef, especially bulgogi. Now, with prosperity high and the price of beef reasonable, it isn't uncommon to find bulgogi cooked in a Korean home. Otherwise, there are restaurants a-plenty scattered across the length and breadth of the land that specialize in bulgogi and, like magnets, draw eager customers to their smoke-filled rooms. The marinated and grilled-at-the-table beef strips hiss and sizzle in front of the diners, teasing them with their heavenly aroma.*

# EASY BEEF KEBABS

## *Bo Nuong Cha*

*VIETNAM*

Serves 4

All types of grilled kebabs enjoy great popularity in Vietnam. Here is a very simple version. You could serve this dish with a green salad of lettuce, cucumber, fresh coriander and mint leaves, and encourage guests to make little packages – Vietnamese-style – using the lettuce leaves as wrappings. Fresh rice noodles are generally served on the side in Vietnam. You could serve dried rice noodles or rice itself.

450 g (1 lb) rump steak or beef skirt
4 cloves garlic
50 g (2 oz) onions
2 tablespoons fish sauce
1½ teaspoons Chinese light soy sauce

TO SERVE
4 tablespoons crushed Roasted Peanuts (see page 223)
Fish Sauce with Vinegar and Lime Juice (see page 217)

■ Hold a large knife at a 135° angle to your work surface (45° for left-handers) and cut the piece of meat against the grain into very thin slices (ie on a slight diagonal). Cut these slices into 2.5 cm (1 inch) long pieces and put them in a bowl.

■ Peel the garlic and onions and chop them very finely. Add these to the meat together with the fish sauce and soy sauce. Mix well and set aside for 1-2 hours.

■ Preheat an indoor grill or an outdoor charcoal grill. Thread the meat fairly tightly on to 2-4 skewers depending on their length. Grill about 13 cm (5 inches) from the heat source for about 5 minutes on one side, then turn and cook on the other side for 3-4 minutes.

■ Serve the meat on or off the skewers, sprinkled with some crushed roasted peanuts and accompanied by the Fish Sauce with Vinegar and Lime Juice. Each diner pours a little of the seasoned fish sauce over their meat.

*What really distinguishes Vietnam's food from its neighbours' is its use of fresh herbs. Mounds are used for each meal. Every mouthful becomes a little perfumed package. If, say, a piece of fish cooked in coconut milk is to be eaten, a portion is put into a piece of lettuce. This is topped with fresh coriander, mints, basils, spring onions and peanuts. It is wrapped up, dipped in a sauce and then eaten. The same happens to a piece of meat that has been marinated with garlic, shallots and perhaps lemon grass; and to small, bite-sized spring rolls. Aromatic herbs keep exploding in the mouth, each fresher than the last.*

# NAPOLEON BEEF ON A SKEWER

## *Thit Bo Lui*

*VIETNAM*

Serves 4

Many Vietnamese in Hanoi refer to this dish either as *boeuf brochette or boeuf Napoleon.* (I suppose it is the sort of thing an army on the move might cook!) Thin slices of meat are marinated in a mixture of fried spices, skewered and then grilled over charcoal or wood.

The meat is then taken off the skewer and put on to a plate. It is eaten, as many other Vietnamese dishes are, in little packages. You take a soft lettuce leaf and put a few pieces of meat on it. On top of the meat you put a few fresh mint leaves, a few small sprigs of fresh coriander, a few fresh bean sprouts, some sliced spring onion, some cucumber slices, some fried shallots and some crushed roasted peanuts. Next you wrap the lettuce leaf round all this to form a bundle, dip the bundle into Fish Sauce Seasoned with Lime Juice – and eat it.

If you do not feel like making packages, there is another way of serving the meat, a method that I use quite frequently. I put only ½ teaspoon of salt in the marinade. When the meat is cooked, I take it off the skewers and put it on a plate. I drizzle Fish Sauce Seasoned with Lime Juice over it generously, then scatter crushed roasted peanuts and some crisp-fried shallot flakes on the top. With this I serve a side salad of lettuce, cucumbers, ripe tomatoes, fresh mint and fresh coriander.

All the cooking in north Vietnam seems to be done in lard. I have used vegetable oil here, but use lard if you wish.

**1 stick fresh lemon grass**
**90 g (3½ oz) onion**
**75 g (3 oz) red pepper**
**1 teaspoon salt**
**freshly ground black pepper**
**¼ teaspoon chilli powder, or to taste**
**4 tablespoons vegetable oil**
**450 g (1 lb) lean steak, about 2.5 cm (1 inch) thick**

TO SERVE

**about 12 crisp inner leaves of iceberg, cos, or other crisp lettuce (optional)**
**some sliced spring onion (optional)**
**cucumber slices (optional)**
**few fresh mint leaves (optional)**
**few small fresh coriander sprigs (optional)**
**few fresh bean sprouts (optional)**
**Crisply Fried Shallot Flakes (page 227)**
**Roasted Peanuts (page 223), crushed**
**Fish Sauce Seasoned with Lime Juice (page 216)**

■ Slice the fresh lemon grass crossways as thinly as possible, starting at the bulbous end and going up about 15 cm (6 inches). Discard the straw-like top.

■ Peel and coarsely chop the onion. Deseed and coarsely chop the red pepper. Combine the lemon grass, onion, red pepper, salt, black pepper and chilli powder in an electric blender. Blend to a smooth paste, adding a few tablespoons of water if necessary.

■ Put the oil in a medium, preferably non-stick, frying pan and set it over a fairly high heat. When the oil is hot, add the paste from the blender. Stir and fry for 6-8 minutes or until the paste has darkened in colour; lower the heat towards the end of this cooking time to avoid over-browning if necessary. Leave the paste to cool.

■ Hold a large knife at a 135° angle to your work surface (45° for left-handers) and cut the piece of meat against the grain into very thin slices (ie at a slight diagonal). Cut these slices into 2.5 cm (1 inch) pieces and put into a bowl.

■ Add the paste and oil from the frying pan and mix well. Cover and set aside to marinate for at least 1 hour, or up to 24 hours if possible, refrigerating as necessary. (You may put the meat on its skewers before you set it aside, if that is more convenient.)

■ Wash and dry the salad leaves and herbs, if using. Wash the bean sprouts and immerse in a bowl of cold water until ready to use, then drain thoroughly. Arrange the salad and herbs, if using, on a serving plate.

■ Preheat an indoor grill or an outdoor charcoal grill. Thread the meat fairly tightly on to 2-4 skewers – the number of skewers required will depend upon their length. Grill the meat about 13 cm (5 inches) from the heat source for about 5 minutes on one side, then turn and cook on the opposite side for 3-4 minutes. Serve as suggested (above, left).

# MEATBALL SOUP

## *Wanja Kuk*

*KOREA*

Serves 4-5

A soupy dish in Korea is not always a soup, as we understand it. This meatball soup, for example, is fairly substantial and is usually served as one of the main dishes at a meal that might also include grilled and stir-fried foods. The meatballs here are quite delicate and light. The reason is bean curd – lots of it – which is mashed and combined with minced beef. This results in soft meatballs, the softest you will probably ever encounter.

When I want a light meal, I serve this mild, gentle soup by itself, with just a green salad on the side for added balance and crunch.

**150-175 g (5-6 oz) bean curd**
**2 cloves garlic**
**4 spring onions**
**225 g (8 oz) minced lean beef**
**1 tablespoon Japanese soy sauce (*shoyu*)**
**2 teaspoons sesame oil**
**2 teaspoons roasted sesame seeds (see page 263)**
**1 cm (½ inch) cube fresh root ginger**
**1.1 litres (2 pints) chicken or beef stock**
**salt**
**65 g (2½ oz) plain flour**
**1 egg**

■ Put the bean curd in the centre of a muslin cloth. Gather the ends together and squeeze out as much moisture from it as you can. Then mash the bean curd with a fork or push it through a sieve.

■ Peel the garlic and chop it very finely. Cut 2 spring onions crossways into very fine rounds.

■ In a bowl, combine the bean curd, garlic, sliced spring onions, minced beef, soy sauce, sesame oil and sesame seeds. Mix thoroughly. With dampened hands, shape the mixture into about 20 meatballs.

■ Cut the remaining spring onions into 5 cm (2 inch) lengths. Peel the ginger and cut into thin slices. Put the stock in a large pan and add the spring onions and ginger. Bring to the boil, lower the heat and simmer gently for 8-10 minutes. Season the stock with salt to taste and leave it simmering very gently.

■ Put the flour on to a plate. Break the egg into a shallow bowl and beat lightly. Roll each meatball first in the flour and then in the egg, and finally drop it into the simmering soup. Once all the meatballs are added, continue to simmer for another 5 minutes.

■ Remove the ginger slices before serving if wished.

# BEEF CHUNKS COOKED IN COCONUT MILK

## *Kaliyo or Rendang Daging* — *INDONESIA*

Serves 4

This is perhaps the most loved dish in Muslim West Sumatra, indeed in all of Indonesia. Large chunks of beef (sometimes water buffalo) are cooked slowly in a mixture of coconut milk and spices until all the liquid disappears and the meat takes on an inviting, dark, dry look. No wedding or festive occasion is ever without a *rendang*. Indeed, every time I was feted it appeared on the menu, much to my delight. Once it was even cooked over wood, which gave it a deliciously complex flavour.

Almost a sister to *rendang* is *kaliyo*. It is exactly the same dish, only in a slightly earlier stage of preparation when the meat still has a nicely thickened sauce clinging to it. I love *rendang*, but I have a passion for *kaliyo*. Its sauce goes so well with the accompanying rice. It also takes less time to cook! This recipe is for both *kaliyo* and *rendang*.

*Rendang is cooked for Indonesian weddings and feasts. It also keeps well and is often taken by Sumatran travellers on long journeys. Made with lots of coconut milk and flavoured with lemon grass and chillies, it cooks long and slow until most of the liquid is gone. It is a quite outstanding dish and the best example of West Sumatra's spicy style of food.*

**4-6 dried hot red chillies**
**5 cm (2 inch) stick cinnamon**
**12-14 cloves**
**2 sticks fresh lemon grass**
**7.5 cm (3 inch) cube fresh galangal**
**90 g (3½ oz) shallots or onions**
**2.5 cm (1 inch) cube fresh root ginger**
**7-8 cloves garlic**
**100 g (4 oz) red pepper**
**12 fresh or dried curry leaves, or 4 dried bay leaves**
**8 fresh or dried kaffir lime leaves**
**1.6 litres (2¾ pints) coconut milk (see page 258)**
**1 kg (2 lb) stewing beef**
**1¼ teaspoons salt**

■ Crumble or break the dried red chillies and cinnamon into a bowl, add the cloves and enough water to cover. Leave to soak for 30 minutes.

■ Cut off and discard the straw-like top of the fresh lemon grass, leaving about 15 cm (6 inches) of the stalk. Lightly crush the bulbous end with a mallet or other heavy object and set aside.

■ Peel and coarsely chop the fresh galangal, shallots, ginger and garlic. Core, deseed and chop the red pepper.

■ In an electric blender, combine the soaked spices and their liquid, the red pepper, galangal, shallots, ginger and garlic. Blend until smooth.

■ Put the paste from the blender, the fresh lemon grass, curry leaves and kaffir lime leaves into a wide, preferably non-stick, pan. Stir the coconut milk until smooth, then add that too. Bring just to the boil, stirring occasionally. Turn the heat to medium and cook for 15 minutes, stirring now and then to prevent the sauce curdling.

■ Cut the meat into 4-5 cm (1½-2 inch) cubes. Add to the sauce with the salt and bring back to the boil. Reduce the heat to medium. Cook, uncovered, for 1 hour, stirring from time to time. Turn the heat up to medium-high and continue to cook, stirring now and then, for 30 minutes or until the sauce is very thick and brown and the meat tender. (If the sauce begins to splatter too much at any stage, partially cover the pan for that period.) At this stage you have *kaliyo*.

■ To make *rendang*, continue to stir and cook until all of the sauce has disappeared.

# SICHUAN SHREDDED BEEF WITH CARROTS AND CHILLIES

## *Gongbao Niuliu*

*HONG KONG*

Serves 3-4

In this spicy, slightly sweet, slightly sour dish, beef and carrot shreds are fried until they turn a bit crisp. They are then stir-fried with hot chillies and spring onions and doused with a light mixture of vinegar, soy sauce and sugar. The result is quite spectacular.

350 g (12 oz) lean beef steak

FOR THE MARINADE
2½ teaspoons Chinese light soy sauce
1 small egg white
1 teaspoon cornflour
1½ teaspoons sesame oil

YOU ALSO NEED
350 g (12 oz) carrots
2 cloves garlic
3-4 fresh hot red or green chillies
4 spring onions
2½ teaspoons Chinese rice wine or dry sherry
1½ teaspoons distilled white vinegar
2½ teaspoons sugar
1 teaspoon Chinese light soy sauce
2 teaspoons Chinese dark soy sauce
vegetable oil for deep-frying
1 teaspoon cornflour

**1** Cut the beef against the grain into wafer-thin slices about 1.5 mm (1/16 inch) in width. Then stack a few slices at a time together and cut the meat into thin strips about 6-7.5 cm (2½-3 inches) long. Put the meat in a bowl. Add all the marinade ingredients and mix well, ensuring that you break up the egg white. Cover and leave to marinate for 1-2 hours, refrigerating if necessary.

**2** Peel the carrots and cut them into long thin julienne strips, the same size as the beef. Peel and finely chop the garlic. Cut the chillies lengthways into fine strips. Cut the spring onions into 7.5 cm (3 inch) lengths, then shred them lengthways with the tip of a sharp knife into long fine strips.

Combine the rice wine, vinegar, sugar, light and dark soy sauces in a cup. Mix well and set aside.

**3** Heat a 4 cm (1½ inch) depth of oil in a wok on a medium heat. Add the carrots and stir-fry for 5 minutes or until slightly crisp; remove with a slotted spoon. Add the beef, turn off the heat and stir until the pieces are separate and just turned white. To achieve this you may need a low heat. With a slotted spoon transfer the meat to a bowl. Sprinkle with the cornflour and toss well. Increase the heat to high. Return the meat to the wok and stir-fry for 30 seconds. Turn into a strainer set over a bowl; reserve the oil. Drain the meat on kitchen paper.

**4** Put 2 tablespoons of the reserved oil into the cleaned wok or large frying pan and set it on a high heat. When hot, add the garlic. Stir and fry for 30 seconds or until it is lightly browned. Put in the chillies, stir once, then add the spring onions. Stir quickly, then add the meat and carrots. Stir-fry for 30 seconds, then add the rice wine sauce. Stir rapidly for about 30 seconds. Serve at once.

# AROMATIC AND SPICY BEEF STEW

## *Thit Bo Kho*

*VIETNAM*

Serves 6

Although we may not associate hearty stews with East Asia, they are, of course, cooked and eaten there. This stew is, perhaps, Vietnam's *boeuf bourguignon*. Familiar seasonings include black pepper and cinnamon – technically cassia bark, a member of the cinnamon family that is used in China and Vietnam. Flavourings such as lemon grass, star anise and yellow bean sauce are not ones we usually add to stews, but they give this recipe its Eastern aroma and taste. The yellow bean sauce used here is the one sold as whole or crushed yellow bean sauce.

In Vietnam, this stew is eaten either with rice or with hunks of crusty French bread that is sold in all markets.

**1.5 kg (3 lb) stewing beef**
**2 medium onions**
**5 cloves garlic**
**10-12 medium shallots or pickling onions**
**1 stick fresh lemon grass**
**7 tablespoons vegetable oil**
**6 tablespoons yellow bean sauce**
**½-1 teaspoon chilli powder**
**4 whole star anise**
**2.5 cm (1 inch) stick cinnamon**
**½ teaspoon black peppercorns**
**2 tablespoons sugar**

■ Cut the beef into 2.5 cm (1 inch) cubes and set aside.

■ Peel and finely chop the onions and garlic. Peel the shallots, but leave whole. Cut the lemon grass into 5 cm (2 inch) sections, from the bottom to about 15 cm (6 inches) from the top; cut off and discard the straw-like top. Crush each section lightly with a mallet or other heavy object.

■ Heat 3 tablespoons of the oil in a non-stick frying pan over a medium-high heat. Add the onions, garlic and shallots, and stir-fry for 2 minutes. Add the lemon grass and continue to fry, stirring, until the onions are lightly browned. Turn off the heat. Take the shallots out of the pan and set aside.

■ Heat the remaining 4 tablespoons oil in a large, wide, preferably non-stick pan over a high heat. When hot, quickly fry the meat cubes in batches, turning to brown them on all sides. Remove with a slotted spoon. Brown all the meat in this way.

■ Return all the meat to the large pan. Add 1 litre (1¾ pints) water and the garlic mixture. Coarsely chop the beans in the yellow bean sauce (if not already crushed) and add them too. Also put in the chilli powder, star anise, cinnamon, peppercorns and sugar. Bring to the boil, then cover, lower the heat and simmer gently for 1¼ hours.

■ Add the reserved shallots, cover again and simmer for a further 15 minutes. Remove the lid, increase the heat to medium and cook for a further 15-20 minutes or until the sauce has thickened a little and the meat is tender. Skim the fat off the top of the stew before serving.

# EASY BEEF CURRY

## *Kaeng Phet Nua*

*THAILAND*

Serves 4

This is a perfect dish to serve at a small dinner party. I use beef skirt to make it, as it is such a tender cut of meat and requires very little cooking. I stand at the cooker for about 12 minutes only, 8 minutes of which are spent frying the spices, and the other 4 minutes cooking the beef. If you cannot get kaffir lime leaves use a 7.5 x 1 cm (3 x ½ inch) strip of lemon rind, cut into fine julienne strips. Put it into the curry at the same time as the mint and basil leaves.

**450 g (1 lb) beef skirt**
**120-150 g (4½-5 oz) red pepper**
**100 g (4 oz) onions**
**4 large cloves garlic**
**1 teaspoon shrimp or anchovy paste**
**½ teaspoon chilli powder**
**8 tablespoons vegetable oil**
**2 tablespoons fish sauce**
**250 ml (8 fl oz) coconut milk (see page 258)**
**½ teaspoon salt**
**4 fresh or dried kaffir lime leaves, or lemon rind (see above)**
**10-15 fresh basil leaves**
**10-15 fresh mint leaves**

■ Cut the beef against the grain into pieces 5-7.5 cm (2-3 inches) long, 2.5 cm (1 inch) wide and 2-3 mm (1/10-1/8 inch) thick. If you have bought the meat in a long, thin, continuous piece, first cut it into 7.5 cm (3 inch) segments, then cut each of these against the grain, holding the knife at a 135° angle to your work surface. This will give you the required width.

■ Core, deseed and coarsely chop the red pepper. Peel and coarsely chop the onions and garlic. Combine the red pepper, onions, garlic, shrimp paste and chilli powder in an electric blender. Blend to a smooth paste, adding a tablespoon or so of water to mix if necessary.

■ Heat the oil in a wide shallow saucepan or frying pan over a medium-high heat. When hot, put in the spice paste from the blender. Stir and fry for 7-8 minutes or until the paste turns dark and separates from the oil. Add the meat and the fish sauce. Stir and cook for 2 minutes.

■ Stir the coconut milk and add that, together with the salt. Add the kaffir lime leaves – tearing them in half and removing the central vein before adding if the leaves are fresh. Coarsely tear the basil and mint leaves, and add these too. Stir once, turn off the heat and serve.

*Thai curries are exquisite and vary throughout the country. The North, where pork reigns supreme, serves a dark and hearty Indo-Burmese-style curry, filled with large chunks of meat, which is eaten with little balls of hard glutinous rice. The South softens its curries with coconut milk, uses many more fresh herbs and cuts its meats (or prawns or chicken) into small pieces.*

# BEEF AND ONION CURRY

## *Daging Nasi Kandar* — *MALAYSIA*

Serves 4

This origin of this dish is interesting. *Daging* is beef, *nasi* is rice and as far as *kandar* is concerned – well, therein lies a tale. Early Indian settlers often turned to hawking as a means of living. They would suspend two baskets from each end of a pole and balance the pole across their shoulders or kandar. Among the most popular items sold from these baskets was a combination of dishes known as *nasi kandar* or 'rice meal on a shoulder'. There was rice, of course, a fish curry, hard-boiled eggs and this beef curry which provided a thick sauce to ladle over the eggs too. You are unlikely to find these vendors today, but *nasi kandar* is still a speciality in restaurants.

This curry is ideal for preparing ahead of time – simply reheat to serve. You can make it as mild or hot as you like by adjusting the number of chillies.

**1 kg (2 lb) stewing beef**
**6-16 dried hot red chillies**
**2 sticks fresh lemon grass**
**750 g (1½ lb) onions**
**150 ml (¼ pint) vegetable oil**
**5 tablespoons black bean sauce**
**5 cm (2 inch) stick cinnamon**
**20 curry leaves (optional)**
**3 tablespoons tamarind paste (see page 264), or 2 tablespoons lime or lemon juice**
**1 tablespoon sugar**
**salt**

■ Cut the beef into 4 cm (1½ inch) cubes and set aside.

■ Crumble the chillies into a small bowl. Add 4 tablespoons hot water and leave to soak for 30 minutes. Put the chillies and soaking liquid into a blender and blend until smooth.

■ Cut the lemon grass sticks into 15 cm (6 inch) lengths, starting from the bottom. Discard the straw-like top. Crush the bulbous bottoms of the lemon grass lightly.

■ Peel and finely slice the onions. Heat the oil in a large wide pan over a medium-high heat. Add half of the sliced onions and fry, stirring, for about 15 minutes or until the onions are reddish brown and crisp. (You will probably need to turn the heat down to medium after about 4-5 minutes.) Remove the onions with a slotted spoon and spread them out on a plate lined with kitchen paper; set aside.

■ Put the chilli paste from the blender into the pan. Stir and fry for 30 seconds. Add the remaining sliced onions and fry, stirring, for about 5 minutes or until they are soft. Add the black bean sauce and stir for 30 seconds.

■ Add the meat, cinnamon stick, curry leaves (if using), tamarind paste (or lime or lemon juice), sugar, lemon grass sticks and 900 ml (1½ pints) water. Stir and bring to the boil. Cover, lower the heat and simmer gently for 1¼ hours or until the meat is almost done. Season with salt to taste.

■ Increase the heat and cook, uncovered, for 10 minutes to reduce the sauce until it is quite thick. Stir in the onions, turn the heat to medium and cook for a further 2 minutes. Remove the lemon grass and cinnamon stick before serving.

# KHEEMA WITH FRIED ONIONS

## *Kheema*

*INDIA*

Serves 6

This is easily my favourite *kheema* recipe. Nutmeg, mace and yogurt are added to the meat for a slight variation. Peas can also be included if you like. Add 1 cup freshly shelled (or frozen) peas to the *kheema* 10 minutes before the end of the cooking time and continue to simmer for 5-10 minutes until the peas are tender.

3 onions
2.5 cm (1 inch) cube fresh root ginger
5 cloves garlic
1 medium tomato
4 tablespoons vegetable oil
2 bay leaves
7.5 cm (3 inch) stick cinnamon
6 cloves
1 tablespoon ground coriander
1 tablespoon ground cumin
1 tablespoon ground turmeric
2 tablespoons yogurt
900 g (2 lb) lean minced lamb or beef
½ teaspoon ground mace
½ teaspoon ground nutmeg
1 teaspoon salt
¼-½ teaspoon cayenne pepper (optional)

■ Peel the onions and finely chop two of them. Peel and finely chop the ginger. Peel and crush the garlic. Peel and chop the tomato.

■ Halve and thinly slice the other onion into half-rings. Heat the oil in a large heavy-based frying pan over a medium heat. Add the sliced onion and fry for about 5 minutes until dark brown, but not burned. Remove with a slotted spoon and drain on kitchen paper; set aside.

■ Add the bay leaves, cinnamon and cloves to the hot oil. When the bay leaves begin to darken and the cinnamon starts uncurling slightly, add the chopped onions, ginger and garlic. Fry, stirring, for 10-12 minutes, until the onions are browned.

■ Lower the heat and add the coriander, cumin and turmeric. Fry for about 2 minutes, stirring all the time. Add the yogurt and cook, stirring, for 1 minute. Add the tomato to the pan and fry, stirring for a further 2-3 minutes.

■ Add the meat, increasing the heat to medium (medium-high if the meat is watery). Fry, breaking up the lumps with the back of a slotted spoon, for about 7-8 minutes.

■ Stir in the mace, nutmeg, salt, cayenne and 150 ml (¼ pint) water. Bring to the boil, cover, lower the heat and simmer for 1 hour, stirring every 10 minutes or so. Stir in the browned onion and remove the cinnamon.

■ Serve with plain boiled rice, Moong Dal (see page 187) and a vegetable dish, such as Cauliflower with Ginger and Coriander (see page 170). This *kheema* is also excellent served with chapatis or pooris instead of rice.

# LAMB WITH SPINACH

## *Palag Gosht*

*INDIA*

Serves 6-8

This is a traditional Moghul dish. I use lamb for the recipe, but you could use beef (chuck or round) if you prefer.

**1.4 kg (3 lb) fresh spinach leaves, or three 340 g (12 oz) packets of frozen spinach**
**3 medium onions**
**2 x 2.5 cm (1 inch) cubes fresh root ginger**
**7-8 cloves garlic**
**1 fresh hot green or red chilli, chopped (optional), or ⅛-½ teaspoon cayenne pepper**
**1.4 kg (3 lb) boneless shoulder of lamb, trimmed of fat**
**8 tablespoons vegetable oil**
**7.5 cm (3 inch) cinnamon stick**
**7 cloves**
**7 whole cardamom pods**
**2 bay leaves**
**2 tablespoons ground coriander**
**1 tablespoon ground cumin**
**1 teaspoon ground turmeric**
**1 medium tomato, peeled and finely chopped**
**2 tablespoons yogurt**
**1 teaspoon salt**
**1 tablespoon garam masala**

■ Bring a large pan of water to the boil. Meanwhile, trim fresh spinach and wash thoroughly in cold water. Blanch the spinach in the boiling water, a third at a time: add to the pan, push down to immerse as necessary and cook until the leaves just wilt. Immediately remove, drain in a colander and refresh under cold running water. (If using frozen spinach, cook according to packet directions and drain.) Squeeze out most of the water from the spinach, then mince or chop finely. Set aside in a bowl.

■ Peel and coarsely chop the onions, ginger and garlic, then place in an electric blender with the fresh chilli (if using) and 5 tablespoons of water. Blend to a smooth paste.

■ Cut the lamb into 2.5-4 cm (1-1½ inch) cubes; pat dry on kitchen paper. Heat the oil in a large, heavy-based cooking pot or flameproof casserole. Brown the meat, 7 or 8 pieces at a time, in the hot oil, turning them to colour on all sides. Remove with a slotted spoon and set aside.

■ Add the cinnamon stick, cloves, cardamom pods and bay leaves to the oil remaining in the pan and fry, stirring, for 10-20 seconds until the bay leaves begin to darken. Add the paste from the blender and continue to fry, stirring, for about 10 minutes until the mixture darkens (if it sticks to the bottom, sprinkle in a teaspoon of water at a time, as you fry).

■ Lower the heat and, continuing to stir and fry constantly, add the coriander, cumin and turmeric; 2 minutes later put in the chopped tomato; about 5 minutes later add the yogurt; finally 2 minutes later return the meat to the pan. Stir well, then add the spinach and salt.

■ Bring to the boil, cover, lower the heat and simmer gently for 50 minutes, stirring occasionally. (It shouldn't be necessary to add liquid, but if you find that the meat is sticking, you can add up to 150 ml (¼ pint) of warm water during cooking.)

■ At the end of the cooking time, uncover, increase the heat and cook rapidly for a few minutes if necessary – to reduce the liquid to a thick sauce. Sprinkle in the garam masala and stir gently, being careful not to break up the meat pieces.

■ Transfer to a warm dish and serve with plain boiled rice, Moong Dal (see page 187) and a vegetable dish, such as Cauliflower with Ginger and Coriander (see page 170).

# LAMB STEW WITH OLIVES, POTATOES AND PEPPERS

## *Caldereta*

*PHILIPPINES*

Serves 4-5

One version or another of *caldereta* is cooked throughout the Philippines, but here it is prepared in the slightly spicy style well loved in the Western Visayas region. Again, as with many dishes from this former Spanish colony, the Mediterranean influence is very evident in the use of tomato paste, red pepper and olives. Incidentally, bay leaves, cinnamon sticks and peppercorns – typical seasonings for stews – are sold here in a combined version and are known collectively as *ricado*.

**1 kg (2 lb) boneless lamb or goat meat**
**3 tablespoons distilled white vinegar**
**salt**
**freshly ground black pepper**
**5 cloves garlic**
**100 g (4 oz) onions**
**4 tablespoons olive oil**
**3 dried hot red chillies**
**1 teaspoon black peppercorns**
**5 cm (2 inch) stick cinnamon**
**2 bay leaves**
**4 teaspoons tomato paste**
**350 g (12 oz) potatoes**
**75 g (3 oz) red pepper**
**8 whole stuffed green olives, or other olives of your choice**

■ Cut the meat into 4 cm (1½ inch) cubes; place in a bowl. Add the vinegar, salt and pepper. Toss to mix and set aside for 30-40 minutes. Drain the meat, reserving the marinade, and pat dry. Peel and finely chop the garlic and onions.

■ Heat the oil in a large, heavy-based pan over a medium-high heat. Add the chillies and stir for a few seconds until they swell and darken. Remove with a slotted spoon and set aside.

■ Brown the meat cubes in the pan in batches, turning them to colour on all sides, then remove with a slotted spoon. Brown all the meat in this way.

■ Add the garlic and onion to the oil remaining in the pan. Stir and cook for 2 minutes, scraping up any sediment from the base of the pan. Add the peppercorns, cinnamon and bay leaves and cook, stirring, for another minute.

■ Now put in the meat and its accumulated juices, reserved marinade, the chillies and tomato paste. Cook, stirring, for 1 minute. Add 450 ml (¾ pint) water and bring to the boil. Cover the pan, turn the heat to low and simmer gently for about 15 minutes.

■ Meanwhile, peel the potatoes and, if large, cut into 4 cm (1½ inch) pieces. Add the potatoes to the pan, re-cover and cook for further 45 minutes-1 hour or until the meat is tender.

■ Deseed the red pepper and cut into 5 mm (¼ inch) wide strips. When the meat is tender, add the pepper strips and olives. Stir and cook for another 3-5 minutes, then serve.

# LAMB COOKED IN DARK ALMOND SAUCE

## *Badami Roghan Josh*

*INDIA*

Serves 4-6

Roghan josh is a traditional North Indian Muslim dish. It has a thick, dark, nutty sauce made with almonds and roasted cumin, coriander and coconut. Shoulder of lamb is used here, but you could use leg, neck or shank if you prefer. Stewing beef may also be substituted.

**900 g (2 lb) boneless shoulder of lamb, trimmed of fat**
**6 tablespoons vegetable oil**
**10 cloves**
**1-2 whole dried hot red peppers (optional)**
**12 black peppercorns**
**6 whole cardamom pods**
**6 cloves garlic**
**2.5 cm (1 inch) cube fresh root ginger**
**3 tablespoons blanched almonds**
**1 tablespoon ground cumin**
**2 tablespoons ground coriander**
**1 tablespoon desiccated unsweetened coconut**
**½ teaspoon ground turmeric**
**¼ teaspoon ground nutmeg**
**¼ teaspoon ground mace**
**2 medium onions**
**3 tablespoons yogurt**
**3 medium tomatoes, peeled**
**salt**

■ Cut the meat into 2.5 cm (1 inch) cubes and dry well with kitchen paper.

■ Heat the oil in a large frying pan. When hot, add the cloves, red peppers, peppercorns and whole cardamom pods. Stir for a few seconds until the cardamom pods puff up and darken.

■ Now brown the meat in the pan, 7 or 8 pieces at a time, turning to colour them on all sides. As each batch is browned, transfer to a large flameproof casserole, with a slotted spoon, leaving the spices in the frying pan. Brown all the meat in this way, then cover the casserole and set aside.

■ Peel and coarsely chop the garlic and ginger; set aside. Roughly chop the almonds.

■ Heat a small cast-iron frying pan. Add the cumin, coriander, coconut and almonds and dry-roast over a medium heat, stirring, for about 5 minutes or until the spices turn a coffee colour. Transfer the roasted spices and nuts to a blender. Add the chopped garlic and ginger.

■ With a slotted spoon, lift out the fried spices from the frying pan and add these to the blender too. Add the turmeric, nutmeg, mace and 8 tablespoons water. Blend to a smooth, thick paste.

■ Peel and mince or finely chop the onions. Heat the oil remaining in the frying pan (in which the lamb was fried). Add the onions and fry over a high heat, stirring and scraping up the juices, for about 5 minutes or until they are tinged brown.

■ Lower the heat to medium and add the paste from the blender. Stir and fry for a further 5 minutes, gradually adding the yogurt, a tablespoon at a time.

■ Roughly chop the tomatoes and add them to the pan. Cook, stirring, for a further 2-3 minutes. Stir in 300 ml (½ pint) water and bring to the boil. Cover, lower the heat and simmer gently for 15 minutes.

■ Put the meat into this sauce and season with salt. Bring to a simmer. Cover, lower the heat and simmer gently for 1 hour, stirring occasionally.

■ Transfer to a warm serving dish. Serve with plain rice or Rice with Spinach (see page 199) and chapatis if you like. A yogurt dish, such as Cucumber Raita (see page 224), and a cauliflower side dish, such as Cauliflower with Ginger and Coriander (see page 170) are also suitable accompaniments.

# LAMB WITH WHOLE SPICES AND ONIONS

## *Pyazwala Khare Masale Ka Gosht* *INDIA*

Serves 4-6

This is one of the first meat recipes I learnt to cook. It is little changed from the original, passed on to me by my mother. When the meat is cooked, it should be nicely browned, and the only liquid should be the sauce clinging to it and the oil it is cooked in. In India, this is how the dish is served, but in this country people may be put off by the quantity of oil in the serving dish, so I suggest you lift out the meat and spices with a slotted spoon and transfer them to another dish. The spices serve as a garnish; they are not to be eaten.

**900 g (2 lb) boneless shoulder of lamb, trimmed of fat**
**4 onions**
**4 cm (1½ inch) cube fresh root ginger**
**9 tablespoons vegetable oil**
**10 whole green cardamom pods**
**4 whole large black cardamom pods (if available)**
**6-7 bay leaves**
**1 teaspoon cumin seeds**
**1-4 whole hot dried red peppers (optional)**
**5 black peppercorns**
**salt**

■ Cut the meat into 2.5-4 cm (1-1½ inch) cubes and pat dry thoroughly with kitchen paper. Peel the onions, cut in half, then slice thinly into half-circles. Peel and grate the ginger.

■ Heat the oil in a large heavy-based cooking pot or flameproof casserole over a medium heat. When hot, add the onions and fry, stirring occasionally, for 15 minutes or until brown and crisp, but not burned. Lift out the onions with a slotted spoon and spread out on kitchen paper to drain.

■ Add all of the cardamoms, the bay leaves, cumin, red peppers, peppercorns and ginger to the oil remaining in the cooking pot. Stir for 1 minute until the bay leaves darken and the ginger is sizzling.

■ Add the meat and ½-1 teaspoon salt. Cook, stirring, for about 5 minutes until the liquid begins to bubble vigorously. Cover, lower the heat and simmer very gently for 1 hour, 10 minutes or until the meat is tender.

■ Add the onions and cook, uncovered, over a medium heat for a final 3-5 minutes, stirring gently. Take care not to break up the meat. Any excess liquid should have boiled away, leaving the meat only with the sauce that clings to it, and the fat left in the pot. Serve as suggested above.

# LAMB WITH SPRING ONIONS

## *Cong Bao Yang Roll*

*HONG KONG*

Serves 4

Beijing (Peking) may be best known in the West for its roast duck but Hong Kong's knowledgeable residents often opt for simpler and equally delicious dishes when they go to northern-style restaurants. Here is a simple dish that is as good to eat as it is easy to make. The only effort required is in slicing the meat and spring onions. The cooking itself takes just a few minutes.

I use leg of lamb for this recipe. I buy a whole leg, asking the butcher to bone it and remove most of the fat. I cut off the amount I need and freeze the rest for future use. In order to make this dish successfully, it is important that you do not overcook the spring onions – they should barely wilt.

350 g (12 oz) lean tender lamb

FOR THE MARINADE

2 teaspoons Chinese light soy sauce

2 teaspoons Chinese rice wine or dry sherry

2 teaspoons sesame oil

½ teaspoon roasted and ground Sichuan peppercorns (see page 264), or coarsely ground black peppercorns

FOR THE SAUCE

1 tablespoon Chinese rice wine or dry sherry

4 teaspoons Chinese dark soy sauce

1 tablespoon sesame oil

1 teaspoon distilled white vinegar

YOU ALSO NEED

2 cloves garlic

150 g (5 oz) spring onions

2 tablespoons fresh coriander leaves

4 tablespoons vegetable oil

TO GARNISH

fresh coriander leaves

**1** Cut the lamb against the grain into very thin slices. Cut the slices into very thin slivers, about 7.5 cm (3 inches) long. Put them into a bowl and add all of the marinade ingredients. Toss well, cover and set aside to marinate for 20 minutes.

**2** Combine the ingredients for the sauce in a small bowl. Stir to mix and set aside. Wash the coriander and pat it dry.

**3** Peel the garlic and chop it finely. Cut the spring onions, including the green section, into 7.5 cm (3 inch) lengths. Then cut each piece lengthways into very fine strips.

**4** Heat the oil in a wok or a large frying pan over a high heat until it is almost smoking, then add the garlic. Stir once or twice, then put in the lamb. Stir-fry for about 1 minute or until the lamb is no longer pink on the outside. Pour in the sauce and stir briefly. Add the coriander and spring onion. Stir for 20-30 seconds or until the spring onions just wilt. Serve immediately, garnished with coriander leaves.

*Pork is a much-loved meat in the Philippines and is eaten often by those who can afford it. The national dish is probably adobo. Even though chicken and squid adobos are very popular, pork is the universal favourite. This dish, originally of Spanish extraction, now involves marinating pork pieces in soy sauce and vinegar with garlic, bay leaves and peppercorns, and then cooking them until they brown in their own juices. It is uncommonly good – and lasts well because of the vinegar. (In my house, however, it does not last at all. It is eaten the minute it's made!)*

# PORK COOKED IN A PICKLING STYLE

## *Adobong Baboy* — *PHILIPPINES*

Serves 4

One of the most popular pork dishes in the Philippines is *adobo*. It originated well before the age of refrigeration. Meat needed to be preserved and the tastiest way to do it was to cook it with a mixture of vinegar, soy sauce and garlic, thus pickling it into the bargain.

Normally belly pork is used, but thin-cut pork loin chops, about 1 cm (½ inch) thick, make a successful substitute. If you wish to use the more authentic belly pork, cut it crossways into 2.5 cm (1 inch) cubes.

Pork *adobo* may be prepared a day ahead of time, refrigerated, then reheated to serve. It is best served with plain rice.

**12 large cloves garlic**
**6 tablespoons Chinese dark soy sauce**
**6 tablespoons distilled white vinegar**
**3 bay leaves**
**1 teaspoon black peppercorns**
**1 kg (2 lb) thin-cut pork loin chops**
**3 tablespoons vegetable oil**

■ Peel and finely chop the garlic cloves. Set aside two thirds of the chopped garlic. Put the rest in a large bowl with the soy sauce, vinegar, bay leaves and peppercorns; mix well. Add the pork chops and toss so that they are well coated with the marinade. Cover the bowl and set aside to marinate for 1 hour, turning the chops occasionally.

■ Heat the oil in a wide saucepan or large frying pan over a medium-high heat. When hot, add the reserved chopped garlic and fry, stirring, until light gold in colour. Add the pork chops, together with their marinade and 120 ml (4 fl oz) water. Bring to the boil. Cover, turn the heat to low and simmer gently for 30 minutes, turning the chops a few times during cooking.

■ Remove the lid from the pan and turn the heat to medium-high. Cook for another 10-15 minutes or until the sauce is thick and the meat is tender.

# STIR-FRIED PORK WITH RED PEPPER

## *Twaeji Bokkum* — *KOREA*

Serves 4

Easy to prepare and spicily delicious, this dish is best served with plain rice.

**350 g (12 oz) boneless loin of pork**
**1 spring onion**
**1 large clove garlic**
**2.5 x 1 cm (1 x ½ inch) piece fresh root ginger**
**2 tablespoons Hot Fermented Bean Paste (see page 218)**
**75 g (3 oz) red pepper**
**75 g (3 oz) onions**
**3 tablespoons vegetable oil**

■ Cut the pork against the grain into slices about 5 x 2.5 cm x 3 mm (2 x 1 x ⅛ inch). Cut the spring onion into very fine rounds. Peel and finely chop the garlic and ginger.

■ Combine the pork, spring onion, garlic, ginger and Hot Fermented Bean Paste in a bowl. Mix well. Cover and set aside for 30 minutes or longer, refrigerating if necessary.

■ Deseed the red pepper and cut into 1 cm (½ inch) squares. Peel the onions and cut into 1 cm (½ inch) cubes, then separate the layers.

■ Shortly before serving, heat the oil in a large non-stick frying pan over a high heat. When hot, add the pork together with its marinade. Stir-fry for 3 minutes or until the pork is white all the way through.

■ Add the red pepper, onion and 6 tablespoons of water. Stir and cook on a high heat for a further 2 minutes or until the pork is cooked through. Serve at once.

# PORK WITH LONG BEANS AND CHIVES

## *Sijidou Chao Zhuliu*

*HONG KONG*

Serves 4

This particular Cantonese-style dish was once made for me with onions and chives, another time with garlic. Each time it was superb and different, which just goes to show that there is great flexibility in Chinese cooking and you should never be afraid to make changes and adjustments.

A note about the ingredients: in Hong Kong, long beans come in two shades of green, light and dark. The darker variety is crisper. Use any type of long beans that you can find – most Chinese and Indian grocers stock them. If you cannot obtain long beans, use any tender green beans, cooking them so that they retain their crispness. If you buy Chinese chives from a market or grow chives, as I do, and they happen to be budding, do use them – young bud and all.

**200 g (7 oz) pork tenderloin, well-trimmed**
**salt**
**4 teaspoons sesame oil**
**2½ teaspoons cornflour**
**200 g (7 oz) long or green beans**
**1 medium onion**
**2 cm (¾ inch) cube fresh root ginger**
**1 large clove garlic**
**1 tablespoon oyster sauce**
**2 teaspoons Chinese light soy sauce**
**1 tablespoon Chinese rice wine or dry sherry**
**5 tablespoons vegetable oil**
**20 g (¾ oz) fresh Chinese chives (if available), or ordinary fresh chives**

■ Cut the pork tenderloin into very thin slices, about 5 cm (2 inches) long and 1 cm (½ inch) wide. Place in a small bowl. Add about ⅛ teaspoon salt, 2 teaspoons of the sesame oil, 1 teaspoon cornflour and 2 teaspoons water. Mix well. Cover and set aside to marinate for an hour or so, refrigerating if necessary.

■ Trim the beans and cut into 5-7.5 cm (2-3 inch) pieces. Cut the chives into 5 cm (2 inch) lengths. Peel the onion and cut in half crossways, then quarter each half and separate the different layers. Peel the ginger and garlic and chop very finely.

■ In a small bowl, combine the oyster sauce, soy sauce, the remaining 2 teaspoons sesame oil, the rice wine and 5 tablespoons water. Mix well and set aside.

■ In a cup, mix the remaining 1½ teaspoons cornflour with 2 tablespoons water and set aside.

■ Shortly before serving, heat 1 tablespoon oil in a wok or frying pan over a high heat. When hot, add half the ginger, stir once or twice, then add the onion and stir briefly. Add the green beans with ¼ teaspoon salt, and stir-fry for 1 minute. Put in 4 tablespoons water and cover immediately. Lower the heat and cook for 4-6 minutes or until the beans are just tender; turn into a bowl. Clean and dry the wok.

■ Heat the remaining 4 tablespoons oil in the wok. When hot, add the pork, then turn off the heat and toss the pork pieces until they just turn white. (You may need to turn the heat on again to achieve this, but keep it on low.) Remove the pork with a slotted spoon and put it into a clean bowl.

■ Pour off all but 1 tablespoon of the oil, then set the wok over a high heat. When the oil is hot, add the remaining ginger and the garlic; stir-fry for 15-30 seconds. Put in the pork and stir-fry for 1 minute. Add the green beans and onion and stir for 30 seconds. Add the sauce and stir for 1 minute.

■ Take the wok off the heat and make a well in the middle of the pork mixture. Stir the cornflour mix, then pour into the well. Return the wok to a low heat and cook, stirring, until the sauce has thickened. Stir in the chives, toss to mix and serve.

# GLAZED GINGERY SPARERIBS

## *Hong Shao Leigu*

*HONG KONG*

Serves 4

There really could not be a simpler way to prepare these braised Shanghai-style pork ribs. As an alternative to spareribs, you could make this dish with thin-cut pork loin chops.

- 1 kg (2 lb) pork spareribs
- 6 tablespoons Chinese dark soy sauce
- 6 tablespoons sugar
- 2 x 2.5 cm (1 inch) cubes fresh root ginger
- 3 spring onions
- 3 tablespoons Chinese rice wine or dry sherry

■ Separate the spareribs, then cut them into 7.5 cm (3 inch) lengths. (Persuade your butcher to do this for you if possible.)

■ Put the spareribs in a wide, preferably non-stick, pan. Add the soy sauce and sugar. Peel and lightly crush the ginger cubes and add them to the pan. Add the spring onions too.

■ Pour in the rice wine and 1 litre (1¾ pints) water. Bring to the boil, then cover the pan and turn the heat to medium-low. Simmer steadily for 45 minutes, turning the meat every 10 minutes or so to ensure it colours evenly.

■ Remove and discard the ginger and spring onions, then increase the heat to high. Cook, uncovered, for a further 20 minutes or so, until the liquid is thick and syrupy, turning the ribs a few times. Once cooked, the ribs should be coated evenly with a dark glaze.

*Much of north-western Thailand not only borders Burma but has also been ruled by it in previous centuries. The cultural give-and-take can still be seen in the lacquered baskets used for storing cooked glutinous rice (this is the rice eaten for breakfast, lunch and dinner), in the cheroot-smoking women of the villages, and in this curry. Those of you who are familiar with India's hot, sweet and sour vindaloo will find that this is almost a sister curry. After all, Burma borders India and the ripple effect of cultural exchanges can be quite far-reaching.*

# THAI PORK CURRY IN THE BURMESE STYLE

## *Kaeng Hunglay*

*THAILAND*

Serves 4-6

Even before I got to Chiang Mai, I had heard of this northern dish from friends in Bangkok. 'Try and eat it in someone's home,' I had been advised. I need not have worried about how I would manage this: Thais are the most hospitable people I know. Within a day of arriving in Chiang Mai, I was seated with a Thai family, devouring not just curry but a tableload of northern delicacies, including black button mushrooms and freshly plucked lychees.

You can use boneless pork from the loin or shoulder for this recipe – a little fat in the meat will keep it more succulent. The curry paste can be made ahead of time and frozen if required; it will need to be defrosted and brought to room temperature before it is used.

875 g (1¾ lb) boneless loin or shoulder of pork

FOR THE CURRY PASTE

3-8 dried hot red chillies, according to taste

90 g (3½ oz) shallots or onions

10 large cloves garlic

2 cm (¾ inch) cube fresh galangal, or fresh root ginger

2 sticks fresh lemon grass

1 teaspoon shrimp or anchovy paste

1 tablespoon ground coriander seeds

2 teaspoons ground cumin seeds

½ teaspoon ground turmeric

YOU ALSO NEED

1½ tablespoons Japanese soy sauce (*shoyu*)

3 x 2.5 cm (1 inch) cubes fresh root ginger (preferably young)

10-12 shallots or small pickling onions

10-15 small cloves garlic

2 tablespoons tamarind paste (see page 264) or lemon juice, or more to taste

2 tablespoons dark brown sugar, or to taste

salt (optional)

TO GARNISH

shredded fresh red chilli and spring onion (optional)

**1** First make the curry paste. Put 250 ml (8 fl oz) water in a small bowl and crumble in the dried red chillies. Leave to soak for 30 minutes. Peel and coarsely chop the shallots, garlic and galangal or ginger. Finely slice the lemon grass from the base to 15 cm (6 inches) from the top; discard the straw-like top. Put the chillies and their soaking liquid into a blender with the chopped flavourings, lemon grass and all the remaining curry paste ingredients. Blend until smooth.

**2** Cut the pork into 4 cm (1½ inch) cubes and place in a bowl. Add the curry paste and soy sauce and toss the meat to coat well. Cover and leave to marinate for 30 minutes, turning the meat occasionally.

**3** Meanwhile, peel the ginger and cut it into very thin slices. Stack a few slices at a time together and cut them into matchstick strips. Peel the shallots and garlic, leaving them whole.

**4** Transfer the pork and marinade to a wide heavy, ideally non-stick, pan. Bring to a simmer over a medium-low heat and simmer gently for 15-20 minutes or until the meat starts to release its fat. Turn heat to medium-high and fry, stirring, for 10 minutes or until the spice mixture begins to dry and brown. Add 450 ml (¾ pint) water, the ginger, whole shallots and garlic. Bring to a simmer and cook, covered, for 45 minutes or until the meat is tender. Add the tamarind paste, sugar and salt to taste. Cook for a further 2-3 minutes. Serve garnished with shredded chilli and spring onion if you wish.

# KNOCKOUT KNUCKLE

## *Patang Bawang*

*PHILIPPINES*

Serves 4

Pork is a much-loved meat in the Philippines, as it is in many Pacific Islands, and what often adds to the status of the meat itself is the crispness of the skin on top of it. In this recipe the meat is juicy and tender and the skin is crackling crisp. This is achieved by a combination of slow braising and double-frying. My children declared that this was the best pork they had ever tasted.

It is quite easy to make this dish, but harder to find the right cut of meat! What you need is the 1.5 kg (3 lb) front leg of a pig that – in the words of the chef – 'has not been around'. This, when translated, means a 3-4-month-old pig. I had great trouble finding the front leg of a pig, let alone that of a pig that had not been around! You have two choices here: you can either buy what is sold as a pork half-leg knuckle; or put in a special order at your butchers for a front leg of a young pig. When I did this it came in weighing 2.5 kg (5½ lb), so I asked the butcher to cut it in two and took both pieces home, one to cook immediately and the thicker end to store in the freezer for later use.

**1.65 kg (3½ lb) pork half-leg knuckle, or portion of front leg of pork**
**1 medium onion**
**2 carrots**
**2 sticks celery**
**1 teaspoon black peppercorns**
**3 bay leaves**
**1 tablespoon salt**
**9 cloves garlic**
**6 fresh hot green chillies**
**150 ml (¼ pint) vegetable oil, plus extra for deep-frying**

■ Put the pork joint, skin-side up, into a large pan and add 4.5 litres (8 pints) water. Bring to a simmer and keep at a very gentle simmer for a few minutes, skimming as much scum from the surface as you can.

■ Peel the onion and carrots. Add to the pan with the celery, peppercorns, bay leaves and salt. Cover partially and simmer gently for about 3 hours or until the meat is tender. Remove the meat and leave to drain and cool.

■ Peel the garlic and cut lengthways into thin slices. Cut the green chillies into thin rings. Heat the 150 ml (¼ pint) oil in a frying pan set over a medium-low heat. Add the garlic and fry, stirring, until it just begins to turn golden, then add the chillies. Continue to stir and fry until the garlic is golden brown and the chillies are slightly crisp. Remove the garlic and chillies with a slotted spoon and spread them on kitchen paper to drain. Reserve the garlicky oil.

■ Heat a 4 cm (1½ inch) depth of oil in a large wok to about 160°C (325°F). When hot, carefully put in the pork joint, skin-side down. Cover and cook for 5 minutes. Turn the pork over carefully, cover again and cook the second side for 3 minutes. Transfer the pork to a plate. (You can prepare to this stage 2 hours ahead; do not refrigerate the meat.)

■ Just before serving, heat the oil again, this time to a high temperature, around 200°C (400°F). When it is hot, put in the meat, skin-side down, and fry, uncovered, for 2-3 minutes or until the skin is crisp and brown. Turn the meat and fry the opposite side for 1 minute. Turn the meat again and fry the skin side for a further 1 minute. Make sure that the skin on the sides of the meat browns properly too.

■ Lift the meat out carefully and drain it briefly. Put it on a plate, then cut the meat off the bone lengthways in long strips. Lay the strips back over the bone, forming a kind of tent over it. Pour a little of the reserved garlicky oil over the meat. Scatter the fried garlic and chillies on top and serve.

*It was fiesta time when I visited the small Negros village. Long tables had been set under shady trees and covered over with banana leaves. A whole pig (lechon) roasted to a turn on a spit, its skin crackling-crisp, was stretched across the centre like an edible epergne. It had been stuffed in the old traditional manner with sour tamarind leaves, then basted as it cooked in the new traditional manner, with bottled American-style ginger ale.*

*On either side of the pig were whole steamed and roasted chickens. They had been boned, then marinated overnight in soy sauce and the juice of the small kalamansi lime. Before cooking the chickens were stuffed with minced meats – such as pork, veal, Chinese ham and Spanish sausage – as well as olives, pimentoes, several American-style pickles, sultanas and Parmesan cheese. There were also generous platters of paella, chock-full of prawns, chicken pieces and sausage.*

# PORK WITH CALF'S LIVER AND CHICKPEAS

## *Menudo*

*PHILIPPINES*

Serves 4

This is an easy stew – hearty, nourishing and comforting all at once. It is, quite clearly, of Mediterranean origin. It may be eaten with a salad and also, if you like, with rice.

I use the meat from 3-4 thin pork loin chops for this dish. If you wish to cook your own chickpeas rather than use canned ones, you will need to soak about ½ teacup dried chickpeas overnight in cold water. The following day, drain, place in a pan, cover with 1.1 litres (2 pints) fresh cold water and bring to the boil. Lower the heat, cover and simmer for 45 minutes. Add ½ teaspoon salt and cook for a further 30 minutes-1 hour or until tender. (Older chickpeas take longer to cook.) Drain and weigh them before use.

**150 g (5 oz) calf's liver**
**salt**
**freshly ground black pepper**
**350 g (12 oz) lean pork loin**
**225 g (8 oz) potatoes**
**275 g (10 oz) canned peeled tomatoes**
**3 cloves garlic**
**1 medium onion**
**4 tablespoons vegetable oil**
**150 g (5 oz) canned or cooked chickpeas**
**1 teaspoon paprika**

■ Cut the liver into 1-2 cm (½-¾ inch) cubes and season lightly with salt and pepper. Cut the pork into 1-2 cm (½-¾ inch) cubes, discarding most of the fat.

■ Peel the potatoes and cut into 1-2 cm (½-¾ inch) cubes; place them in a bowl of water and set aside. Crush the tomatoes lightly, leaving them in their liquid. Peel the garlic and cut into fine slivers. Peel and thinly slice the onion.

■ Heat the oil in a large, preferably non-stick, frying pan over a high heat. When hot, add the liver and fry, stirring, until browned on the outside but still soft and slightly rare inside. Remove with a slotted spoon and set aside.

■ Add the garlic and onion to the oil remaining in the pan and fry, stirring, for 1 minute. Then put in the diced pork and stir-fry for 3 minutes. Add the tomatoes with their liquid and continue to stir and cook on a high heat for 1 minute.

■ Cover the pan, lower the heat and simmer for 15 minutes. Drain the potatoes and add them to the pan, with the chickpeas, salt and black pepper, the paprika and 150 ml (¼ pint) water. Stir and bring to a simmer. Cover and cook for 15-25 minutes, or until the potatoes and pork are tender.

■ Add the liver, together with any accumulated juices, and heat through to serve.

# vegetables and salads

# AUBERGINE IN A THICK, HOT, SWEET AND SOUR CHILLI SAUCE

## *Pacheri Terong*

*MALAYSIA*

Serves 4

Another dish of Indian-Malay ancestry, this hot, sweet and sour *pacheri* may be made with fresh pineapple cubes rather than aubergines for a change.

**200 g (7 oz) onions**
**2.5 cm (1 inch) cube fresh root ginger**
**2 teaspoons cumin seeds**
**2 teaspoons ground coriander seeds**
**3-5 dried hot red chillies**
**4 cloves**
**5 cm (2 inch) stick cinnamon**
**450 g (1 lb) aubergines**
**6 tablespoons vegetable oil**
**1 tablespoon paprika**
**3-4 tablespoons tamarind paste, or 3 tablespoons lime juice mixed with 2 tablespoons dark brown sugar**
**1-2 tablespoons dark brown sugar**
**1½-2 teaspoons salt**

■ Peel and finely slice the onions. Peel the ginger and cut it into fine shreds.

■ Put the cumin, ground coriander, dried chillies, cloves and cinnamon into a clean coffee grinder or spice grinder and grind as finely as possible.

■ Cut the aubergines into 2.5 cm (1 inch) cubes, leaving the skin on.

■ Heat the oil in a large, preferably non-stick, frying pan or large wok set over a medium-high heat. When the oil is hot, add the onions and ginger. Stir and fry for about 4 minutes until softened and fairly dry, but not browned. Add the spices from the spice grinder and fry, stirring, for 1 minute.

■ Immediately pour in 300 ml (½ pint) water and turn the heat down a little. Add the paprika, tamarind (or lime juice and sugar), sugar and salt. Stir to mix. Put in the cubed aubergines and bring to a simmer. Cover and cook gently for 20-30 minutes, stirring now and then, until the aubergines are tender. Remove the lid and increase the heat. Cook until most of the remaining liquid has evaporated, leaving a thick sauce clinging to the aubergine pieces. Serve hot.

*Malaysia is one of the world's few true melting pots. The sharp edges of racialism have been softened by the constant rubbing of multi-coloured shoulders, and the sharp differences in the cuisines have been blurred by the constant exchange of techniques and ingredients. Today one finds that, while some foods have kept their original form, most have been modified subtly or drastically, making it hard to fit many dishes into a clear niche or to pinpoint their exact origin.*

# SMOKY AUBERGINES IN A LIME SAUCE

## *Ca Tim Nuong*

*VIETNAM*

Serves 4

This is a superb dish, inspired in every way. Aubergines, all smoky from being charred over a flame, are smothered with stir-fried pork and then submerged in a delicious lime sauce. You may roast the aubergines outdoors over charcoal in the summer, over an open fire indoors during the winter or under your kitchen grill at any time of year. I find that the most convenient way is directly on top of a gas burner. When buying the aubergines, make sure that they have their green sepals and a short length of stalk still attached. This makes the cooking easier and the presentation prettier.

**2 aubergines, each 220-225 g (7-8 oz)**
**65 g (2½ oz) onion**
**1 clove garlic**
**1 spring onion**
**1 tablespoon vegetable oil**
**100 g (4 oz) lean pork, minced**
**¼ teaspoon salt**
**freshly ground black pepper**
**4 tablespoons Fish Sauce Seasoned with Lime Juice (see page 216)**

■ Do not trim the aubergines, but prick them lightly with a fork to prevent them from bursting during cooking. Line a burner on a gas cooker with foil, leaving an opening for the gas. (Line two burners if you wish to cook both aubergines simultaneously.)

■ Hold one aubergine by its stem end and stand it upright, directly on top of a medium-low flame. Let the bottom char. Now lay the aubergine down on top of the flame and let one side char. Keep turning the aubergine until all of it is charred and roasted and the entire vegetable has gone limp. You may need to hold it with a pair of tongs towards the end. Cook the other aubergine in the same way.

■ Peel the charred skin off the aubergines, occasionally picking them up carefully by the stem and holding them under cold running water to wash away small bits of skin. The aubergines should stay intact though they will be somewhat flattened. (If small pieces become detached, the aubergines can easily be reassembled.)

■ Put the aubergines side by side into a serving dish. Pat them dry with kitchen paper. (You can prepare the dish up to this point a day in advance. Cover and refrigerate, but bring to room temperature the following day before proceeding with the next step.)

■ Peel the onion and garlic and chop them finely. Cut the spring onion into very fine rings.

■ Heat the oil in a frying pan over a medium-high heat. When the oil is hot, put in the onion and garlic. Stir once or twice, then add the pork, salt and lots of black pepper. Stir and fry for about 5 minutes or until the meat is cooked through, breaking up any lumps as you do so. Add the spring onion and stir for 10 seconds.

■ Spoon the pork mixture over the aubergines. Pour the Fish Sauce Seasoned with Lime Juice over the top and serve.

# GREEN BEANS AND CARROTS WITH GINGER AND CHILLIES

## *Tumis Bunchis*

*INDONESIA*

Serves 4

When little girls begin to learn how to cook in Indonesia, a *tumis* is frequently one of the dishes they start with. It is simply a stir-fried dish with a little liquid. In Indonesia long beans are used and they are usually combined with bean curd or bean sprouts. If you wish to include either of these, you will need about 1½ cakes of pressed bean curd or about 225 g (8 oz) fresh bean sprouts. Add them to the dish at the same time as the beans. The bean curd should be cut into pieces about the same size as the beans. I have used carrots instead, only because they are more easily available and because the West has so few imaginative carrot dishes. If you cannot get fresh galangal, just do without it.

450 g (1 lb) green beans (preferably long beans)
2 medium carrots
3-4 fresh hot green chillies
2.5 cm (1 inch) cube fresh root ginger
2.5 cm (1 inch) cube fresh galangal (optional)
4-6 cloves garlic
50 g (2 oz) shallots or onions
3 tablespoons vegetable oil
8-10 fresh or dried curry leaves, or 2 bay leaves
¾ teaspoon salt

■ Trim the beans and cut into 2.5 cm (1 inch) pieces. Peel the carrots and cut into 5 cm (2 inch) lengths, then cut each piece lengthways into quarters and halve these.

■ Finely chop the green chillies. Peel the ginger and cut into paper-thin slices. Stack a few slices together at a time and cut them into minute dice. If using fresh galangal, peel and dice it in the same way. Peel and finely chop the garlic and shallots.

■ Set a wok over a high heat and swirl in the oil. When the oil is hot, put in the chillies, ginger, galangal, garlic, shallots and curry (or bay) leaves. Stir and fry briefly until the spices start to brown.

■ Add the green beans, carrots and salt. Stir and fry for 1 minute. Pour in 175 ml (6 fl oz) water and cover with a lid. Turn the heat to medium and cook for about 5 minutes or until the vegetables are just tender.

*In Thailand, vegetables are often cooked with small amounts of meat, generally pork. In one northern village I was treated to cauliflower stir-fried with minced pork. In Bangkok I often took myself for a cheap meal of green beans, stir-fried with minced pork and chillies, served behind my ritzy hotel; and I remember buying a quite scrumptious dish of gai lan, a green leafy vegetable, stir-fried with smoked pork. Pork lubricates the vegetable and gives it an added dimension.*

# STIR-FRIED GREEN BEANS WITH PORK AND CHILLIES

## *Moo Pad Prik Sai Tua Fak Yao* *THAILAND*

Serves 4

Versions of this dish are to be found in many parts of South-east Asia. I met an official in Hanoi who often lunches on this in his office. In the Sichuan province of China, beans are cooked with similar seasonings, but soy sauce is used instead of fish sauce. This particular recipe comes from a lady with a food stall ensconced in the middle of the weekend market in Bangkok. She served it to me for lunch along with a plate of plain rice. It was a simple but quite memorable meal.

You may make these beans as hot as you like by increasing the number of chillies. In Thailand fresh hot red chillies are used and they not only contrast stunningly in flavour with the green beans and brown pork, but add bright flecks of colour as well. I tend to use green chillies as they are easier to find at my grocers. If you like, you can throw in a small amount of finely diced red pepper for the last 5 minutes of cooking, to add colour. In Thailand long beans are preferred; if you cannot obtain them, use ordinary stringless beans instead.

**500 g (1¼ lb) green beans**
**12-16 cloves garlic**
**6-9 fresh hot green or red chillies**
**5 tablespoons vegetable oil**
**275 g (10 oz) lean pork, minced**
**½ teaspoon paprika**
**1 teaspoon dark brown sugar**
**3 tablespoons fish sauce, or salt to taste**

■ Wash and trim the beans, then cut into 1 cm (⅓-½ inch) pieces. Peel the garlic and chop it finely. Cut the chillies into very thin slices.

■ Heat the oil in a wok set over a medium-high heat. When it is hot, add the garlic and chillies. Stir-fry until the garlic turns golden, then add the pork. Stir and fry, breaking up any lumps, until the pork no longer looks raw.

■ Put in the green beans, paprika, sugar, fish sauce and 300 ml (½ pint) water. Stir and cook on a medium-high heat for about 8-10 minutes or until the beans are tender and most of the water has been absorbed.

# GREEN BEANS WITH SESAME DRESSING

## *Sando Mame No Goma Aye* *JAPAN*

Serves 4

You may choose from long beans, French beans and runner beans to make this dish. It may be served as an appetizer or as an accompanying vegetable with any meat or fish dish. If required, it can be made ahead of time and refrigerated; take out of the refrigerator at least 20 minutes before serving.

**350 g (12 oz) green beans**
**salt**
**300 ml (½ pint) Japanese Soup Stock (see page 255), or chicken stock at room temperature, lightly salted to taste**
**2½ tablespoons sesame seeds**
**1½ tablespoons Japanese soy sauce (*shoyu*), or to taste**
**1 tablespoon mirin, or 1½ teaspoons sugar**

■ Trim the beans. Cut French beans into 4 cm (1½ inch) lengths. Slice other green beans diagonally, or first cut into 5 cm (2 inch) lengths and then into thin slivers.

■ Bring a large pan of salted water to a rolling boil. Add the beans and boil rapidly for 2-5 minutes or until they are just tender but still crisp. Drain and quickly plunge them into cold water to set the colour. Drain again and put the beans into a bowl. Pour the stock over them and set aside for 30 minutes or longer.

■ Now prepare the dressing. Put the sesame seeds in a small cast-iron frying pan set over a medium-high heat. Stir the seeds about for a few minutes until they are roasted and give out a nutty aroma. Set aside about ½ tablespoon of the roasted sesame seeds for the garnish. Tip the rest into a clean coffee grinder and grind finely, then turn into a bowl.

■ Add the soy sauce, mirin and 1 tablespoon stock taken from the beans. (If using sugar rather than mirin, dissolve it in 1½ teaspoons of the stock, then add to the dressing.) Mix well.

■ Drain the beans thoroughly. (Save the stock for a soup.) Put the beans into a bowl, add the dressing and toss to mix.

■ To serve, Japanese-style, pile the beans in a little hillock in the centre of each of 4 small bowls or plates. Sprinkle the reserved roasted sesame seeds over the top of each serving.

*The Japanese like to stress the seasons in their meals. In summer a moss-eating fish may be served to you on a bed of cool-looking pebbles. In autumn chrysanthemum petals could be added to your salad. Winter brings steaming savoury custards and warmth-retaining bean curd casseroles. Spring might produce fiddlehead ferns, young bamboo shoots and hillocks of green beans.*

# BRAISED BROAD BEANS

## *Shengbian Candou*

*HONG KONG*

Serves 3-4

You can make this Shanghai-style dish with fresh or frozen broad beans. Here the hard outer skin around each individual bean is not peeled away before cooking. Instead, it is popped open by the diner, just before being devoured.

**1 spring onion**
**275 g (10 oz) fresh broad beans (shelled weight), or frozen broad beans**
**3 tablespoons vegetable oil**
**½ teaspoon salt**
**150 ml (¼ pint) chicken stock**
**½ teaspoon sugar**
**1 tablespoon sesame oil**

■ Cut the spring onion into very thin rounds. Wash fresh broad beans and drain well. If using frozen beans, defrost fully in a bowl of lukewarm water, then drain thoroughly.

■ Put the oil in a wok or large frying pan and set it over a high heat. When the oil is hot, put in the broad beans. Stir briskly for about 30 seconds, then add the salt, stock and sugar. Cover and cook on a high heat for 6-7 minutes or until the beans are just tender.

■ Remove the lid and boil for a minute or two to evaporate the liquid. Add the spring onion and sesame oil. Toss to mix and serve immediately.

*A few words about etiquette. The Chinese invented chopsticks and use the 'nimble brothers' with masterful ease. Chopsticks should never be left in a crossed position (except after eating dim sum to indicate that you have finished). Soup spoons are used not only for soup but also for the liquid in stews. All foods, except the individual bowls of rice, are communal and placed in the centre of the table. Rice bowls should be brought near the mouth when you eat from them, not left on the table. When eating a whole cooked fish, you should never turn it over to get at the flesh on the other side (if you do, a fishing boat will tip over!). And yes, you may slurp your soup!*

# BEAN SPROUTS WITH A SPICY COCONUT DRESSING

## *Kerabu Tawgeh*

*MALAYSIA*

Serves 4-6

Here is a very simple refreshing vegetable dish-cum-salad. It has an unusual dressing of lime juice, tomatoes and roasted coconut. If you cannot get fresh coconut, use unsweetened desiccated coconut and roast before soaking it in hot water.

**3 tablespoons uncooked rice**
**100 g (4 oz) fresh coconut, grated (see page 258), or 50 g (2 oz) unsweetened desiccated coconut**
**75 g (3 oz) red pepper**
**2 teaspoons shrimp or anchovy paste (optional)**
**3 tablespoons lime or lemon juice**
**2 peeled plum tomatoes (fresh or canned, lightly drained)**
**¼ teaspoon chilli powder, or to taste**
**1½ teaspoons salt**
**1½ teaspoons sugar**
**2 cm (¾ inch) cube fresh root ginger**
**65 g (2½ oz) onions**
**450 g (1 lb) fresh bean sprouts**
**175 g (6 oz) cabbage**

TO GARNISH (OPTIONAL)

**6 cherry or very small tomatoes**
**2 spring onions**
**few celery leaves**
**5-6 fresh hot green or red chillies**

■ Set a small cast-iron frying pan over a medium heat. When hot, put in the rice and stir until it is golden and roasted. Empty the rice out on to a plate.

■ Put the coconut into the same frying pan. Stir and fry until it is tinged golden brown. Empty it on to a separate plate (if using fresh coconut). Or if using desiccated coconut put it in a small bowl with 120 ml (4 fl oz) hot water and leave to soak for 30 minutes; it will absorb most of the liquid.

■ Put the rice into a clean coffee grinder or spice grinder and grind until it is powdery.

■ Deseed and coarsely chop the red pepper. Place in a blender with the shrimp or anchovy paste (if using), lime juice, tomatoes, chilli powder, salt and sugar. Blend until smooth.

■ Peel the ginger and grate it finely. Peel and finely slice the onions. Break off the thread-like tails at the end of the bean sprouts, if required. Cut the cabbage into fine long shreds.

■ Set a large pan of water over a high heat. When it comes to a rolling boil, drop in the bean sprouts and cabbage. Let the water return to the boil, then boil for about 1 minute or until the cabbage is barely limp. Drain and rinse under cold running water. Drain thoroughly again and place in a bowl.

■ For the garnishes, if required, halve the tomatoes; slice the spring onions into fine rings; finely chop the celery leaves.

■ Just before serving, add the ground rice, roasted coconut, grated ginger and sliced onions to the bean sprout mixture and toss well. Add the sauce from the blender and toss to mix. Transfer to a serving dish. Sprinkle with the spring onions and celery leaves and garnish with the tomato halves and whole chillies if using.

# CABBAGE STIR-FRIED WITH RED PEPPER PASTE

## *Sala Lobak*

*INDONESIA*

Serves 4

I discovered this absolutely delicious dish in the remote hills of Western Sumatra. Even though there was an array of fine foods laid out on the floor-cloth – curries of beef, chicken and fish – all hands went first to the cabbage and it was, indeed, the dish that was finished first.

Only the dark, outer leaves of the cabbage were included, and a small flat piece of dried fish had been fried and added to the seasoning. For my version I often add some of the inner cabbage and use a small amount of shrimp or anchovy paste instead of the dried fish.

You may serve this dish with any Eastern meal. It goes particularly well with roast pork and lamb, as well as chops and cutlets.

**450 g (1 lb) bok choi, other cabbage, cabbage greens or spring greens**
**100 g (4 oz) red pepper**
**50 g (2 oz) shallots or onions**
**2 large cloves garlic**
**½ teaspoon shrimp or anchovy paste (optional)**
**¼ teaspoon chilli powder**
**6 tablespoons vegetable oil**
**½ teaspoon salt**

■ Wash the cabbage leaves and drain. Stacking several of them together, cut them crossways into long, fine, 3 mm (⅛ inch) wide shreds.

■ Core and deseed the red pepper, then chop coarsely. Peel and coarsely chop the shallots and garlic. Put the red pepper, shallots, garlic, shrimp paste, chilli powder and 3 tablespoons water in an electric blender. Blend until a coarse paste results – it should not be too smooth.

■ Set a wok over a high heat. When hot, add the oil. Once the oil is hot, put in the spice paste. Stir and fry for about 5 minutes or until the oil separates and the mixture is dark red in colour.

■ Add the cabbage and salt and cook, stirring, for 30 seconds. Cover tightly, turn the heat to medium-low and cook for 8-10 minutes or until the cabbage is just cooked. (No water should be needed, but check after 5-6 minutes and add a little if the mixture appears dry.) Turn into a warmed dish and serve at once.

# CAULIFLOWER AND CARROTS WITH A COCONUT DRESSING

## *Gudangan*

*INDONESIA*

Serves 4

This Javanese dish, eaten with slight variations throughout much of Indonesia, consists of blanched mixed vegetables tossed with an exquisite dressing that includes lime juice, coconut and red pepper. It is an inspired mixture. The main ingredient here is cauliflower, but it could equally well be greens of various sorts, or long beans or bean sprouts.

You may serve the dish hot, at room temperature, or cold, though I feel that it is best to mix the dressing in while the vegetables are still hot.

**50 g (2 oz) fresh coconut, or 25 g (1 oz) unsweetened desiccated coconut**
**425 g (15 oz) cauliflower florets**
**100 g (4 oz) carrots**
**50 g (2 oz) red pepper**
**1 clove garlic**
**4 teaspoons lime or lemon juice**
**1 teaspoon dark brown sugar**
**¼ teaspoon chilli powder**
**salt**

■ If you are using fresh coconut, grate it finely. If using desiccated coconut, soak it in 4 tablespoons boiling water for 30 minutes; most of the water will be absorbed.

■ Cut the cauliflower into slim delicate florets – no wider than 2.5 cm (1 inch), with stems no longer than 5 cm (2 inches). Peel the carrots and cut into 5 cm (2 inch) lengths. Quarter the thick pieces lengthways; halve the thinner pointed ends.

■ Deseed and coarsely chop the red pepper. Peel and chop the garlic. In an electric blender combine the red pepper, garlic, lime juice, sugar, chilli powder and ¼ teaspoon salt. Blend until smooth. Taste the dressing and add a little more salt if required.

■ Bring a large pan of salted water to a rolling boil. Add the cauliflower and carrots and boil rapidly for several minutes or until the vegetables are just tender but still retain a hint of crispness.

■ Drain them quickly and turn into a serving bowl. Add the dressing and toss to mix. Sprinkle in the coconut and toss the vegetables again. Serve immediately, or allow to cool.

# STIR-FRIED COURGETTES WITH SESAME SEEDS

## *Hobak Namul* — *KOREA*

Serves 6

This superb, gently flavoured dish may be served with almost any Asian meal as well as with Western-style roast and grilled meats, sausages and hamburgers. It may be served hot, or cold as a salad.

**1 kg (2 lb) medium courgettes**
**2 teaspoons salt**
**2½ tablespoons sesame seeds**
**4 cloves garlic**
**1 spring onion**
**3 tablespoons vegetable oil**
**1 tablespoon sesame oil**

■ Trim the courgettes, halve lengthways, then cut each piece crossways into 5 mm (¼ inch) thick slices and place in a large bowl. Sprinkle with 1½ teaspoons salt, toss to mix and set aside for 30-40 minutes. Rinse under cold running water and drain thoroughly, then pat dry.

■ Meanwhile, put the sesame seeds in a small cast-iron frying pan set over a medium-high heat. Stir the seeds about for a few minutes until they are roasted and give out a nutty aroma. Set aside.

■ Peel the garlic and chop it finely. Cut the entire spring onion into very fine rounds.

■ Set a wok over a high heat. When hot, add the vegetable oil. When the oil is hot, add the garlic and stir once or twice until it begins to colour. Add the courgettes and fry, stirring, for 4-5 minutes or until the courgettes are just done.

■ Season with salt to taste. Add the spring onion and sesame oil. Stir once or twice, then add the roasted sesame seeds. Stir once and serve. (Or allow to cool and serve cold as a salad.)

*It is said that the birth of Korea was the direct result of a union between the son of the divine creator, a bear and twenty cloves of garlic. The bear wanted to become human so the god gave it the garlic, suggesting that it retire for 100 days. It emerged as a woman and had a son by the god. This child, Tan'gun, then went on to found Korea. The Koreans may or may not have divinity in their blood. They certainly have a lot of garlic in it. They eat it morning, noon and night, sometimes raw, sometimes grilled, sometimes pickled, and almost always as a seasoning for their marinated and grilled meats and stews. I find it rather amusing that Western nutritionists are now telling us what Asian folk wisdom has known for centuries – that garlic cleanses the blood and keeps it flowing freely.*

# COURGETTES WITH PORK AND PRAWNS

## *Bau Xao*

*VIETNAM*

Serves 4

When I asked a government official in Hanoi what he had eaten for his lunch that day, he said that he had brought it from home and that it consisted of green beans stir-fried with a little pork and some rice. Vegetables are nearly always cooked with pork or seafood, or both, in Vietnam. The amount of flesh is not necessarily large, but just enough to flavour the vegetables. For this recipe, I buy one large thin-cut pork chop and then take the meat off the bone.

**500 g (1¼ lb) courgettes**
**½ teaspoon salt**
**100 g (4 oz) uncooked unpeeled prawns**
**100 g (4 oz) lean pork**
**7-8 tablespoons fresh coriander leaves**
**65 g (2½ oz) onions**
**1 clove garlic**
**1 spring onion**
**2 tablespoons vegetable oil**
**freshly ground black pepper**
**2 tablespoons fish sauce, or salt to taste**

**1** Trim the courgettes and cut them into quarters lengthways. Cut away and discard most of the seeded area. Now cut the courgette shells into fingers that are roughly 6 cm (2½ inches) long, 1 cm (½ inch) wide and 5 mm (¼ inch) thick. Put these into a bowl. Add the salt and toss to mix. Set aside for 30 minutes. Wash the courgettes under cold running water and pat them as dry as possible.

**2** Peel and de-vein the prawns and split them in half lengthways. Cut the pork into 3 mm (⅛ inch) thick slices, about 6 cm (2½ inches) long and 5 mm-1 cm (¼-½ inch) wide.

**3** Chop the coriander leaves coarsely. Peel and finely chop the onions and garlic. Cut the spring onion into fine rings along its entire length, including the green section.

**4** Put the oil in a large frying pan or wok and set it over a high heat. When hot, add the garlic and onion, and stir-fry for 1 minute. Add the pork and prawns. Stir and cook for 2 minutes. Then put in the courgettes, pepper and fish sauce. Stir and fry for about 3 minutes. Add the coriander and spring onion. Stir and cook for 30 seconds. Serve hot.

# CAULIFLOWER WITH GINGER AND CORIANDER

## *Gobi Ki Bhaji*

*INDIA*

Serves 6-8

When an Indian housewife buys vegetables, the shopkeeper, if friendly, will often throw in a handful of green chillies and a bunch of fresh coriander free. These two items are essential to Indian cooking and they feature strongly here.

**6 x 2.5 cm (2½ x 1 inch) piece fresh root ginger**
**1 large cauliflower**
**8 tablespoons vegetable oil**
**½ teaspoon ground turmeric**
**1 fresh hot green chilli, finely sliced, or ¼ teaspoon cayenne pepper (optional)**
**1 teacup (firmly packed) coarsely chopped fresh coriander leaves**
**1 teaspoon ground cumin**
**2 teaspoons ground coriander**
**1 teaspoon garam masala**
**1 tablespoon lemon juice**
**salt**

■ Peel and coarsely chop the ginger, then put into a blender with 4 tablespoons of water. Blend until smooth.

■ Cut off the thick, coarse stem of the cauliflower and remove all leaves. Break the cauliflower into florets, with your hands, or a sharp knife if it is tightly packed. Slice the lower part of the stems into fairly thin rounds, then cut the cauliflower into slim delicate florets – no wider than 2.5 cm (1 inch), with stems no longer than 4 cm (1½ inches). Wash the florets and stem slices in a colander and leave to drain.

■ Heat the oil in a large frying pan over a medium heat. Add the ginger paste and turmeric and fry, stirring constantly, for about 2 minutes. Add the green chilli or cayenne pepper and green coriander. Cook, stirring, for another 2 minutes.

■ Add the cauliflower and continue to cook, stirring, for 5 minutes. (If the mixture begins to stick to the pan, sprinkle with 1 teaspoon warm water from time to time.)

■ Add the cumin, coriander, garam masala, lemon juice, salt and 3 tablespoons warm water. Cook, stirring, for 3-4 minutes. Cover the pan, lower the heat, and cook slowly for 35-40 minutes, stirring gently every 10 minutes. The cauliflower is ready when it is tender with just a faint trace of crispness along its inner spine.

■ Transfer to a shallow serving bowl. Serve with hot chapatis, or parathas, or any kind of lentil dish and plain boiled rice.

*Indian vegetable markets are an absolute delight to the eye and a source of great anticipatory glee to the palate. India produces most of the vegetables and fruit found in this country and many more but, of course, everything is seasonal. For example, you can expect to buy corn from August through to October, mangoes in the summer, cauliflower in the winter, and fresh mushrooms only during the humid monsoons. As a consequence our menu changes considerably with the seasons.*

# SALAD OF CUCUMBER, CARROTS, CELERY AND HAM

## *Liang Ban Yangcai*

*HONG KONG*

Serves 4

This Shanghai-style salad is normally made with the addition of vermicelli-like strands of agar-agar, a vegetable form of gelatine. Although powdered agar-agar is available in this country, it is difficult to find the stranded version, so I have excluded it here. If you can find it, cut about 12 g (⅓ oz) into 5 cm (2 inch) lengths with a pair of scissors, then soak it in 450 ml (¾ pint) water for 30 minutes. Drain, pat it dry and add it to the salad ingredients. The dressing should, in any case, be mixed in only at the last minute.

**100 g (4 oz) carrots**
**65 g (2½ oz) celery**
**165 g (5½ oz) cucumber**
**25 g (1 oz) lean ham**

**FOR THE DRESSING**
**1 tablespoon Chinese light soy sauce**
**1 tablespoon distilled white vinegar**
**1 tablespoon sesame oil**
**¼ teaspoon sugar**

■ Peel the carrots and cut them into fine julienne strips, about 5 cm (2 inch) long. Cut the celery into 5 cm (2 inch) lengths, then into fine julienne strips.

■ Bring a medium pan of water to a rolling boil. Drop in the carrots and celery and leave for 30-40 seconds. (The water may not even come to the boil again during this time.) Drain the vegetables and immediately refresh under cold running water. Drain again and put them into a bowl.

■ Peel the cucumber, cut it into fine, 5 cm (2 inch) long julienne strips and add to the carrots and celery. Cut the ham into fine, 5 cm (2 inch) long julienne strips as well. Wrap in cling film and refrigerate if necessary.

■ For the dressing, mix the soy sauce, vinegar, sesame oil and sugar together in a small bowl and set aside.

■ Just before serving, add the ham to the vegetable julienne and toss together. Stir the dressing, pour it over the salad and toss to mix.

*You will find certain staples in most Hong Kong kitchens: rice; soy sauces, light and dark; vinegars of varying hues; oil for cooking (peanut) and flavouring (sesame); as well as preserved and pickled foods. The spice rack may hold red chillies, Sichuan peppercorns, star anise, cassia bark and sesame seeds. Other ingredients are bought fresh and often on a daily basis from markets. Shoppers are choosy about their vast selection of vegetable produce – including bean curd, bamboo shoots, fungi, gourds, cabbages and radishes – and fresh herbs and seasonings, such as fresh coriander, chives and ginger.*

# GREENS WITH GARLIC AND OYSTER SAUCE OR 'FLYING' GREENS

## *Pak Bung Loy Fa*

*THAILAND*

Serves 4

Swamp morning glory, also known as swamp cabbage and water spinach (*pak bung* and *kangkung*) are cheap in Thailand, nourishing and utterly delicious. They grow in or near water, and are eaten throughout South-east Asia.

Most of us cannot get swamp morning glory, but luckily any greens will do – young spring greens, spinach, Swiss chard, the Chinese *choi sam* and *gai lan*.

In Chiang Mai, where I saw these greens being prepared, the ingredients were combined on a plate and then emptied into a very hot wok encircled by billowing flames. Because most of us cannot expect to get this sort of intense heat in our kitchens at home, I add the ingredients to the wok in my own slower order.

**350 g (12 oz) spring greens (trimmed weight)**
**3 cloves garlic**
**2 tablespoons meat, poultry or vegetable stock, or water**
**1 tablespoon oyster sauce**
**2 teaspoons crushed yellow bean sauce, or soy sauce**
**3 tablespoons vegetable oil**

■ Separate and trim the greens. Bring a large pan of water to a rolling boil. Drop in the greens and boil rapidly for a few minutes or until just tender. Drain immediately and plunge them into cold water to set the colour. Drain thoroughly.

■ Peel the garlic and chop it finely. Combine the stock, oyster sauce and yellow bean sauce in a small bowl.

■ Set a wok over a high heat and add the oil. When hot, add the garlic, stir quickly until golden brown, then add the greens. Stir for a brief minute. Add the stock mixture and cook, stirring, on a high heat, for another minute or so. Pour out any liquid into a serving dish. Give the greens a final stir, then lift out and lay them over the liquid in the dish. Serve at once.

*One day, or so this recent legend goes, a young chef in an open-air restaurant in the northern town of Phitsanulok, stir-fried this recipe in a wok, then tossed the greens into the air a few times before transferring it to a serving plate. He noticed that he had an audience. He threw it higher the next time, then higher and higher until he made an act out of it. Soon he was not content with throwing the greens 20 feet into the air and catching them. He decided to throw them across the street where an acrobatic second chef ran to catch them on a serving plate. Of course, a few strands did end up on telephone wires and in trees, but the dining audience was hooked! Nowadays members of the same family do their 'act' in Chiang Mai and Pattaya as well, to great acclaim. Fortunately the greens taste good even if they are not air-borne before being eaten.*

*Kohlrabi belongs to the cabbage family. You have probably seen it in Indian or South-east Asian grocers' shops, if not in your local supermarket. It consists of a pale green or purple turnip-shaped ball from which grow long edible leaves. Only the ball itself is required for this recipe.*

# KOHLRABI SALAD

## *Nom Su Hao*

*VIETNAM*

Serves 4

This popular and delicious salad is served at most weddings in north Vietnam. It calls for kohlrabi, a vegetable that is probably still unfamiliar to many Westerners. When I was a child growing up in India, we, the four daughters, insisted that our father grow it in our vegetable garden. We loved it with a passion and devoured it raw while it was still young and tender. I did not care for it in its cooked version then, though I have since changed my mind.

If you cannot obtain kohlrabi, use the larger stems from heads of broccoli. Peel them before cutting them into julienne strips; you will need 225 g (8 oz) peeled stems. The taste of the two is very similar. When cutting kohlrabi, you will notice that almost a quarter of the bottom end is fibrous and very hard – this should be cut away and discarded.

400 g (14 oz) kohlrabi with leaves – peeled weight 225 g (8 oz), or broccoli stems (see above)
50 g (2 oz) carrot
salt
4 teaspoons distilled white vinegar
1 teaspoon sugar
⅛ teaspoon chilli powder
10-12 fresh mint leaves
2-3 tablespoons fresh coriander leaves

TO SERVE
1 fresh hot red or green chilli (optional)
40 g (1½ oz) Roasted Peanuts (see page 223)

**1** Peel the kohlrabi and cut it lengthways into 1.5 mm (1/16 inch) thick slices. Stacking a few slices at a time together, cut lengthways into 1.5 mm (1/16 inch) julienne strips.

**2** Peel the carrot and cut into 4-5 cm (1½-2 inch) lengths. Cut these into 1.5 mm (1/16 inch) thick julienne strips.

**3** Put the kohlrabi and carrot into a bowl. Add 1 teaspoon salt and mix thoroughly with your hands. Set aside for 10-15 minutes. The kohlrabi will begin to sweat. Squeeze out as much moisture as you can and pat dry with kitchen paper. Wipe the bowl dry and put the vegetables back into it.

**4** Add the vinegar, sugar, chilli powder and a pinch of salt. Toss to mix. Taste the salad and adjust the seasoning if necessary. Tear the mint leaves into pieces and add them, with the coriander leaves, to the salad. Toss to mix. Cut the chilli into fine shreds, if using. Chop the peanuts coarsely. Just before serving, add the peanuts to the salad and toss well. Serve the salad garnished with chilli shreds.

# BEAN CURD WITH OYSTER SAUCE

## *Haoyou Doufu*

*HONG KONG*

Serves 4-6

This dish is made with fried bean curd. Bean curd turns spongy when it is fried and is better able to absorb sauces.

- **6-8 dried Chinese mushrooms, or large fresh mushroom caps**
- **450 g (1 lb) firm bean curd (*tofu*)**
- **oil for deep-frying**
- **1 teaspoon cornflour**
- **120 ml (4 fl oz) chicken stock, plus 1 tablespoon**
- **1 clove garlic**
- **1 teaspoon Chinese light soy sauce**
- **2 teaspoons Chinese dark soy sauce**
- **3 tablespoons oyster sauce**
- **2 teaspoons sugar**
- **120 g (4½ oz) fresh peas (shelled weight), or frozen peas (defrosted)**
- **1 tablespoon sesame oil**

■ Put the dried mushrooms in a bowl, add warm water to cover and leave to soak for 30 minutes or until soft. Remove them from the water and cut off the hard stems.

■ Cut the bean curd into slices, ½ x 4 x 5 cm (½ x 1½ x 2 inches). Place on a sheet of kitchen paper and cover with another piece of kitchen paper to dry them.

■ Heat the oil in a wok or deep-fat fryer over a medium-high heat; it should be about 5 cm (2 inches) deep in the centre of the wok if you are using one. When the oil is hot, fry the bean curd until golden brown on both sides. Remove and leave to drain on a plate lined with kitchen paper.

■ Mix the cornflour with 1 tablespoon chicken stock in a cup. Peel and finely chop the garlic.

■ Combine the light and dark soy sauces, oyster sauce, sugar and 120 ml (4 fl oz) chicken stock in a small bowl. Stir to mix.

■ Put 2 tablespoons oil in a wok or large frying pan and set it over a high heat. When the oil is hot, add the garlic and stir-fry for 30 seconds. Add the Chinese mushrooms or fresh mushroom caps and continue to stir and fry for about 1 minute. Now add the bean curd and toss it gently with the mushrooms.

■ Pour in the oyster sauce mixture. Cover, turn the heat to low and simmer very gently for 8 minutes. Then add the peas. Simmer, covered, for a further 2 minutes. Remove the lid and take the wok off the heat.

■ Stir the cornflour mixture and pour it into the wok. Return to the heat and add the sesame oil. Stir gently and cook on a low heat until the sauce has thickened. Serve at once.

# MANGETOUT STIR-FRIED WITH PRAWNS

## *Sitsaro Guisado*

*PHILIPPINES*

Serves 4

Many vegetables in the Philippines are cooked with just a few chopped prawns or cockles, or snippets of pork, in order to flavour them gently. This exquisite dish fits just as successfully into Western meals as it does into Eastern ones.

**350 g (12 oz) mangetout**
**3 cloves garlic**
**25 g (1 oz) onion**
**4 medium uncooked unpeeled prawns**
**3 tablespoons olive oil**
**½ teaspoon salt**
**4 tablespoons chicken, duck or pork stock**
**freshly ground black pepper**

■ Trim the mangetout. Peel and finely chop the garlic and onion.

■ Peel and de-vein the prawns. Wash them and pat dry. Cut the prawns into 5 mm (¼ inch) pieces.

■ Heat the oil in a large wok or frying pan set over a medium-high heat. When the oil is hot, add the garlic and onion and stir-fry for about 30 seconds or until golden.

■ Add the prawns and stir-fry for 30 seconds. Put in the mangetout and stir-fry for another 30 seconds. Add the salt and stir to mix.

■ Add the stock and cover the pan immediately. Cook on a medium-high heat for about 1½ minutes or until the mangetout are just cooked but still crisp. Season with black pepper and serve.

# SEASONED SPINACH

## *Sigumchi Namul* — *KOREA*

Serves 4

Although this recipe comes from Korea, a very similar dish is eaten in Japan. Both are offered at room temperature in relatively small quantities and serve as appetizers. The Koreans tend to put the entire amount on to a single plate while the Japanese divide it up into individual portions and serve it mounded up into tiny hillocks.

**275 g (10 oz) fresh spinach**
**salt**

FOR THE DRESSING
**1½ tablespoons sesame seeds**
**1½ tablespoons Japanese soy sauce (*shoyu*)**
**1 teaspoon sugar**
**1 tablespoon sesame oil**

■ Trim any coarse stems from the spinach, separate the leaves, and wash them thoroughly. Bring a large pan of lightly salted water to a rolling boil and drop in the spinach. Boil rapidly until the leaves have wilted. Drain well and immediately plunge the spinach into cold water to set the colour. Drain and squeeze out as much water as possible. Cut the spinach into 5 cm (2 inch) lengths.

■ To make the dressing, put the sesame seeds into a small cast-iron frying pan set over a medium-high heat. Stir the seeds about for a few minutes until they are roasted and impart a nutty aroma. Transfer to a clean coffee grinder or mortar and grind coarsely. Turn the ground sesame seeds into a bowl. Add the soy sauce, sugar and sesame oil and stir well.

■ Pour the dressing over the spinach and toss to mix. Taste and adjust the seasoning if necessary, adding more soy sauce if you think it is needed, then serve.

# SPINACH WITH GARLIC AND FISH SAUCE

## *Pad Pak Bung* — *THAILAND*

Serves 4-6

Here is a simple and delicious way to cook spinach Thai-style.

**750 g (1¾ lb) fresh spinach**
**3 cloves garlic**
**5 tablespoons vegetable oil (preferably groundnut)**
**4-5 teaspoons fish sauce, or salt to taste**

■ Pull the spinach leaves apart and wash them well; drain. Bring a large pan of water to a rolling boil. Drop in the spinach. Bring the water to the boil again, and boil rapidly for 2 minutes or until the spinach is barely cooked. Drain and rinse under cold running water to set the bright green colour. Drain again.

■ Peel the garlic and chop it finely. Heat the oil in a wok or large frying pan set over a medium-high heat. When the oil is hot, add the garlic and stir-fry for 30 seconds or until it turns golden.

■ Add the spinach and cook, stirring, for 3 minutes. Add the fish sauce or salt to taste. Cook for a further minute, stirring frequently. Serve at once.

# MUSHROOMS IN A SPRING ONION DRESSING

## *Kinoko No Aemono*

*JAPAN*

Serves 4

The mushrooms in this recipe are eaten raw so it is essential to use very fresh unblemished ones. If you haven't any Japanese rice vinegar, use 3 tablespoons distilled white vinegar mixed with 1 tablespoon water and ¼ teaspoon sugar.

**400 g (14 oz) large fresh mushrooms – preferably with 5 cm (2 inch) caps**

**5 spring onions**

**3 tablespoons sake**

**2 tablespoons Japanese soy sauce (*shoyu*)**

**4 tablespoons Japanese rice vinegar**

**½ teaspoon salt**

**TO GARNISH (OPTIONAL)**

**finely shredded spring onion**

■ Wipe the mushrooms with a damp cloth. If they are large, quarter them; otherwise halve them. Finely chop the spring onions.

■ Put the mushrooms and spring onions in a bowl. Add all the remaining ingredients and toss to mix. Leave the mushrooms to marinate in their dressing for 5 minutes, then toss again and set aside for another 5 minutes.

■ Toss the mushrooms once more before serving, garnished with spring onion shreds if you like.

*The national drink in Japan is undoubtedly sake. These days, however, whisky or beer may be drunk right through a meal, and French wines, too, are encroaching.*
*For an informal meal, a family might serve grilled fish, a salad-like dish of spinach or beans dressed with sesame seeds, and perhaps carrots braised in stock, or a dish of mushrooms. There would be soup, rice, pickles and tea to round off the meal.*

# SPICED MUSHROOMS IN A PACKET

## *Pepes Jamur*

*INDONESIA*

Serves 4

In Indonesia fresh straw mushrooms are steamed in banana leaves to delicious effect. Although these mushrooms are not yet available fresh to us in the West, I find that ordinary white mushrooms make a good substitute here. Instead of steaming in banana leaves, I bake my mushrooms in foil packets, unless I am able to buy banana leaves.

**50 g (2 oz) fresh coconut, or 25 g (1 oz) unsweetened desiccated coconut**
**1 large clove garlic**
**2 tablespoons lime or lemon juice**
**1-2 fresh hot green or red chillies**
**½ teaspoon shrimp or anchovy paste**
**⅛ teaspoon chilli powder**
**¾ teaspoon salt**
**225 g (8 oz) fresh mushrooms**

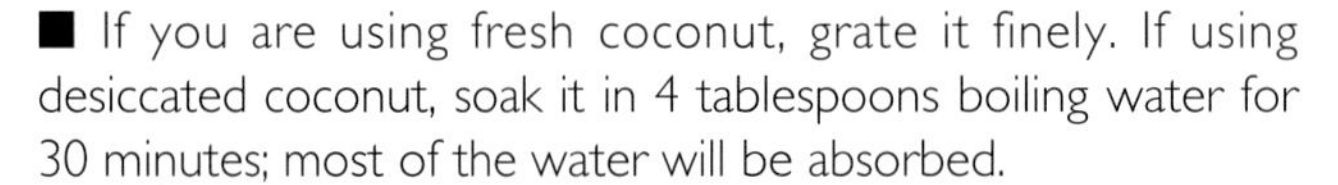

■ If you are using fresh coconut, grate it finely. If using desiccated coconut, soak it in 4 tablespoons boiling water for 30 minutes; most of the water will be absorbed.

■ Peel and crush the garlic. Mix the crushed garlic with the lime juice in a large bowl. Chop the chillies very finely. Add them to the garlic-lime juice mixture with the shrimp paste, coconut, chilli powder and salt. Mix well.

■ Preheat the oven to 180°C (350°F) gas mark 4. Wipe the mushrooms with a damp cloth and cut into 5 mm (¼ inch) thick slices. Add them to the bowl containing the coconut mixture. Toss well.

■ Lay a large piece of foil about 45 cm (18 inches) long, or a few banana leaves on a work surface. Empty the tossed mushrooms and all the spices in the centre of the foil (or banana leaves). Fold the foil (or leaves) over the mushrooms and seal to make a neat packet. Place the packet in the oven and bake for 30 minutes. Open carefully and empty the mushrooms into a serving bowl.

*I was driving through Jogyakarta's university area with Sri Owen, the noted Indonesian food specialist, when she brought the car to an abrupt halt. She pointed to a lone vendor on a bicycle, saying, 'There, there he is,' and hopped out, only to return with several banana leaf packets of some of the tastiest mushrooms I had ever eaten. Fresh straw mushrooms had been tossed with a spicy coconut mixture, wrapped up in banana leaves and steamed.*

# SPICY YELLOW SPLIT PEAS

## *Parpu*

*MALAYSIA*

Serves 4-6

This was originally a South Indian dish, as its Tamil name attests. It changed, just very slightly, as it moved through Malaysia. Here, even though the traditional Indian *toovar dal* is preferred, it is harder to find and more expensive. Hence yellow split peas are commonly used instead. This dish may be served with rice, or with naan or pitta bread.

**280 g (10½ oz) yellow split peas**
**2 x 5 cm (2 inch) sticks cinnamon**
**4-8 dried hot red chillies**
**½ teaspoon ground turmeric**
**225 g (8 oz) potatoes**
**1 large clove garlic**
**1 cm (½ inch) cube fresh root ginger**
**1½ teaspoons salt**
**200 ml (7 fl oz) coconut milk (see page 258)**
**40 g (1½ oz) onion**
**1 teaspoon mustard seeds (black or yellow)**
**½ teaspoon fennel seeds**
**6-8 fresh or dried curry leaves (optional)**
**4 tablespoons vegetable oil or ghee**

■ Wash the split peas, drain and put them in a heavy-based pan. Add the cinnamon, half the red chillies, the turmeric and 900 ml (1½ pints) water. Bring to a simmer. Partially cover and simmer gently for about 45 minutes or until the peas are almost tender.

■ Meanwhile, peel the potatoes and cut into pieces about ½ inch (1 cm) thick and about 2 cm (¾ inch) long. Peel the garlic and ginger and cut them into very fine strips.

■ Add the potatoes, garlic, ginger, salt and 120 ml (4 fl oz) water to the peas. Bring back to a gentle simmer and cook, covered, for a further 20 minutes, stirring now and then to prevent sticking. Stir the coconut milk and pour it in. Bring back to a simmer, stirring. Cover and turn off the heat; keep warm.

■ Peel and finely slice the onion. Mix the mustard seeds, fennel seeds, remaining chillies and curry leaves together in a small bowl.

■ Heat the oil or ghee in a small frying pan. When it is hot, add the onion and fry stirring, until brown. Add the mustard seed mixture and stir briefly over the heat.

■ Add the spice and onion mixture to the peas, replacing the lid of the pan immediately to hold in the aromas. Serve hot.

# VEGETABLE SALAD WITH A PEANUT DRESSING

## *Gado-gado*

*INDONESIA*

Serves 4 as a main course, or 8 as a first course or salad

My family's idea of a perfect lunch is *gado-gado*. It is light and meatless, which suits us in the middle of the day. It also happens to be mouth-watering and totally satisfying in a way that many so-called 'light' salads are not.

It may be described as a composed salad: vegetables of various humble sorts – cabbage, cauliflower, green beans, bean sprouts, carrots, potatoes, cucumbers – as well as hard-boiled eggs, are all neatly laid out on individual plates. Then a kind of cooked vinaigrette, rich with crushed peanuts, is poured over the top. The result is as magical as it is nutritious.

Although I have suggested vegetables to include, you may vary them or their quantities according to what is to hand. It is the perfect way to use up the odd few carrots or the remaining quarter of a cabbage!

All the parts of this salad may be prepared several hours ahead. It can also be assembled in advance and covered with cling film until you are ready to eat. The dressing should, however, be poured on at the last minute. In Indonesia, Prawn Wafers (see page 40) are always served on the side.

**250 g (9 oz) new potatoes (or 'salad' potatoes)**
**3 eggs**
**100 g (4 oz) green beans**
**75 g (3 oz) carrots**
**150 g (5 oz) cauliflower**
**100 g (4 oz) cabbage**
**100 g (4 oz) bean sprouts**
**150 g (5 oz) cucumber**
**salt**

FOR THE PEANUT DRESSING

**100 g (4 oz) Roasted Peanuts (see page 223)**
**2 cloves garlic**
**25 g (1 oz) shallots or onion**
**2 tablespoons vegetable oil**
**½ teaspoon chilli powder**
**½ teaspoon salt**
**2 teaspoons dark brown sugar**
**4-5 teaspoons lime or lemon juice**
**freshly ground black pepper**

■ Cook the potatoes in boiling salted water until tender. Drain, then leave until cool enough to handle. Peel them and cut into 5 mm (¼ inch) thick slices. Hard-boil the eggs. Shell them and cut lengthways into quarters.

■ Keep all the raw vegetables separate as you prepare them. Trim the green beans and cut into 5 cm (2 inch) lengths. Peel the carrots, cut into 5 cm (2 inch) lengths, then halve or quarter these sections lengthways (so the carrots are a similar size to the beans).

■ Cut the cauliflower into small delicate florets. Cut the cabbage into long, fine shreds. Break off and discard the thread-like tails of the bean sprouts, then rinse well in a bowl of cold water; drain. Peel and slice the cucumber into rounds.

■ Place a sieve over a large bowl near the hob. Also set out several plates to hold the different vegetables as they are cooked.

■ Bring a pan of salted water to a rolling boil. Add the green beans and carrots, bring back to the boil and boil rapidly for about 3 minutes or until the vegetables are just cooked. Drain the vegetables in the sieve; return the water to the pan. Immediately refresh the vegetables under cold running water, drain thoroughly and put them on a plate.

■ Bring the water to a rolling boil again. Add the cauliflower, return to the boil and boil rapidly for about 1½ minutes or until just tender, but retaining a hint of crispness. Drain and refresh under cold running water (as above); put on a plate.

■ Cook the cabbage and bean sprouts in the same way, boiling the cabbage for about 1 minute and the bean sprouts for 30 seconds. Drain each and refresh under cold running water. Squeeze any excess moisture from the cabbage and bean sprouts and separate the strands before putting them on separate plates.

■ To make the dressing, grind the peanuts in a clean coffee grinder or spice grinder as finely as possible. Peel and finely chop the garlic and shallots. Heat the oil in a small frying pan over a medium heat. When hot, add the garlic and shallots and fry, stirring, until golden brown.

■ Add 450 ml (¾ pint) water, the chilli powder, salt, sugar and ground peanuts. Stir and bring to the boil. Turn the heat to medium-low and simmer, stirring occasionally, for 15-20 minutes or until the sauce has thickened (to the consistency of a creamy salad dressing). Allow to cool slightly, then add the lime juice and pepper to taste.

■ Arrange the potatoes, eggs, green beans and carrots, cauliflower, cabbage, bean sprouts and cucumber side by side on 4 large individual plates or shallow serving dishes. Just before serving, pour about a quarter of the dressing evenly over each serving. Allow diners to toss their own salad.

# CHICKPEAS WITH GARLIC AND GINGER

## *Aloo Chole*

*INDIA*

Serves 6

This makes a tasty, substantial snack meal, served with Indian bread, such as naan, and a relish, such as Cucumber Raita (see page 224) or Fresh Coriander and Yogurt Chutney (see page 224). It is also an excellent accompaniment to almost any meat or chicken dish. You will need to remember to put the chickpeas to soak the night before.

**175 g (6 oz) chickpeas (large chanas)**

**¼ teaspoon bicarbonate of soda**

**4 medium potatoes**

**10 cloves garlic**

**2 x 2.5 cm (1 inch) cubes fresh root ginger**

**3 medium tomatoes (canned or peeled fresh)**

**5 tablespoons vegetable oil**

**pinch of ground asafetida, or a tiny lump asafetida**

**½ teaspoon ground turmeric**

**salt**

**freshly ground black pepper**

**¼-½ teaspoon cayenne pepper (less if desired)**

**2 tablespoons lemon juice**

■ Put the chickpeas in a bowl, add the bicarbonate of soda and pour on 900 ml (1½ pints) cold water. Leave to soak overnight.

■ The following day, transfer the chickpeas and any remaining liquid to a large pan or cooking pot. Add 600 ml (1 pint) water. Bring to the boil and skim off any froth from the surface. Cover, lower the heat and simmer gently for about 1 hour or until the chickpeas are tender. Turn off the heat.

■ Meanwhile, peel the potatoes and cook in boiling salted water until tender. Drain and cut into quarters; set aside.

■ Peel and chop the garlic and ginger. Put the garlic, ginger and tomatoes in a blender with 2 tablespoons water and blend to a smooth paste.

■ Drain the cooked chickpeas, reserving 300 ml (½ pint) of the liquid.

■ Heat the oil in a large frying pan or flameproof casserole over a medium heat, then add the asafetida. As soon as it sizzles and expands, after a few seconds, add the paste from the blender, keeping your face averted, and sprinkle in the turmeric. Fry, stirring, for 1-2 minutes.

■ Pour in the reserved 300 ml (½ pint) liquid and put in the chickpeas and potatoes. Add 1 teaspoon salt, black pepper and cayenne to taste, and the lemon juice. Bring to the boil, cover, lower the heat and simmer gently for 30 minutes. Check the seasoning before serving.

# NORTH INDIAN MOONG DAL

## *Moong Dal*

*INDIA*

Serves 6

This is North India's most popular dal. It is eaten with equal relish by toothless toddlers, husky farmers and effete urban snobs! The simple recipe given below can also be used for the white *urad dal*, the salmon-coloured *masoor dal*, and the large *arhar* or *toovar dal*.

**285 g (10 oz) moong dal, hulled and split**
**2 cloves garlic**
**2 slices fresh root ginger, 2.5 cm (1 inch) square and 3 mm (1/8 inch) thick**
**1 teaspoon chopped fresh coriander leaves**
**1 tablespoon ground turmeric**
**1/4-1/2 teaspoon cayenne pepper (optional)**
**salt**
**1 1/2 tablespoon lemon juice**
**3 tablespoons vegetable oil or ghee**
**pinch of ground asafetida, or a tiny lump asafetida**
**1 teaspoon cumin seeds**
**lemon or lime wedges, to serve**

■ Wash the dal thoroughly and place in a large heavy-based pan or cooking pot. Add 1.1 litres (2 pints) water and bring to the boil. Remove the froth and scum that collects on the surface.

■ Meanwhile, peel the garlic and ginger. Add the garlic, ginger, coriander, turmeric, and cayenne pepper if using, to the pan. Partially cover, lower the heat and simmer gently for about 1 1/2 hours, stirring occasionally. When the dal is cooked, the consistency should be thicker than pea soup, but thinner than porridge. Add salt to taste and the lemon juice. Transfer to a serving dish.

■ Heat the vegetable oil or ghee in a small cast-iron frying pan over a medium-high heat. When hot, add the asafetida and cumin seeds and fry for a few seconds until the asafetida sizzles and expands and the cumin seeds darken.

■ Immediately pour the oil and spices over the dal and serve, with lemon or lime wedges and rice or bread. Dal is an excellent side dish to accompany most meat and chicken dishes. For a simple meal, serve the dal with plain rice, *Kheema* (see page 136), and a vegetable.

*Pulses – dried beans, peas and lentils – are a staple in India and are eaten in some form or other on a daily basis in almost every Indian home. For those who are poor, they are often the only source of protein. While we talk of earning our 'bread and butter', Indians speak of earning their 'dal roti' – roti meaning bread.*

# rice, pancakes and noodles

# PLAIN LONG-GRAIN RICE

Serves 4-6

In this recipe and all those using rice, you will see that the rice is measured by volume rather than by weight. I prefer to do it this way because the ratio of rice to cooking liquid is crucial and this method makes for greater accuracy. Simply measure the rice in a standard measuring jug.

**450 ml (¾ pint) long-grain rice**

■ Put the rice in a bowl and fill the bowl with cold water. Rub the rice gently with your hands. When the water turns milky, pour it off. Do this several times in quick succession until the water runs clear. Now fill the bowl with fresh water and leave the rice to soak for 30 minutes. Drain.

■ Put the drained rice into a heavy-based medium pan. Add 600 ml (1 pint) water and bring to the boil. Cover with a tight-fitting lid. (If your lid is not tight-fitting, cover the pan first with foil, crimping the edges, and then cover with the lid.) Turn the heat to very low and cook for 25 minutes.

■ If left covered in a warm place, this rice will retain its heat for up to an hour.

# BASMATI RICE

## *Basmati Chaaval*

*INDIA*

Serves 6

I was brought up with this fine long-grained rice. It is grown in the foothills of the Himalayas and has a very special aroma and flavour. It can be served with almost any Indian dish; I particularly love it with Moong Dal (see page 187) and Lamb with Whole Spices and Onions (see page 141).

**350 g (12 oz) basmati rice**
**salt**
**1 tablespoon butter**

■ Put the rice in a bowl and wash well in several changes of cold water. Fill the bowl with 1.1 litres (2 pints) fresh water, add ½ teaspoon salt and leave to soak for 30 minutes. Drain.

■ Melt the butter in a heavy-based pan over a medium heat. Add the rice and stir for 1 minute. Add 550 ml (18 fl oz) water and ¾ teaspoon salt. Bring to the boil, cover, lower the heat and cook gently for 20 minutes.

■ Fork through the rice gently to separate the grains. Re-cover and cook for a further 10 minutes, or until the rice is tender.

# PLAIN JAPANESE AND KOREAN RICE

## *Gohan, Pab*

*JAPAN, KOREA*

Serves 4-6

The rice in Japan and Korea is a plump short-grain variety which develops a most pleasing stickiness when it is cooked. The grains adhere to each other, making them easy to pick up with chopsticks in small lumps. They can also be easily rolled into ovals and rounds – all the better to be devoured with neat slivers of raw fish or roasted sesame seeds.

The brand to look for in Asian grocers' shops is *Kokuho Rose*. If you cannot find it, use a Thai or American long-grain rice and cook it according to the recipe for Plain Long-Grain Rice (see left). Aromatic rices, such as basmati, are quite unsuitable for Japanese and Korean meals.

If you wish to cook more or less rice than suggested in the recipe below, note that the proportion of rice to water, in volume, is 1:1¼. The cooking time remains the same.

**450 ml (¾ pint) Japanese rice**

■ Put the rice in a bowl and add water to cover generously. Swish the rice around gently with your hand, kneading it lightly as you do so. Pour off the water when it has turned milky. Do this several times in quick succession, until the water remains almost clear.

■ Drain the rice through a sieve. Leave the rice in the sieve for 30 minutes-1 hour to allow it to absorb the moisture that clings to it.

■ Put the rice into a heavy-based pan. Add 550 ml (18 fl oz) water and bring to the boil. Cover, turn the heat to very low and cook for 20 minutes. Turn the heat to high for 30 seconds, then turn it off. Let the pan sit, covered and undisturbed, for 10-15 minutes.

# GLUTINOUS RICE

Serves 4-6

Glutinous rice is also known as sticky rice and sweet rice. The grains are short and white and, when cooked, they turn translucent and slightly glutinous. Throughout much of the Far East this rice is used for both sweets and stuffings. In the region around northern Thailand, however, it is the staple grain. At each meal it is served from a large basket. Each diner forms the rice into a little ball, combines that ball with a bit of meat and a bit of vegetable and then pops the morsel into his or her mouth.

This rice is best steamed, or cooked in a double-boiler. Here is the double-boiler method.

**450 ml (¾ pint) glutinous rice**

■ Wash the rice in several changes of water and drain. Put it in a bowl, cover with plenty of water and leave to soak for 6 hours. Drain, wash again, then drain thoroughly.

■ Heat some water in the bottom of a double-boiler. When it starts to boil, fit the top of the double-boiler and put in the rice and enough water to come 1 cm (½ inch) above the level of the rice. When this water begins to boil, cover the pan and cook on a medium heat for 25 minutes.

*Rice is always served in Japan, even at the most formal of dinners. I have known Japanese men to eat for three hours at official banquets but refrain from devouring that final triumvirate. 'My wife will be waiting up,' they say. 'I will have my rice with her.' Rice symbolises the meal, and the man who has his rice at home is eating his meal with his wife. Symbols mean a lot in Japan.*

# JAPANESE MIXED RICE

## *Kayaku Gohan*

*JAPAN*

Serves 4-6

This delightful mixture of rice, chicken and vegetables may be served as a meal in itself with accompanying salads (and beer!). Alternatively, if you leave the chicken out, it may be served with all manner of simply grilled meats and fish. You may substitute any cubed white fish fillets for the chicken, in which case omit the blanching stage. The rice will probably develop a slightly brown crustiness at the bottom; this is as it should be.

**450 ml (¾ pint) Japanese rice**
**2 boned chicken thighs, or 1 boned chicken leg**
**1 carrot**
**8-12 green beans**
**4 mushrooms**
**550 ml (18 fl oz) Japanese Soup Stock (see page 255), or chicken stock**
**3 tablespoons Japanese soy sauce (*shoyu*)**
**2 tablespoons mirin (or 1 tablespoon sugar dissolved in 1 tablespoon sake or water)**
**about 15 mangetout**
**salt**
**2 tablespoons sake (optional)**
**fresh coriander sprigs, to garnish (optional)**

■ Put the rice in a bowl and add water to cover generously. Swish the rice around gently with your hand. Pour off the water when it turns milky. Do this several times in quick succession, until the water remains almost clear. Drain the rice through a sieve and leave it in the sieve for 30 minutes-1 hour to allow it to absorb the moisture that clings to it.

■ Skin the chicken and cut into 5 mm (¼ inch) dice. Drop into a pan of boiling water for 10-15 seconds. Drain quickly, rinse briefly under cold running water, then drain thoroughly.

■ Peel the carrot and cut into 2.5 cm (1 inch) lengths, then into fine julienne strips. Trim the green beans and cut into 2.5 cm (1 inch) lengths, then into fine julienne strips. Wipe the mushrooms with a damp cloth, then slice thinly.

■ Put the rice, chicken, carrot, green beans, mushrooms, stock, soy sauce and mirin in a heavy-based pan. Bring to the boil, cover tightly, turn the heat to very low and cook for 20 minutes.

■ Meanwhile, cut the mangetout into fine strips. Drop into a pan of lightly salted boiling water and boil rapidly for 15-20 seconds. Drain, refresh under cold running water and drain again.

■ Add the mangetout and sake to the cooked rice. Take off the heat, immediately cover the pan with a clean tea-towel and then with the lid. Set aside for 10-15 minutes before serving; any excess moisture will be absorbed by the tea-towel. Serve garnished with coriander, if you like.

*Rice is the staple grain in Japan. This country has very little arable land and rice is made to grow on every available patch, however small it may be. The Japanese pay a lot for their short-grain, somewhat glutinous rice. They could import it; it would be far cheaper that way. But the Japanese are fiercely independent and do not wish to rely on others for a basic foodstuff. Besides, they like the flavour of their own grain.*

# BASMATI RICE WITH SPICES AND SAFFRON

## *Zaafraani Chawal*

*INDIA*

Serves 6

Although this recipe calls for basmati, any long-grain, fine-quality rice can be used instead. I particularly like to serve this fragrant rice with Chicken Moghlai (see page 107).

1 teaspoon saffron threads
2 tablespoons warm milk
350 g (12 oz) basmati or long-grain rice
salt
2 tablespoons vegetable oil
5 cardamom pods
2 x 7.5 cm (3 inch) cinnamon sticks

■ Dry-roast the saffron in a cast-iron frying pan, cool slightly, then crumble into the warm milk and leave to soak for about 30 minutes.

■ Put the rice in a bowl and wash well in several changes of cold water. Fill the bowl with 1.1 litres (2 pints) fresh water, add ½ teaspoon salt and leave to soak for 30 minutes. Drain.

■ Heat the oil in a heavy-based pan or cooking pot over a medium heat. Put in the cardamom pods and cinnamon sticks, and stir over the heat a few times. Add the rice and fry, stirring, for about 1 minute.

■ Add 550 ml (18 fl oz) water and ¾ teaspoon salt. Bring to the boil, cover with a tight-fitting lid, reduce the heat to very low and cook for 20 minutes.

■ Gently but quickly fork through the rice to separate the grains. Drizzle the saffron-infused milk over the rice to form streaks of colour. Re-cover and cook for a further 10 minutes or until the rice is done. Turn the rice on to a serving platter with a fork. Serve at once.

*Saffron not only imparts its enticing yellow-orange colour, but a delicious flavour to rice as well. I'll never forget my first introduction to saffron. I was in my early teens and on my first visit to Kashmir. We were riding through a valley and past a hill that were completely purple from all the crocuses growing there. I remarked on their beauty and was told by my Kashmiri companions that the flowers meant more than just beauty to them. One of the boys got off his horse, plucked a flower and brought it to me. He pulled the petals apart to reveal the orange stigma, which – on drying – become saffron. He told me that thousands of stigmas were needed to obtain a single tablespoon of saffron threads. No wonder this prized spice is expensive.*

# SPICED RICE WITH CASHEW NUTS

## *Caju Pullao*

*INDIA*

Serves 6

This dish can be found with interesting local variations, all over India. It is not hot – just lightly, fragrantly spiced. Use unsalted raw cashew nuts, not roasted ones.

The cooked rice will retain its heat for a good half hour after you remove it from the oven, as long as the pan is kept covered and in a warm place.

**450 ml (¾ pint) long-grain rice or Indian basmati rice**

**1 medium onion**

**1 clove garlic**

**4 tablespoons vegetable oil**

**2 tablespoons cashew nuts, split**

**1 teaspoon grated fresh root ginger**

**½ teaspoon finely chopped fresh hot green chilli, or pinch of cayenne pepper**

**¾ teaspoon garam masala**

**750 ml (1¼ pints) hot vegetable stock or water**

■ Put the rice in a bowl and add water to cover. Rub the rice grains gently with your hands. When the water turns milky, pour it off. Repeat several times until the water runs clear. Drain the rice and return to the bowl. Cover with 1 litre (1¾ pints) fresh water and leave to soak for 30 minutes. Drain, leaving the rice in a strainer.

■ Preheat the oven to 170°C (325°F) gas mark 3. Peel the onion, halve lengthwise, then slice very thinly. Peel and finely chop the garlic.

■ Heat the oil in a heavy ovenproof frying pan or flameproof casserole over medium heat. Add the cashew nuts and fry for a few seconds, stirring all the time, until they turn golden brown. Remove with slotted spoon and leave on kitchen paper to drain.

■ Fry the onion slices in the oil remaining in the pan for 2-3 minutes or until tinged brown at the edges. Add the drained rice, the garlic, ginger, green chilli, garam masala and salt. Turn the heat to medium-low. Fry, stirring, for 7-8 minutes or until the rice is translucent and well coated with the oil.

■ Pour in the hot stock and cook, stirring, on a medium-low heat for a further 5-6 minutes until the surface of the rice starts to look dry. Cover with a well-fitting lid (see note) and cook in the oven for 20-25 minutes until the rice is cooked.

■ Remove the rice pan from the oven and leave to stand, covered, in a warm place for 10 minutes.

■ Using a slotted spoon, gently transfer the rice to a warmed serving platter, breaking up any lumps with the back of the spoon. Garnish with the cashew nuts and serve at once.

NOTE If the pan lid isn't tight-fitting, improve the seal by placing a piece of crumpled foil underneath it, around the rim.

# SPECIAL FRIED RICE WITH BEEF AND PRAWNS

## *Nasi Goreng Istimewa* *INDONESIA*

Serves 4

This tempting fried rice can be a meal in itself if it is served with Prawn Wafers (see page 40) and either of the Red Pepper Sauces (on page 219).

In Indonesia hot chillies and cucumbers – cut to resemble tropical flora – decorate the rice plate like bunting, along with Egg Strips (see page 223). You may prefer a simpler garnish of finely sliced spring onions and/or chopped hard-boiled eggs and cucumber slices.

Cooked prawns may be used if raw ones are unavailable; if they are small, increase the quantity recommended. Simply add cooked prawns with the cooked rice to heat through.

It is a good idea to cook the rice well ahead, so it has time to cool off completely before it is stir-fried. For optimum flavour, the rice should be stir-fried with all the other ingredients just before eating.

**300 ml (½ pint) long-grain rice**
**100 g (4 oz) red pepper**
**25 g (1 oz) shallots or onion**
**1 teaspoon shrimp or anchovy paste**
**½-1 teaspoon salt**
**¼ teaspoon chilli powder**
**100 g (4 oz) lean beef steak**
**4 uncooked unpeeled prawns**
**2 cabbage leaves**
**4 tablespoons vegetable oil**

**1** Put the rice in a bowl and wash in several changes of water, then drain. Cover it generously with fresh water and leave to soak for 30 minutes; drain again. Put the rice into a heavy-based pan. Add 375 ml (13 fl oz) water and bring to the boil. Cover the pan tightly, turn the heat to very low and cook for 25 minutes. Turn off the heat. Keep covered and let the rice cool to room temperature.

**2** Core, deseed and coarsely chop the red pepper. Peel and coarsely chop the shallots. Combine the red pepper, shallots, shrimp paste, salt and chilli powder in an electric blender. Blend to a smooth paste.

**3** Cut the steak across the grain into very thin slices, then cut the slices into 5 mm (¼ inch) wide strips. Peel and de-vein the prawns. Cut into 5 mm (¼ inch) wide segments. Cover both and set aside, refrigerating if necessary. Cut the cabbage leaves into very fine long shreds.

**4** Shortly before serving, set a wok over a medium-high heat, then put in the oil. When the oil is hot, add the spice paste from the blender. Fry, stirring, for 3-4 minutes until the paste turns dark red and the oil separates. Add the beef and prawns; stir and fry for 1 minute. Add the cabbage and fry, stirring, for a further 1 minute. Now put in all the rice, breaking up any lumps with the back of a slotted spoon. Stir and fry for 4-6 minutes or until the rice is heated through. Garnish as suggested (see recipe introduction), and serve.

*Spices are often a clue to the origin of a recipe. Like so many Malaysian dshes, nasi tomat is of mixed Chinese and Indian origin. Star anise is the dried, unripened fruit of a small tree belonging to the magnolia family, which is native to China. It has a strong, pungent flavour, reminiscent of anise, and is an ingredient in Chinese five-spice powder. Cinnamon originally came from Sri Lanka, but is now used throughout Asia and further afield. This spice is the bark peeled from thinner branches of a small evergreen tree. Cinnamon bark is dried in the sun to form the curled-up scrolls or sticks that are familiar to us. The best quality cinnamon is pale in colour, with a distinctive flavour.*

# TOMATO RICE

## *Nasi Tomat* — *MALAYSIA*

Serves 4-6

This fragrant rice dish can be served with almost any Malaysian meal. The rice is simmered slowly in a mixture of yogurt and tomatoes, enriched with spices and aromatics. When rice is cooked in a thick liquid, there is a tendency for the grains on top to remain slightly underdone. The solution is to turn the rice over halfway through cooking. This must be done quickly to minimize the amount of steam lost.

**450 ml (¾ pint) long-grain rice**
**4 canned peeled plum tomatoes, lightly drained**
**4 tablespoons yogurt**
**50 g (2 oz) shallots or onions**
**2.5 cm (1 inch) cube fresh root ginger**
**8-10 fresh mint leaves**
**3 tablespoons vegetable oil**
**5-6 whole cardamom pods**
**5 cm (2 inch) stick cinnamon**
**½ teaspoon cumin seeds**
**5 cloves**
**1 star anise**
**salt**

■ Wash the rice in several changes of water. Drain and put into a bowl. Cover generously with water and leave it to soak for 30 minutes. Drain.

■ Meanwhile, mash the tomatoes to a pulp. Put the yogurt in a measuring jug and beat with a fork until smooth and creamy. Add the tomatoes and enough water to make up to 600 ml (1 pint). Stir well.

■ Peel the shallots and cut into fine slices. Peel and finely dice the ginger. Chop the mint leaves coarsely.

■ Heat the oil in a heavy-based pan over a moderate heat. When hot, put in the cardamom pods, cinnamon, cumin, cloves and star anise. Stir once or twice, then add the shallots. Fry, stirring, until the shallots are reddish-brown. Add the ginger and stir once.

■ Add the rice and stir for 2 minutes, lowering the heat slightly if the rice starts to stick to the base of the pan. Pour in the tomato-yogurt mixture, season with salt and add the mint. Bring to the boil. Cover well, first with foil and then with a lid. Turn the heat to very low and cook for 15 minutes.

■ Lift the lid, gently turn the rice with a slotted spoon so that the top layer is well buried at the bottom, re-cover and cook for a further 15 minutes or until the rice is done.

# RICE WITH SPINACH

## *Saag Pullao* — *INDIA*

Serves 6

Buy a long-grain rice for this recipe – patna rice is ideal and inexpensive. Don't buy quick-cooking or partially cooked rice. If fresh spinach is not available, substitute a 350 g (12 oz) packet chopped frozen spinach.

This dish is best served straight from the oven, but you can, if necessary, cook it 3-4 hours earlier. When cooked, let stand covered with foil for 5 minutes, then put on a tight-fitting lid, but do not refrigerate. Fifteen minutes before serving, reheat in the oven (at the same setting) for 15 minutes.

**350 g (12 oz) long-grain rice**
**salt**
**675 g (1½ lb) fresh spinach**
**2 medium onions**
**6 tablespoons vegetable oil**
**1 teaspoon garam masala**

■ Wash the rice thoroughly in a colander. Turn into a large bowl, add cold water to cover and 1 teaspoon salt. Leave to soak for 2 hours.

■ Bring a large pan of water to the boil with 1 teaspoon salt added. Trim and thoroughly wash the fresh spinach. In 3 or 4 batches, blanch the spinach in the boiling water until just wilted. Quickly drain, cool slightly and press between the palms of your hands to squeeze out excess moisture. Chop the cooked spinach very finely.

■ Peel and finely chop the onions. Heat the oil in a large flameproof casserole or cooking pot. Add the onions and sauté on a medium heat for about 5 minutes until golden. Add the chopped spinach and garam masala. Sauté for about 30 minutes.

■ Preheat the oven to 150°C (300°F) gas mark 2. Drain the rice and add to the spinach with 600 ml (1 pint) water and 1 teaspoon salt; bring to the boil. Lower the heat and simmer for 15 minutes, stirring occasionally.

■ Cover the casserole or cooking pot with foil, cutting a hole, about 1 cm (½ inch) in diameter, in the middle (to let the steam escape and allow the to rice dry out). Place in the middle of the oven and bake for 30 minutes. Check to see if the rice is done; if not, cook for 5 minutes longer. Serve hot.

# PERFUMED RICE WITH VEGETABLES NONYA-STYLE

## *Nasi Ulam*

*MALAYSIA*

Serves 4-6

This unusual rice dish is first perfumed with fresh herbs, then flavoured with a little fish and finally topped with crunchy raw vegetables. It is exquisite, both in taste and appearance. Rather like fried rice, to which it is a very superior cousin, it may be eaten with other foods or all by itself. Use any tender green beans other than runner beans; in Malaysia long green beans would be used.

Try to get fresh lemon grass and kaffir lime leaves as dried equivalents cannot be used in this dish. However, if you can't get these fresh herbs, all is not lost. Western herbs, such as basil, chervil and summer savory, may be substituted. The dish will taste very different but still interesting.

In Malaysia, where the climate is generally balmy, this rice is served at room temperature. I prefer to serve it hot or warm.

**450 ml (¾ pint) long-grain rice**
**salt**
**4-5 fresh kaffir lime leaves, or 1½ tablespoons grated lemon rind**
**1 stick fresh lemon grass (or 15 fresh basil leaves)**
**65 g (2½ oz) cucumber**
**65 g (2½ oz) long beans or other tender green beans (not runner beans)**
**3 medium shallots, or ½ small onion**
**50 g (2 oz) uncooked unpeeled prawns**
**4 tablespoons vegetable oil**

■ Wash the rice in several changes of water. Drain and place in a bowl. Add plenty of water to cover and leave to soak for 30 minutes.

■ Meanwhile, cut out the central vein from the kaffir lime leaves, then cut the leaves crossways into the thinnest possible strips. Trim the lemon grass, discarding the end of the base and the straw-like top. Cut the rest, approximately 15 cm (6 inches), into very fine rounds. Place in a bowl with the lime leaves and cover.

■ Halve and peel the cucumber, then scoop out the seeds. Cut the flesh into 3 mm (⅛ inch) dice. Trim the ends of the beans, then cut crossways into 3 mm (⅛ inch) pieces. Blanch the beans in boiling water for 30 seconds, then drain and set aside with the cucumber.

■ Drain the rice and place in a medium heavy-based pan with 600 ml (1 pint) water and 1 teaspoon salt. Bring to the boil, cover, turn the heat to very low and cook for 25 minutes.

■ Peel the shallots and cut into paper-thin slices. Peel and de-vein the prawns, then cut into 5 mm (¼ inch) segments.

■ Heat the oil in a frying pan over a medium heat. When the oil is hot, add the shallots and fry, stirring, until they turn medium brown and crisp. Remove with a slotted spoon and spread out on a plate lined with kitchen paper to drain.

■ Fry the prawns in the oil remaining in the pan, stirring constantly, for about 1 minute or until they are cooked. Remove with a slotted spoon, drain and sprinkle very lightly with salt. Reserve the oil in the pan.

■ When the rice is cooked, it may be kept covered in a warm place for a short while.

■ Just before serving, turn the rice into a serving bowl, breaking up any lumps with the back of a slotted spoon. Add the prawns, reserved oil, kaffir lime leaves and lemon grass. (If using basil leaves and lemon rind, add these now.) Toss to mix. Scatter the cucumber and beans over the top, then sprinkle with the fried shallots and serve.

# PAELLA WITH SEAFOOD, CHICKEN AND SAUSAGES

## *Paella*

*PHILIPPINES*

Serves 6

One of the glories of Spain, *paella* now also decks the tables at fiestas and banquets all over the Philippines. While the main ingredients, rice and a touch of saffron, remain the same (the less affluent use colouring from caper-shaped Mexican *achuete* seeds instead), all other ingredients are left to the whim, and pocket, of the cook. In the poorer *barrios*, chicken, green peas and tomatoes suffice, while in the mansions of the rich, *paellas* come with prawns, squid, clams and mussels peeping invitingly out of the rice.

Traditionally a *paella* was cooked on a *paellera*, and in some homes it still is. A *paellera* is a very large, round tray. Rice is cooked in it rather in the manner of an Italian risotto with frequent additions of hot stock and much stirring. Raw, partially cooked and fully cooked meats and seafood are embedded in the rice at frequent intervals and in a sequence that only practised chefs have mastered. All ingredients must be ready at the same time.

Since most of us do not have *paelleras*, here is a delicious *paella* that is cooked in a saucepan. You do need a large, wide, heavy pan with a tight-fitting lid. If you are unsure of the fit of the lid, cover the pan first with foil.

**2 spicy Italian or Spanish sausages, such as chorizo, about 175 g (6 oz) in total**
**2 whole chicken legs, each cut into 3-4 pieces**
**salt**
**freshly ground black pepper**
**6 tablespoons olive oil**
**8 fresh clams in shells**
**8 fresh mussels in shells**
**large pinch of saffron threads**
**about 450 ml (¾ pint) chicken stock**
**12 uncooked unpeeled prawns**
**75 g (3 oz) red pepper**
**75 g (3 oz) green pepper**
**90 g (3½ oz) onions**
**3 cloves garlic**
**175 g (6 oz) fresh peas (shelled weight) or frozen peas**
**750 ml (1¼ pints) long-grain rice**

■ Prick the sausages with a fork. Put them in a frying pan with 150 ml (¼ pint) water and bring to the boil. Cover, turn the heat to medium and cook for 5 minutes. Uncover and continue to cook until the water boils away. Brown the sausages in the fat, that they have exuded. Let cool, then cut into 5 mm (¼ inch) slices.

■ Dust the chicken lightly with salt and pepper. Heat the olive oil in a clean frying pan over a medium heat. When the oil is hot, put in the chicken pieces and fry, turning frequently, for about 10 minutes or until brown on both sides. Remove with a slotted spoon. Reserve the oil.

■ Scrub the clams and mussels clean with a stiff brush under cold running water, pulling off any beards that may still be attached to the mussels. Put the clams and mussels into a pan with 750 ml (1¼ pints) water and bring to the boil. Cover the pan and simmer vigorously over a medium heat for 4-5 minutes or until the shells open. Lift out with a slotted spoon and discard any molluscs that remain closed. Cool, cover and set aside. Strain the cooking liquid through a muslin-lined sieve into a large measuring jug or bowl. Add the saffron and enough chicken stock to make up to 1 litre (1¾ pints).

■ Peel and de-vein the prawns. Rinse and pat them dry. Deseed the peppers and cut lengthways into 5 mm (¼ inch) wide strips. Peel and thinly slice the onions. Peel and finely chop the garlic.

■ If using fresh peas, boil in 600 ml (1 pint) water until just tender. Drain and refresh under cold running water. Drain again and set aside. (If the peas are frozen, cook for just 1 minute; drain, refresh and drain again.

■ Heat 5 tablespoons of the oil in a large, wide heavy-based pan over a medium-high heat. When hot, add the onions and garlic and fry for 2-3 minutes or until soft. Add the peppers. Stir and cook for another 2-3 minutes.

■ Now add the rice and fry, stirring, for 2 minutes, lowering the heat slightly if the rice seems to stick. Add the saffron-infused liquor, the sausages, chicken and ½-1 teaspoon salt. Bring to the boil. Cover, turn the heat to very low and cook for 20 minutes.

■ Lift the lid, quickly bury the prawns in the rice and scatter the peas on top. Cover the pan again and cook for a further 5 minutes.

■ Lift the lid and quickly put in the clams and mussels. Cover and cook for another 2 minutes. Serve at once.

# DOSAS WITH MUSTARD SEEDS AND PEPPER

## *Dosai*

*INDIA*

Makes 8 pancakes

The batter for these pancakes is made in a food processor or blender for convenience. It can also be prepared several hours in advance. Before you start to cook the pancakes, make sure you have everything you need: frying pan, cup of oil, a teaspoon, a rounded soup spoon for spreading out the batter, and a small measuring cup for the batter. You also need a plate to hold the pancakes, and a second plate that you can invert over the pancakes to keep them warm and moist.

If you wish to reheat these pancakes, wrap well in foil, and place in the oven at 200°C (400°F) gas mark 6 for 15 minutes.

**115 g (4 oz) plain white flour**
**140 g (5 oz) rice flour**
**1/8-1/4 teaspoon cayenne pepper**
**115 g (4 oz) chopped onion**
**30 g (1 oz) freshly grated coconut**
**1 1/4 teaspoons salt**
**250 ml (8 fl oz) yogurt (the sourer the better)**
**about 7 tablespoons vegetable oil**
**1 teaspoon whole black mustard seeds**
**3/4-1 teaspoon coarsely crushed black peppercorns**

■ Put the white flour, rice flour, cayenne, onion, coconut, salt, yogurt and 175 ml (6 fl oz) water into a food processor or blender. Blend until smooth, then pour into a bowl.

■ Heat 1 tablespoon oil in a small frying pan over a medium heat. When hot, add the mustard seeds. As soon as they begin to pop – almost immediately – pour the mustard seeds and oil on to the batter. Add the crushed black pepper and mix thoroughly.

■ Set an 18-20 cm (7-8 inch) non-stick frying pan over a medium-low heat. Drizzle 1/2 teaspoon oil into it. When the frying pan is hot, take 75 ml (3 fl oz) of batter and plop it right in the centre of the frying pan. Immediately spread the batter outwards, using the rounded base of a soup spoon, and a gentle but continuous spiral motion. You should end up with a pancake 15-18 cm (6-7 inches) in diameter – the thinner, the better. Drizzle 1/2 teaspoon oil over the pancake and another 1 teaspoon oil just outside its edge.

■ Cover and cook for 3 1/2-5 minutes or until the pancake is reddish-gold underneath and slightly crisp around the edge. It may not colour uniformly. Turn the pancake over and cook uncovered for about 4 minutes until the second side is flecked with reddish-gold spots. Remove with a spatula and keep on the nearby plate. Cover with the second inverted plate. Make all the pancakes this way, stacking them all on the same plate.

■ Serve with Fresh Coriander and Yogurt Chutney (see page 224) or vegetables of your choice.

# POTATO PANCAKES

## *Ganja Buchin*

*KOREA*

Makes 8 small pancakes, to serve 2-4

Koreans eat these scrumptious, slightly glutinous pancakes as a snack with a spicy dipping sauce. They can also be served as part of a meal. I often serve them at brunch or at breakfast along with scrambled eggs. Once the potatoes have been grated and the batter mixed, you need to cook the pancakes quite quickly, because the batter will discolour on standing. Use 2 frying pans at the same time if necessary. If you wish to make more than 8 pancakes, make another batch of fresh batter, rather than double the quantities.

**225 g (8 oz) potatoes**
**25 g (1 oz) onion**
**1 egg**
**1½ tablespoons cornflour**
**¼ teaspoon salt**
**3-4 tablespoons vegetable oil**

TO SERVE

**Korean Dipping Sauce (see page 219)**

■ Peel the potatoes and put them into a bowl of cold water. Peel the onion and chop it very finely. Beat the egg in a bowl and set aside. Mix the cornflour with the salt.

■ Just before cooking, grate the potatoes finely to a pulp and place in a bowl. Add the onion, egg and cornflour mixture and mix well.

■ Put just enough oil into 2 large frying pans to coat the bottom and set each over a medium heat. When the oil is hot, drop 1 rounded tablespoon batter into a corner of a frying pan, spreading it out with the back of a spoon until the pancake is about 7.5 cm (3 inches) in diameter. You should be able to fit 4 pancakes into 1 large frying pan. Cook each pancake for 2-3 minutes on the first side, or until it turns reddish-brown. Turn the pancakes over and cook on the second side for another 2-3 minutes, or until that side develops reddish spots.

■ Serve hot, with the Korean Dipping Sauce.

# CELLOPHANE NOODLES WITH BEEF AND VEGETABLES

## *Chapchae*

*KOREA*

Serves 4

Also called transparent bean thread noodles, pea starch noodles and bean sticks, cellophane noodles are made from mung beans. They can be put into soups and combined with almost any meat and vegetable. This is a Korean way of preparing them.

50 g (2 oz) cellophane noodles
5 dried Chinese mushrooms
4 spring onions
4 cloves garlic
150 g (5 oz) tender beef steak
4 teaspoons plus 1 tablespoon soy sauce (preferably Japanese *shoyu*)
4 teaspoons sugar
freshly ground black pepper
1 tablespoon plus 1 teaspoon sesame oil
1 medium carrot
1 small courgette
150 g (5 oz) fresh spinach
5 tablespoons vegetable oil
salt
1 tablespoon roasted sesame seeds (see page 263)

**1** Put the cellophane noodles in a bowl. Pour on warm water to cover and soak for 30 minutes-1 hour or until they are soft. Drain and cut them into 7.5 cm (3 inch) lengths. Soak the dried mushrooms in enough hot water to cover for 30 minutes or until they are soft. Lift them out of the water and cut off their hard stems. Slice the caps into 3 mm (⅛ inch) thick strips. Cut the spring onions into 7.5 cm (3 inch) lengths. Cut each piece lengthways into 2-3 strips. Peel the garlic and chop it finely.

**2** Cut the beef against the grain into very thin slices. Cut these slices, also against the grain, into thin julienne strips, about 7.5 cm (3 inches) long. In a small bowl, combine the beef with 4 teaspoons soy sauce, 2 teaspoons sugar, 1 tablespoon spring onions, 1 teaspoon garlic, some black pepper and 1 tablespoon sesame oil. Toss to mix.

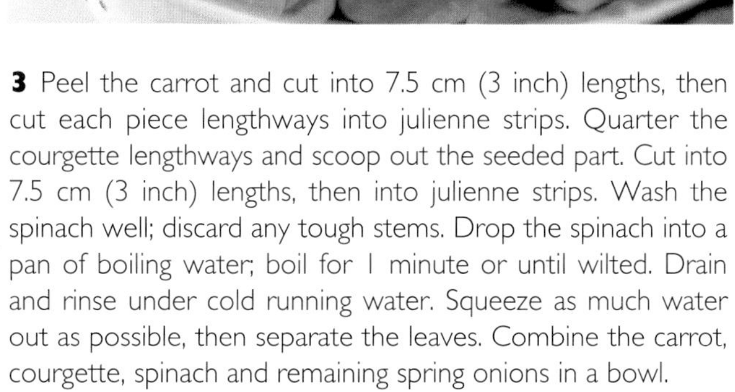

**3** Peel the carrot and cut into 7.5 cm (3 inch) lengths, then cut each piece lengthways into julienne strips. Quarter the courgette lengthways and scoop out the seeded part. Cut into 7.5 cm (3 inch) lengths, then into julienne strips. Wash the spinach well; discard any tough stems. Drop the spinach into a pan of boiling water; boil for 1 minute or until wilted. Drain and rinse under cold running water. Squeeze as much water out as possible, then separate the leaves. Combine the carrot, courgette, spinach and remaining spring onions in a bowl.

**4** Heat 3 tablespoons vegetable oil in a wok over a high heat. Add the remaining garlic and stir-fry for 30 seconds. Add the vegetables and stir-fry for 3-4 minutes until cooked but still crisp. Season lightly and return to the bowl. Heat the remaining vegetable oil in the wok. Add the meat and mushrooms and stir-fry for 1-2 minutes. Using a slotted spoon, transfer to a bowl. Turn the heat to low and add 50 ml (2 fl oz) water, the remaining 1 tablespoon soy sauce and 2 teaspoons sugar. Stir, then turn the heat to medium.

**5** Add the cellophane noodles to the wok. Cook for about 2 minutes or until they are heated through and tender. Add the meat and mushrooms, the vegetables, the remaining 1 teaspoon sesame oil and the roasted sesame seeds. Toss to mix and heat through briefly. Transfer to a serving dish.

# COLD SESAME NOODLES WITH CHICKEN AND VEGETABLES

## *Bon Bon Jihan Banmian* — *HONG KONG*

Serves 3 as a main course, or 6 as a first course

The noodles in this dish can be cooked in advance, rinsed in cold water and tossed with a little sesame oil. The other parts of the dish can be prepared ahead too. All you need to do at the last minute is mix everything together in a large bowl.

**225 g (8 oz) fresh or dried egg noodles (preferably fresh Chinese)**
**1 tablespoon sesame oil**
**100 g (4 oz) chicken breast, skinned and boned**
**salt**
**50 g (2 oz) carrot**
**50 g (2 oz) celery**
**2 spring onions**
**100 g (4 oz) cucumber**

FOR THE SAUCE
**4 tablespoons sesame paste**
**2 tablespoons sesame oil**
**2 teaspoons Chilli Oil (see page 216)**
**2 tablespoons light soy sauce**
**1 tablespoon distilled white vinegar**
**1 teaspoon sugar**
**pinch of chilli powder (optional)**
**5 tablespoons chicken stock**

■ Bring a large pan of water to a rolling boil. Drop in the noodles and cook for 3-5 minutes or until just cooked. Drain, rinse with cold water and drain again. Put them into a bowl, and toss with the 1 tablespoon sesame oil. Cover with cling film and set aside, refrigerating if necessary.

■ Cut the chicken breast lengthways into 2 cm (¾ inch) wide strips. Put these in a medium pan with ¼ teaspoon salt and enough water just to cover the chicken. Slowly bring to a simmer and simmer gently for 2-4 minutes or until the meat turns white all the way through. Drain the meat and allow it to cool. With your hands, pull the cooked chicken into fine long shreds. Put the shredded chicken into a bowl.

■ Peel the carrot and cut into 5 cm (2 inch) long, very fine julienne strips. Cut the celery and spring onions into similar julienne strips. Bring a medium pan of water to a rolling boil. Add the carrot and celery, bring back to the boil and boil rapidly for 40 seconds. Drop in the spring onions and boil for a further 10 seconds. Drain the vegetables and refresh under cold running water. Drain again and pat dry. Add most of the vegetables to the chicken, keeping a few aside for the garnish.

■ Peel the cucumber, cut into 5 cm (2 inch) chunks, then into fine julienne strips. Add most of these to the chicken, reserving a few for garnish. Cover with cling film. Wrap the garnish vegetables in cling film and set aside, refrigerating if necessary.

■ To make the sauce, put the sesame paste in a bowl and stir well. Slowly mix in all the other ingredients. Set aside.

■ Just before serving, put the noodles in a bowl. Add the chicken and vegetables. Stir the sauce and pour it over the top. Toss well and check the seasoning. Transfer to a serving dish or individual plates. Garnish with the reserved vegetables.

# RICE NOODLES IN SOUP WITH BEEF

## *Pho*

*VIETNAM*

Serves 4-6

In Vietnam this soupy dish which derives its name *pho* from the fresh rice noodles that are in it, is a meal in itself.

I am told by Vietnamese who have left Vietnam that true *pho* is made only with beef and beef stock and that the use of chicken is a change brought about by harder times. Here I give the more traditional recipe. Incidentally, even though *pho* is a much loved breakfast food, it is also eaten for lunch and dinner and as a snack.

The fresh *pho* (pronounced 'far') noodle isn't easy to find in this country except where there is a Far Eastern or Chinese population. Use any fresh flat rice noodle, if you can find it. Just heat it briefly in boiling water.

Dried *pho* noodles, usually sold as *banh pho*, are available at many Chinese and Thai food shops. They need to be soaked in water for 2 hours, then cooked very briefly in boiling water. If you cannot find any rice noodles, use flat egg noodles as a last resort, cooking them just before serving.

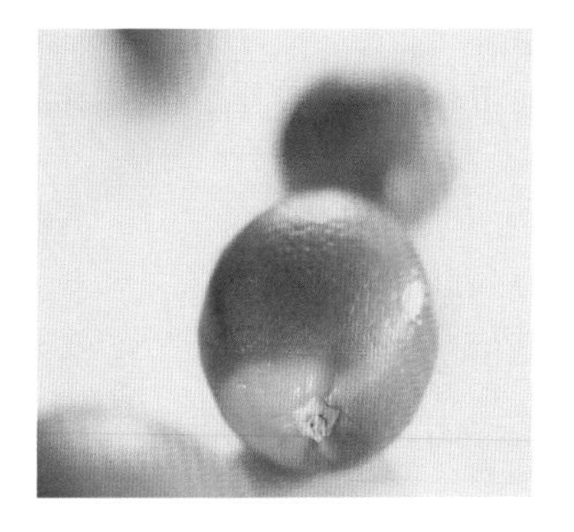

*Millions of Vietnamese eat pho for breakfast at the crack of dawn as they sit hunched in small restaurants, their chopsticks digging in with gusto. It is quite a sight. In Hanoi I saw huge cauldrons of all-purpose stock boiling away in the fronts of restaurants. A peep inside revealed beef and pork bones, chicken carcasses, chunks of fresh root ginger and onions. As orders came in – and at dawn they come fast – slithery white noodles were dipped in hot water to be heated and then divided into several bowls at the same time. They were topped with slices of cooked chicken, or rare beef for those who could afford it. A veritable salad of fresh green herbs and seasonings, rich in vitamins, went in next: mints, coriander, spring onions and hot green chillies. Finally, a healthy ladle of the boiling stock wilted the greens and released their varying aromas.*

*That was not all. At the table were more seasonings in the form of sauces – fish sauce, a sauce of hot red chillies and a third one of vinegar and chillies. There were lime wedges, too, for those who wanted to add a generous squeeze of lime. Pho is eaten with chopsticks and a Chinese-style spoon.*

**275 g (10 oz) dried flat rice noodles (preferably *banh pho*), or flat egg noodles**

**225 g (8 oz) tender beef steak, about 2.5 cm (1 inch) thick**

**2-3 fresh hot red or green chillies**

**1 spring onion**

**6 tablespoons fresh coriander leaves**

**6 tablespoons small fresh mint leaves**

**1.5 litres (2½ pints) Beef Stock (see page 254) plus ⅓ of the beef brisket used to make it, wrapped tightly and chilled**

TO SERVE

**1 lime**

**Red Pepper Sauce (see page 219)**

**1 small bowl fish sauce**

**Seasoned Vinegar (see page 222)**

■ If using dried rice noodles, soak them in water for 2 hours or more. Drain them before cooking.

■ Cut the beef into paper-thin slices, 2.5 cm (1 inch) wide and 5 cm (2 inches) long. (You will find this easier to do if the meat is partially frozen first.)

■ Cut the chillies into very thin slices and arrange at one end of a large plate. Cut the spring onion, including the green part, into very fine rounds. Place beside the chilli slices. Wash and dry the coriander and mint leaves separately, snipping off their coarse stalks. Put next to the spring onion, then cover the plate with cling film.

■ Cut the lime into wedges. Put the Red Pepper Sauce, fish sauce, Seasoned Vinegar and lime wedges in separate bowls and set these on the dining table.

■ Cut the cold brisket against the grain into thin slices, 2.5 cm (1 inch) wide and 5 cm (2 inches) long.

■ If using dried rice noodles, bring a large pan of water to the boil and drop the drained noodles into it. They will cook very quickly – possibly within 1 minute – so keep testing them. When cooked, drain and immediately rinse the noodles under cold running water. Keep the noodles in a bowl of cold water until needed.

■ Just before serving, heat the stock and keep hot. Drain the noodles and plunge them into hot water for a few seconds to heat through. (Fresh rice noodles need only to be dropped into boiling water for a few seconds, then drained. If using egg noodles, cook according to the packet instructions).

■ Divide the noodles among 4-6 individual serving bowls. Arrange a layer of cooked brisket slices over them, then top with a layer of raw beef slices. Sprinkle with chilli and onion slices, coriander and mint. Ladle some hot stock over the top and serve. Diners add sauces and freshly squeezed lime juice to taste.

# NOODLES WITH PORK IN HOT AND SOUR SOUP

## *Suanla Zha Jiangmian*

*HONG KONG*

Serves 2 as a meal, or 4 as a soup

I enjoyed this spicy Sichuan speciality in a very humble restaurant on Hong Kong's Diamond Hill. It is not quite a soup, though you may certainly serve it as one. It really makes a meal in itself, especially when served with a Chinese-style vegetable on the side. All the different parts of the soup may be prepared in advance, but you should only assemble them just before you intend to eat the soup.

FOR THE NOODLES

- 225 g (8 oz) fresh or dried egg noodles (preferably fresh Chinese)
- 1 tablespoon sesame oil

FOR THE PORK

- 3 spring onions
- 2 cloves garlic
- 1 tablespoon vegetable oil
- 225 g (8 oz) lean pork, minced
- 1½ tablespoons hoisin sauce
- 1 teaspoon chilli bean sauce, or ¼-½ teaspoon chilli powder
- 1 teaspoon Chilli Oil (see page 216)
- 1 teaspoon sugar
- 1 tablespoon Chinese dark soy sauce
- 150 ml (¼ pint) chicken stock, chicken and pork stock, or water

FOR THE SOUP

- 475 ml (16 fl oz) chicken or chicken and pork stock
- 3 tablespoons sesame paste
- 1-2 teaspoons Chilli Oil (see page 216)
- 1 tablespoon distilled white vinegar
- 4 teaspoons Chinese light soy sauce

TO GARNISH

- 1 spring onion

■ First prepare the noodles. Bring a large pan of water to a rolling boil. Drop in the noodles and cook for 3-5 minutes or until just done. Drain and put them into a bowl. Add the sesame oil and toss. Let the noodles cool slightly, then cover the bowl with cling film. Set aside, refrigerating if necessary.

■ For the pork, cut the spring onions, including the green part, into very fine rounds. Peel and finely chop the garlic.

■ Put the oil in a wok or frying pan and set over a high heat. When the oil is hot, add the garlic and spring onions and stir-fry for 1 minute. Add the pork and fry, stirring to break up the lumps, until the meat is no longer pink.

■ Add the hoisin sauce, chilli bean sauce, chilli oil, sugar and dark soy sauce. Stir and fry for 30 seconds. Add the stock, cover and simmer for 10 minutes.

■ For the soup, combine all of the ingredients in a pan (stirring the sesame paste well before adding it). Mix well, taste and adjust the seasoning if necessary.

■ For the garnish, cut the spring onion into very fine rounds.

■ To serve, bring a large pan of water to the boil. Heat the pork and soup in separate pans. When the soup is boiling, divide between individual soup bowls. Plunge the noodles into the boiling water for 10-20 seconds to heat them through. Drain in a colander, then divide among the soup bowls, piling them up in the centre. Top with the pork, scatter with the spring onion and serve.

# RICE NOODLES IN A COCONUT CURRY SOUP

## *Curry Mee*

*MALAYSIA*

Serves 4 as a light meal or snack, or 6 as a soup course

Curry Mee is the finest curry soup I have ever eaten. Filled with slithery rice noodles, this coconut-enriched soup is permeated with the very Malay aromas of lemon grass and galangal. Even though there are many parts to this dish, it is easy to make. If you prepare the coconut milk from fresh coconut, use only the thick milk which rises to the top.

**275 g (10 oz) dried flat rice noodles (preferably *banh pho*), or flat egg noodles**
**1 stick fresh lemon grass**
**100 g (4 oz) onions**
**2.5 cm (1 inch) cube fresh galangal**
**2.5 cm (1 inch) cube fresh root ginger**
**4 cloves garlic**
**175 g (6 oz) red pepper**
**1 tablespoon paprika**
**1½ tablespoons shrimp or anchovy paste**
**½ teaspoon ground turmeric**
**¼-½ teaspoon chilli powder**
**8 tablespoons vegetable oil**
**1.1 litres (2 pints) chicken stock**
**300 ml (½ pint) thick coconut milk (see page 258)**
**salt**
**freshly ground black pepper**
**120 g (4½ oz) chicken breast, skinned and boned**
**75 g (3 oz) fresh bean sprouts**
**1 stick celery (preferably from the middle of the bunch)**
**4 tablespoons Crisply Fried Shallot Flakes (see page 227; optional)**
**lime wedges, to serve**

■ If using dried noodles, soak them in water for 2 hours or more.

■ Slice the lemon grass crossways into very thin rounds, starting at the bulbous end and going up about 15 cm (6 inches); discard the straw-like top.

■ Peel and coarsely chop the onions, galangal and ginger.

■ Peel the garlic. Core, deseed and coarsely chop the red pepper.

■ In an electric blender, combine the lemon grass, onions, galangal, ginger, garlic, red pepper, paprika, shrimp paste, turmeric and chilli powder. Blend until smooth, adding a few tablespoons of water if needed to achieve a paste-like consistency.

■ Heat the oil in a wide heavy pan over a medium-high heat. When hot, put in the paste from the blender. Stir and fry for about 15 minutes until the paste is dark red and reduced, and the oil separates from it. Add the stock, stir and bring to the boil. Turn the heat to low and simmer for 15 minutes.

■ Strain this soup through a sieve, pushing out as much liquid as you can, then return to the clean pan. Stir the coconut milk well, then add it to the pan, stir and bring to a simmer. Season with salt and pepper to taste. The soup is now ready; set it aside until later.

■ Put the chicken breast in a frying pan and add sufficient water just to cover. Add a generous pinch of salt and bring slowly to the boil. Turn the heat to low and simmer for 3-5 minutes, turning a few times, until the chicken is white all the way through. Lift out of the liquid and shred the meat. Cover and set aside.

■ Pluck off the thread-like ends of the bean sprouts, then immerse them in a bowl of cold water. Finely dice the celery. Cover and set aside.

■ Just before you are ready to serve, set the soup on a low heat. Bring a large pan of water to a rolling boil. If using dried rice noodles, drain and drop them into the boiling water. Cook until they are just done – this may take only 1 minute, so watch them carefully. If using egg noodles, cook according to the packet instructions.

■ Drain the noodles and divide between individual soup bowls. Ladle the hot soup over the noodles. Top with the chicken, bean sprouts, diced celery and some crisply fried shallot flakes. Serve accompanied by lime wedges.

*High tea in England was never quite like this one served in Malaysia! At the Ming Court Hotel in Kuala Lumpur, early evening finds tables in the lobby groaning with cakes and pastries, mango sweetmeats, stir-fried noodles and curried soups. The ritual of tea drinking has been reclaimed, albeit in its anglicised form, by the former colony. With the beverage (and even without it) can be had not just the delicacies of the former rulers but also an array of Eastern snacks that no Malay would dream of doing without. Curry Mee is one of them.*

# NOODLES IN BROTH WITH POACHED EGG AND VEGETABLES

## *Sansai Udon*

*JAPAN*

Serves 4

Japan, like all Far Eastern countries, has many types of noodles and they are highly popular – indeed whole restaurants are devoted to them. The Japanese love their noodles and are just as content to have them quite plain and icy cold in the summer with a light dipping sauce as they are to have them topped with an elaborate assortment of vegetables, meats, fish and eggs.

Noodle dishes of this type are entire meals in themselves, hence they are served in rather large, deep, individual bowls. In Japan the only 'cutlery' provided is chopsticks. You are supposed to pick up the noodles with chopsticks, then suck them in with a deep intake of breath that cools them off. Loud noises made in the process are considered normal and indicative of pleasure! All solids are picked up with the chopsticks. To drink the broth, chopsticks are left on rests and the bowl is picked up with both hands and brought directly to the mouth.

Japanese *udon* are thick wheat noodles that are obtainable flat or rounded. Try to find some if you can, as there is no real substitute for them. (Many healthfood shops carry a wholewheat version.) If you cannot get them, use either Italian linguine or flat egg noodles, cooking them according to the packet instructions just before you are ready to serve. After draining linguine or egg noodles, toss them with about 250 ml (8 fl oz) stock just to prevent them from sticking to each other as you arrange the vegetables over them.

If using ready-prepared *dashi-no-moto* instead of Japanese Soup Stock, omit the salt in this recipe entirely or add only a very small amount, tasting as you go.

FOR THE VEGETABLES

**100 g (4 oz) carrots, cooked (see page 229)**

**100 g (4 oz) green beans, cooked (see page 229)**

**8 medium mushrooms, cooked (see page 229)**

**75 g (3 oz) bamboo shoot tips or chunks, cooked (see page 229)**

**12 medium asparagus spears (optional), cooked (see page 228)**

FOR THE SOUP

**3½ pints (2 litres) Japanese Soup Stock (see page 255), or light unsalted chicken stock**

**3 tablespoons sugar**

**4 tablespoons sake**

**6 tablespoons Japanese soy sauce (*shoyu*)**

**salt**

**400 g (14 oz) Japanese *udon* noodles or linguine or flat egg noodles**

**4 eggs**

TO SERVE

**Japanese seven-spice seasoning (*shichimi*), or Sesame Seed Seasoning (see page 263)**

■ Prepare and cook the carrots, beans, mushrooms, bamboo shoots, and asparagus if using, according to their respective instructions. (They may be cooked a day in advance, then covered and refrigerated in their own liquid. Return to room temperature before adding them to the soup.)

■ Put the Japanese Soup Stock in a pan with the sugar, sake, soy sauce and salt to taste. Simmer very gently for 5 minutes. (This can be made a day ahead, covered and refrigerated. Heat it just before you are ready to eat.)

■ If using dried Japanese *udon* noodles, bring a very large pan of water to a rolling boil. (Don't add salt.) Drop in the noodles and, when the water comes back to the boil, add an extra 250 ml (8 fl oz) cold water. Repeat this 3-4 times, each time waiting for the water to come to the boil again. Keep testing the noodles. When they are just done (there should be no hard core left in the centre), drain and rinse under cold running water, rubbing them with your hands to remove the starch. Set aside in a colander until ready to eat. Shortly before serving, drop them into a large pan of boiling water for a few seconds to heat through, then drain quickly.

■ Poach the eggs just before you are ready to eat and when everything else is heated and ready. Pour a 2 cm (¾ inch) depth of water into a medium frying pan and bring to a very low simmer. Break the 4 eggs into the water so they sit side by side. Let the water simmer very gently until the egg whites are almost set. Now turn off the heat and place a loose cover over the pan. As soon as the whites of the eggs have set, remove the cover.

■ Assemble the dish quickly now. Divide the noodles between 4 large individual bowls. Lift the vegetables out of their liquid and arrange them over the noodles, laying them prettily side by side. Pour the hot stock over the top, dividing it among the 4 bowls. Place a poached egg in each bowl and serve at once. Each diner sprinkles the seasoning mixture on their portion to taste, and breaks the egg yolk with chopsticks, allowing it to mix with the broth.

*I first enjoyed this soup for lunch on a spring day in Japan. It was prepared by Keiko Okamoto, the wife of a prestigious potter living in the tea-growing Uji district just outside Kyoto. Needless to say, the soup arrived in exquisite bowls that had been hand-crafted by the master potter himself. Most of the vegetables Keiko used grew wild in the hills around her. Each had been cooked separately and then arranged over the noodles at the last minute. My vegetables, are rather more prosaic, but the dish remains delightful – and very healthy, to boot.*

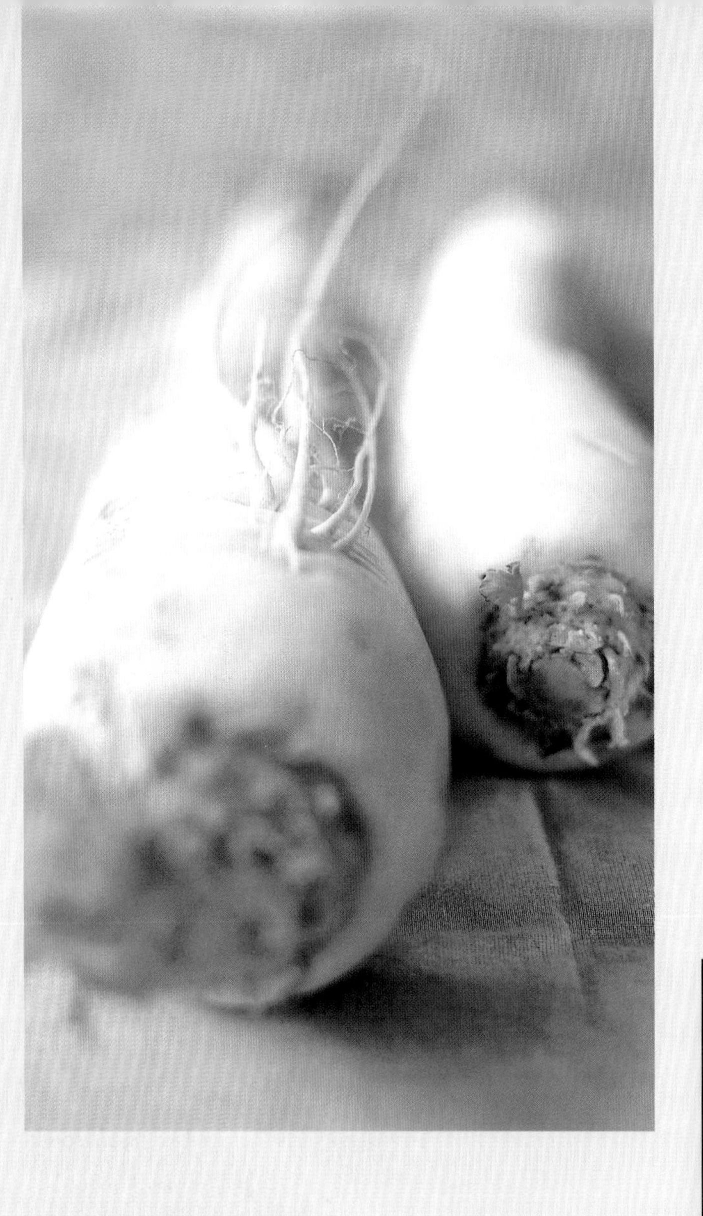

# dips, sauces, pickles and garnishes

# EAST-WEST SAUCE

## *Tonkatsu Sosu*

*JAPAN*

Serves 4-6

This sauce is a mixture of Eastern and Western ingredients. It contains, among other things, tomato ketchup and Worcestershire sauce. We must remember, though, that ketchup is an Asian word for an Asian sauce and that tomato ketchup may well have been an attempt to replicate the kind of sweet and sour sauces found all over the Far East. Also, Worcestershire sauce has ingredients like tamarind in it. Tamarind is very much an Eastern ingredient. This may well be a case of an idea for a sauce travelling from the East to the West and then back to the East in a new incarnation.

East-West sauce is served with Breaded Pork Cutlets (see page 48). You can, however, serve it with any meat, fried chicken or fried fish. Since this sauce is prepared commercially in Japan where it is known as *tonkatsu sosu*, I never could get an exact recipe for it. However, by tasting it again and again I have come up with this reasonable approximation.

**½ teaspoon mustard powder**
**4 tablespoons tomato ketchup**
**4 teaspoons sake**
**4 teaspoons Japanese soy sauce (*shoyu*)**
**4 teaspoons sugar**
**4 teaspoons Worcestershire sauce**
**4 teaspoons distilled white vinegar**
**¼ teaspoon ground allspice**
**pinch of ground cloves**

■ Mix the mustard powder with 4 teaspoons hot water in a small bowl. Add all the remaining ingredients and mix well.

# CHILLI OIL

## *Lajiao You*

*HONG KONG*

Makes about 150 ml (¼ pint)

Orange-coloured chilli oil is offered as a seasoning on the tables of most restaurants in Hong Kong. A few drops, or more liberal doses, are drizzled on to any foods that need extra 'heat'. It is also a common seasoning in Chinese kitchens serving Sichuan-style food. You can buy ready-made chilli oil, but it is easy enough to make at home. I find that it needs to be strained a couple of times for a really clear oil.

**150 ml (¼ pint) vegetable oil (preferably groundnut)**
**1 tablespoon chilli powder**

■ Heat the oil in a small pan over a medium-high heat. When hot, remove from the heat and sprinkle in the chilli powder. Mix and leave to cool.

■ Strain the oil through a clean cloth. It is now ready to be used. You may, however, let it sit for a few hours and strain it a second time into an empty bottle or jar.

# FISH SAUCE SEASONED WITH LIME JUICE

## *Nuoc Mam Toi Ot*

*VIETNAM*

Serves 4

I am told that the popularity of a restaurant often rests with the quality of this ever-present sauce.

**1 clove garlic**
**4 tablespoons fish sauce**
**4 tablespoons lime or lemon juice**
**3 tablespoons sugar, or less to taste**
**3-4 fresh hot red or green chillies**

■ Peel and crush the garlic. Combine it with the fish sauce, lime or lemon juice, sugar and 4 tablespoons water. Mix well and pour into 4 individual bowls. Cut the chillies into very thin rounds and divide them between the bowls.

# FISH SAUCE WITH LIME JUICE AND CHILLI

## *Nam Pla Prik*

*THAILAND*

Serves 4

You may put this sauce on the table when you are serving any Thai meal.

**1 fresh hot green or red chilli**
**4 tablespoons fish sauce**
**2 tablespoons lime or lemon juice**

■ Cut the chilli into very fine rounds and put in a small bowl. Add the fish sauce and lime or lemon juice. Stir to mix.

# FISH SAUCE WITH VINEGAR AND LIME JUICE

## *Nuoc Cham Thong Dung* — *VIETNAM*

Serves 4

This is a wonderful dipping sauce to use with spring rolls and grilled or boiled meats.

**5 tablespoons fish sauce**
**3 tablespoons distilled white vinegar**
**2 tablespoons sugar**
**1½-2 tablespoons lime or lemon juice**
**1-2 fresh hot green or red chillies**

■ Put the fish sauce, 3 tablespoons water, the vinegar, sugar and lime or lemon juice in a jug and mix well. Slice the chillies crossways as thinly as possible and add them too. Divide the sauce equally among 4 small bowls and serve.

# FISH SAUCE SEASONED WITH VINEGAR

## *Nuoc Cham* — *VIETNAM*

Serves 4

When serving this sauce, give each diner an individual bowl. This recipe is enough for 4 small bowls.

**8 tablespoons fish sauce**
**6 tablespoons distilled white vinegar**
**1 tablespoon sugar**
**3-4 fresh hot green or red chillies**

■ Combine the fish sauce, vinegar and sugar. Mix thoroughly. Cut the chillies into fine rounds and put them into the sauce. Divide between 4 small bowls.

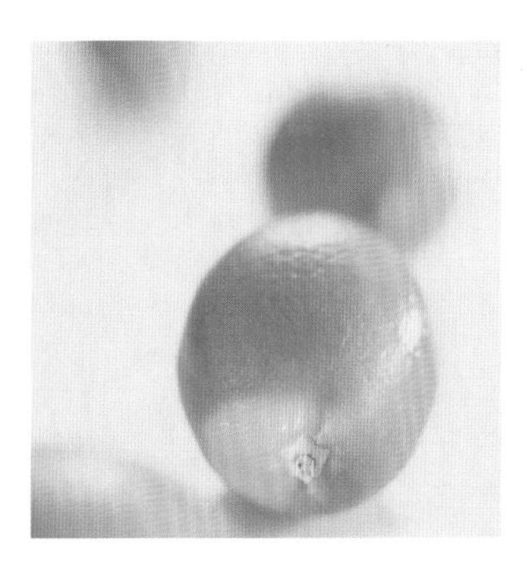

# HOT FERMENTED BEAN PASTE

## *Kochu Chang*

*KOREA*

Makes 4-5 tablespoons

Every household in Korea has a tall earthenware jar of Hot Fermented Bean Paste (*kochu chang*) sitting serenely in a courtyard, on a balcony or in some other convenient nook. It is an essential seasoning and is one of the several bean pastes used with great frequency throughout Korea. It serves as a cross between a chutney and a spice.

Its method of preparation is elaborate and long, calling for barley or glutinous rice powder to be mixed with malt, cooked slowly into a thick paste and then mixed with fermented soya bean powder, chilli powder and salt. The resulting paste is red in colour (because of the chillies) and very thick. It is added to dipping sauces, to meats that are just about to be stir-fried, and to stews. Dollops of it are also served as a kind of salty sweet and hot chutney.

*Kochu chang* is available only in Korean shops. It can, however, be approximated at home with ingredients available to most of us. It is best to buy brown or reddish *miso* for this recipe. This, when mixed with chilli powder, paprika and a little sugar, tastes and looks very much like real *kochu chang*.

**4 tablespoons brown or red miso**
**1½ tablespoons paprika**
**1 teaspoon chilli powder**
**1 tablespoon sugar**

■ Mix all of the ingredients together thoroughly in a bowl.

*I cannot say for sure which country in this world eats the hottest foods, but South Korea must rank easily in the top three. Fiery chilli pods ripen to a rich red colour in the autumn here, at which time they are either cut into hair-thin slices before drying (old women are generally assigned this tedious task) or dried first and then pounded into some of the world's best chilli powder. Its bright carmine colour can be seen smothering squid rings, oysters, meat and all manner of vegetables.*

# KOREAN DIPPING SAUCE

## *Yang Nyum Jang*

*KOREA*

Serves 4

This all-purpose sauce may be served with plain heated bean curd, chicken patties or with potato pancakes.

**I small clove garlic**
**I spring onion**
**4 tablespoons soy sauce (preferably Japanese *shoyu*)**
**2 tablespoons distilled white vinegar**
**I tablespoon sesame oil**
**I teaspoon sugar**
**I teaspoon roasted sesame seeds (see page 263)**
**¼ teaspoon chilli powder (optional)**

■ Peel and crush the garlic. Cut the spring onion into very thin rounds. Combine the garlic, I tablespoon sliced spring onion, the soy sauce, vinegar, sesame oil, sugar, sesame seeds and chilli powder in a small serving bowl and mix well.

# RED PEPPER SAUCE

*VIETNAM, THAILAND, MALAYSIA AND INDONESIA*

Serves 4

In Vietnam, this sauce is made by pounding red chillies and salt in a mortar, cooking the mixture, then passing it through a sieve. Some countries do not bother with the cooking and straining. Others add a little sugar and vinegar. My method is very simple: I let a blender do all the work.

**2-3 dried hot red chillies**
**100 g (4 oz) red pepper**
**¼ teaspoon sugar**
**½ teaspoon distilled white vinegar**
**¼ teaspoon salt, or to taste**

■ Put 3 tablespoons water in a small cup, crumble in the dried red chillies and leave to soak for 30 minutes.

■ Coarsely chop the red pepper, discarding all the seeds. Combine the chillies and their soaking liquid with all the other ingredients in a blender. Blend until smooth.

# RED PEPPER SAUCE WITH SHRIMP PASTE

## *Sambal Terasi*

*INDONESIA*

Makes about 250 ml (8 fl oz)

This spicy relish or sambal may be served with all Indonesian meals. It will keep for at least a week in the refrigerator. Store it in a screw-topped jar.

**225 g (8 oz) red pepper**
**2 teaspoons shrimp or anchovy paste**
**½ teaspoon salt**
**½ teaspoon chilli powder**
**4 tablespoons vegetable oil**
**I teaspoon dark brown sugar**
**2½ tablespoons lime or lemon juice**

■ Dice the red pepper coarsely, discarding all the seeds. Put the red pepper, shrimp paste, salt and chilli powder in an electric blender. Blend until smooth.

■ Set a wok over a medium-high heat. When hot, add the oil. When the oil is hot, put in the paste from the blender. Stir and fry for about 5 minutes, lowering the heat slightly if necessary, until the paste turns dark red and the oil separates. Add the sugar and stir to mix.

■ Turn the paste into a bowl. Beat in the lime or lemon juice. Taste and adjust the seasoning if necessary.

# CARAMEL WATER

## *Nuoc Hang*

*VIETNAM*

Makes about 300 ml (½ pint)

This is used in Vietnamese cooking to add colour and extra flavour to foods.

**3 tablespoons sugar**

■ Put the sugar in a small cast-iron frying pan and warm gently, without stirring, over a very low heat. The sugar will melt and begin to caramelize. Tilt the pan slowly back and forth to move the sugar, but do not stir it.

■ When all the sugar has turned brownish, slowly pour in 150 ml (¼ pint) warm water – it will bubble vigorously, so be careful. Stir to mix. Pour the sauce into a bowl.

■ Stir in another 150 ml (¼ pint) boiling water. Allow to cool, then store in a covered jar in the refrigerator.

# RED CURRY PASTE

## *Nam Prik Kaeng Dang*

*THAILAND*

Makes about 8 tablespoons

This recipe makes enough Thai curry paste to flavour 2 dishes each serving 4 people. You can freeze any of the paste that you do not use immediately, or keep it in a screw-topped jar in the refrigerator for several days.

**7 large or 10 medium dried hot red chillies**
**5 cm (2 inch) cube fresh galangal or fresh root ginger**
**1 stick fresh lemon grass**
**3 cloves garlic**
**6 shallots, or ½ medium onion**
**4-5 stems fresh coriander**
**3 x 1½ inch (7.5 x 1 cm) piece fresh kaffir lime rind (optional)**
**1½ teaspoons shrimp or anchovy paste**
**2 teaspoons paprika**
**½ teaspoon ground coriander seeds**
**½ teaspoon ground cumin seeds**
**¼ teaspoon ground turmeric**
**pinch of ground cinnamon**
**pinch of ground cardamom seeds**
**½ teaspoon salt**

**1** Remove and discard the seeds from the red chillies.

**2** Put the chillies in a small bowl and pour on about 175 ml (6 fl oz) water. Leave to soak for 40 minutes-1 hour.

**3** Peel and coarsely chop the galangal (or ginger).

**4** Cut the lemon grass crossways into very fine slices, going up about 6 inches (15 cm) from the bulbous end. Discard the straw-like top. Peel the garlic and shallots.

**5** Wash the coriander roots well and pat them dry. (Break off the leaves and use for a garnish, or other dish.)

**6** Put the chillies and their soaking liquid, galangal (or ginger), lemon grass, garlic, shallots and coriander roots in an electric blender. Add all the remaining ingredients and blend thoroughly to a paste.

# SWEET GLAZING SAUCE

## *Teriyaki No Tare*

*JAPAN*

Serves 4

This *teriyaki* sauce is sweet and salty at the same time. It is generally made with equal parts of Japanese rice wine (sake), soy sauce, mirin (a sweetened syrupy sake) and a little sugar. I have substituted sugar for the mirin, which isn't always easy to find. If you do manage to obtain it, add 150 ml (¼ pint) of it to the soy-sake mixture and reduce the sugar to 2 teaspoons.

Generally, *teriyaki* sauce is brushed on to grilled foods such as fish, chicken and beef when they are slightly more than half-cooked. It gives them a glorious glaze, as well as the sweet and salty *teriyaki* flavour. You may, if you like, add a little juice from grated fresh ginger to the sauce as well.

**150 ml (¼ pint) Japanese soy sauce *(shoyu)***
**150 ml (¼ pint) sake**
**6 tablespoons sugar**

■ Combine the soy sauce, sake and sugar in a small pan and bring to the boil. Lower the heat to medium and simmer for about 5 minutes or until the sauce turns very slightly syrupy.

■ If the sauce is to be used as a marinade, it should be allowed to cool off first.

# GINGER SHREDS IN SWEET VINEGAR

## *Hari Shoga*

*JAPAN*

Serves 4

Even though this is a Japanese relish, I keep it on hand to serve with Western-style roast lamb and grilled chicken.

**5 cm (2 inch) cube fresh root ginger**
**4 tablespoons distilled white vinegar**
**4 tablespoons sugar**
**¼ teaspoon salt**

■ Peel the ginger and cut it crossways into very thin slices. Stacking a few slices at a time together, cut them into very fine julienne strips.

■ Combine the vinegar, sugar and salt in a bowl and mix well until the sugar is dissolved. Add the ginger julienne and stir. Set aside for at least 10-15 minutes.

■ Lift the ginger shreds out of the liquid before serving.

# SEASONED VINEGAR

Serves 4

This seasoning is found in all the Asian countries where the Chinese have lived or settled – Hong Kong, Vietnam, the Philippines, Malaysia, Thailand and Indonesia. Of course, the actual vinegar varies not only from country to country but often from village to village. Diners usually add just a few drops of the hot vinegar to their food, together with a few of the chilli slices if they wish.

**2 fresh hot green or red chillies**
**4 tablespoons distilled white vinegar**

■ Cut the chillies into very thin rounds. Put the vinegar into a small bowl. Add the chillies and let stand for 30 minutes.

# QUICK SPICY RELISH

## *Nam Prik Num*

*THAILAND*

Serves 4-6

This relish is so good that you will want to eat it with everything – including crisps. It is found only in northern Thailand. In fact Thai visitors from the south buy kilos of it to take back home. It is hot, so serve it in small portions.

**6 shallots**
**3 cloves garlic**
**6 fresh hot green chillies**
**½-1 teaspoon shrimp or anchovy paste**
**6 cherry or baby plum tomatoes**
**1 tablespoon fish sauce, or salt to taste**
**1 tablespoon lime or lemon juice**

■ Preheat the grill. Peel the shallots and garlic. On a foil-lined grill rack, spread out the shallots, garlic and green chillies in a single layer. If using shrimp paste, make a patty of it and place it on the rack as well. (If using anchovy paste, set aside for the time being.) Put the rack under the grill briefly until the ingredients are lightly browned. Turn them and brown the other side.

■ Now either chop the grilled ingredients or put them into an electric blender and blend briefly until to a coarse paste. Turn into a bowl.

■ Chop the tomatoes and add these to the relish. Add the anchovy paste if using, the fish sauce, and lime or lemon juice. Mix well. Taste and adjust the seasoning if necessary.

# ROASTED PEANUTS

Crushed roasted peanuts are a common seasoning throughout most of South-east Asia. They add a nutty taste, a crunchy texture and protein to a dish.

Raw peanuts are sold in every market in this region, usually still covered with their red inner skins. To roast them at home, put them into a hot cast-iron wok or frying pan over a medium heat. Stir the peanuts around until they are roasted, reducing the heat if necessary. The red skins will turn crisp and papery. When the nuts have cooled, rub them with your hands and blow the skins away. To crush them, lightly or finely as required, either whizz them for a few seconds in a clean coffee grinder or, if only a few tablespoons are needed, chop them with a large knife.

# EGG STRIPS

These omelette strips are a popular garnish for rice and noodles in many parts of South-east Asia. They are also used in salads and soups.

**3 eggs**
**1 teaspoon sugar**
**large pinch of salt**
**about 2 teaspoons vegetable oil**

■ Break the eggs into a bowl and add 1 tablespoon water. Beat until evenly combined, but not frothy. Add the sugar and salt and beat lightly to mix.

■ Brush an 18-20 cm (7-8 inch) non-stick frying pan with about ½ teaspoon of the oil and set over a medium heat. When hot, pour in a quarter of the egg mixture. Tilt the pan so that the egg flows evenly to the edges. Let the mixture set, which it will do quite quickly. Turn carefully and cook the second side until it is just firm (a matter of seconds).

■ Transfer the omelette to a plate and cover with greaseproof paper. Make 3 more omelettes in this way, piling them on top of each other with a layer of greaseproof paper in between. Allow to cool.

■ Roll each omelette up and cut into 3 mm (⅛ inch) slices. Use at once as a garnish, or put the egg strips in a bowl, cover and refrigerate until needed.

# FRESH CORIANDER AND YOGURT CHUTNEY

## *Hari Chutney* — *INDIA*

Serves 6

This chutney needs to be eaten on the day it is made. Serve it in a small bowl as a relish with almost any Indian meal, or spooned on to cooked meat, fish or vegetables. If pressed to classify this dish, I would describe it as a 'sour' chutney.

**1 packed teacup chopped fresh coriander leaves**
**1 fresh hot green chilli, sliced, or ¼ teaspoon ground cayenne pepper (optional)**
**300 g (10 oz) yogurt**
**1 tablespoon lemon juice**
**½ teaspoon salt, or to taste**
**large pinch of freshly ground pepper**
**½ teaspoon roasted, ground cumin seeds**

■ Put the chopped coriander and chilli into a blender with 3 tablespoons water. Blend to a smooth paste.

■ In a non-metallic bowl, combine the yogurt, lemon juice, salt, pepper, cumin, and paste from the blender. Stir well to mix, then cover and refrigerate until ready to use.

# CUCUMBER RAITA

## *Kheere Ka Raita* — *INDIA*

Serves 4-6

This familiar, refreshing, cool yogurt and cucumber relish complements nearly all Indian meals. In the hot summer months, it really takes the place of a salad.

**1 cucumber**
**425 g (15 oz) yogurt**
**salt**
**freshly ground black pepper**
**½ teaspoon roasted, ground cumin seeds**
**pinch of cayenne pepper (optional)**
**pinch of paprika**

■ Peel and coarsely grate the cucumber.

■ Turn the yogurt into a serving bowl and beat with a fork until smooth. Add the cucumber, and season with salt and pepper to taste. Reserve a pinch of the roasted cumin for garnish; add the rest to the yogurt with the cayenne. Stir to mix and check the seasoning.

■ Cover and refrigerate until required. Sprinkle with the reserved roasted cumin and paprika to serve.

# TOMATO AND ONION RELISH

## *Timatar Aur Pyaz Ka Cachumbar* — *INDIA*

Serves 4

This relish can be eaten with almost all Indian meals.

**2-3 medium tomatoes**
**1 medium onion**
**1 teaspoon roasted, ground cumin seeds**
**1 tablespoon lemon juice**
**salt**
**freshly ground black pepper**
**⅛-¼ teaspoon cayenne pepper**

■ Cut the tomatoes into 5 mm (¼ inch) cubes. Peel and finely chop the onion. Combine the tomato and onion in a serving bowl.

■ Add the roasted cumin, lemon juice, and salt, pepper and cayenne to taste. Toss to mix. Cover with cling film and refrigerate for 30 minutes.

*No Indian meal is complete without at least one kind of relish. At its simplest this can be a small, fresh chilli, or a hastily chopped onion. The fresh relishes I have included here provide a delicious contrast to spicy Indian dishes. The Indian climate often causes appetites to wilt, especially during the blazing summer months. Relishes are, perhaps, one way of perking up sluggish tastebuds.*

# CABBAGE PICKLE

## *Kimchee*

*KOREA*

Makes enough to fill a 2 litre (3½ pint) jar

In Korea, this popular *kimchee* is made with a long fat cabbage, called long or Peking cabbage. It looks like a very large, overweight head of Chinese leaves and can weigh as much as 2 kg (4½ lb). An extended family of 10 Koreans eats about 200 heads of this pickled cabbage in 3-4 months!

*Korean pickles (kimchee) are a world in themselves and no meal, from breakfast to dinner, is complete without them. There is a kimchee museum in Seoul that lists 160 varieties made of vegetables ranging from ordinary pumpkins to the precious ginseng root. The staple, however, remains the kimchee made of large Chinese cabbages (rather like Chinese leaves).*

*Around late November, when the cabbage and red chilli crops are ready, whole villages fall to the task of making their supply of winter kimchee. On the first day, cartloads of cabbages are trimmed, washed and left overnight in salted water to wilt and soften. The next day they are washed again while another group of workers prepares the stuffing. Large white radishes are julienned, green onions and Chinese celery are cut, ginger is chopped and red chillies crushed. This mixture, along with shelled oysters, salt and tiny salted shrimps, is slapped between each leaf of the cabbages. The cabbage heads are then packed into large, Ali Baba-sized vats where they seethe, bubble and ferment until they turn deliciously sour. In the villages the vats are buried up to their necks in the earth to prevent the pickle from freezing. In city homes all vats stand like sentinels, lined up on balconies.*

**450 g (1 lb) half-head Chinese cabbage or leaves**
**salt**
**450 g (1 lb) long white radish (mooli)**
**7.5 cm (3 inch) cube fresh root ginger**
**8-10 large cloves garlic**
**8 spring onions**
**2 teaspoons chilli powder**
**1 teaspoon sugar**
**10 shelled oysters, or 10 canned anchovy fillets**
**1 tablespoon plain flour**

■ Halve the Chinese cabbage or leaves lengthways. Trim the very base of the stalk end, ensuring the leaves stay attached. (If using a very thick half-head of Chinese cabbage, quarter lengthways; Chinese leaves should be halved only.) Wash the cabbage well, carefully removing the dirt between the leaves.

■ Pour 1.5 litres (2½ pints) water into a large bowl, add 3 tablespoons salt and stir to dissolve. Put the cabbage in the salted water and weigh it down with a clean heavy plate to keep it submerged. Cover loosely and leave for 8 hours.

■ To prepare the stuffing, peel the radish and cut into 5 cm (2 inch) chunks. Cut each chunk lengthways into 3 mm (⅛ inch) slices, then into 3 mm (⅛ inch) julienne strips.

■ Peel and coarsely chop the ginger and garlic. Put them into a blender with 3 tablespoons water. Blend until smooth. Cut the spring onions, including the green part, into fine rounds.

■ In a large bowl, combine the radish, ginger-garlic paste, spring onions, chilli powder, sugar and oysters. (If using anchovy fillets, wipe off the oil and chop them finely before adding.) Mix well, then add 1 tablespoon salt and stir again.

■ Put the flour into a small pan and slowly mix in 350 ml (12 fl oz) water. Bring to a simmer and simmer gently until slightly thickened.

■ Remove the cabbage from the salted water. Rinse thoroughly in cold water several times, keeping the leaves attached. Drain well. Starting with the outside leaves, put some stuffing in between each cabbage leaf. Tuck the largest leaf under so that it will hold the 'package' together. Continue in this way until you have stuffed all the cabbage sections.

■ Fit the cabbage packages tightly inside a clean, wide-mouthed, 2 litre (3½ pint) crock or jar. Pour the flour water over the top. Make sure that there is some space at the top for the fermenting pickle to expand. Cover and set aside for 3-7 days, depending upon the weather; the hotter it is, the quicker the cabbage will pickle. Taste the pickle now and then to see if it has turned sufficiently sour. Once the pickle is ready, it should be refrigerated.

■ To serve, remove just as much of the cabbage from the liquid as you need and put it in a small bowl. In Korea the liquid is used to flavour stews and soups.

# CRISPLY FRIED SHALLOT FLAKES

A young lady in Padang, Indonesia, told me with great authority that shallot flakes turn much crisper if they are soaked in lightly salted water before being fried. This makes sense, as salt draws out some of the moisture. I think that starting the frying at a medium-hot rather than a very hot temperature also helps.

In much of South-east Asia shallots are cheap and used rather as onions are used in the West. These crisp-fried shallot flakes serve both as a garnish and as a seasoning. Often they are fried in bulk and kept in tightly lidded jars to be used as needed. Small amounts of shallots, intended for use the same day, may be fried without first being soaked in salted water.

If shallots are not available, use onions: halve lengthways, then slice into very fine half-rings. Fry as you would shallots.

**200 g (7 oz) shallots, or onions**
**salt**
**vegetable oil for deep-frying**

■ Peel the shallots, cut lengthways into fine slivers and place in a bowl. Add ½ teaspoon salt and toss lightly. Pour on 450 ml (¾ pint) water and leave to soak for 30 minutes. Drain well and pat dry.

■ Heat a 5 cm (2 inch) depth of oil in a wok set over a medium heat, or heat the recommended quantity of oil in a deep-fat fryer to 190°C (375°F). When the oil is hot, add the shallots and fry for 1 minute. Turn the heat down to medium-low, or the deep-fat fryer to 160°C (325°F) and continue to fry until the shallots are reddish-brown and crisp; if using a wok, keep stirring.

■ Remove the shallots with a slotted spoon and spread them out on kitchen paper to drain. Use at once or leave until cool and crisp, then store in a screw-topped jar until needed.

# ASPARAGUS

## *Asupara*

*JAPAN*

Serves 4

The asparagus here may be used as a garnish for meats, fish or chicken, or placed over a dish of noodles in broth. If you are using prepared *dashi-no-moto* instead of the Japanese Soup Stock, omit the salt that is added to the stock.

**12 medium-thick asparagus spears**
**salt**

**150 ml (¼ pint) ice-cold Japanese Soup Stock (see page 255), or light unsalted chicken stock**

■ Break off the woody base of each asparagus spear, then peel the lower half of each stem.

■ Cut the asparagus spears into 4-6 cm (2-2½ inch) sections, on the diagonal if you prefer.

■ Pour a 1 cm (½ inch) depth of water into a medium frying pan and bring to the boil. Add a pinch of salt, and put in the asparagus. Cover the pan, lower the heat and cook for about 3 minutes until the asparagus is just tender.

■ Drain and immediately plunge the asparagus pieces into the ice-cold stock. Add ¼ teaspoon salt and mix gently. Let the asparagus sit in the stock for at least 15 minutes.

■ Drain the asparagus to serve.

# GREEN BEANS

## *Ingen*

*JAPAN*

Serves 4

When Japanese food is presented, a few vegetables are sometimes used as a kind of garnish, or arranged over noodles, often with other similarly prepared vegetables. You could always increase these quantities if you wish to serve the beans as a Western-style accompaniment. If using prepared *dashi-no-moto* or salted chicken stock instead of Japanese Soup Stock, omit the salt that is added to the stock.

**100 g (4 oz) green beans**
**salt**
**120 ml (4 fl oz) ice-cold Japanese Soup Stock (see page 255) or unsalted light chicken stock**

■ Trim the green beans and cut into 6 cm (2½ inch) lengths. Bring 600 ml (1 pint) water to the boil in a pan. Add salt, put in the beans and cook briskly for about 4 minutes until they are tender, but retain some crispness.

■ Drain and immediately drop into the ice-cold stock. Add ¼ teaspoon salt and stir. Let the beans sit in the stock for at least 15 minutes. Lift the beans out of the liquid to serve.

# CARROTS

## *Ninjin*

*JAPAN*

Serves 4

Small quantities of carrots often provide a colourful accent, and a third dimension, to plates of chicken or fish in Japan. These carrots can also be arranged along with other vegetables over a bowl of noodles. You could easily double or triple the quantities below to serve the carrots, Western-style, as a vegetable accompaniment. If using prepared *dashi-no-moto* instead of Japanese Soup Stock, omit the salt.

**100 g (4 oz) carrots**
**2 teaspoons sugar**
**¼ teaspoon salt**
**4 tablespoons Japanese Soup Stock (see page 255) or light unsalted chicken stock**

■ Peel the carrots. Cut into 6 cm (2½ inch) chunks, then cut lengthways into 3 mm (⅛ inch) thick slices. Either use these slices, or cut lengthways into fine julienne strips.

■ Put the carrots, sugar, salt and stock in a small pan. Bring to the boil and boil for about 1 minute; the carrots should retain some crispness. Immerse the pan in a bowl of cold water to cool off the carrots quickly. To serve, lift the carrots out of their liquid and arrange as required.

# BAMBOO SHOOT TIPS

## *Takenoko*

*JAPAN*

Serves 4

Since the bamboo shoots in this recipe need to look as good as they taste, only the tips are used. These are sometimes available in cans (labelled 'winter bamboo shoots'). Tender bamboo shoot chunks can be used as a substitute, but don't buy sliced bamboo shoots. If you are using prepared *dashi-no-moto* instead of Japanese Soup Stock, omit the salt.

**75 g (3 oz) canned bamboo shoot tips, or chunks**
**150 ml (¼ pint) Japanese Soup Stock (see page 255), or light unsalted chicken stock**
**1 tablespoon sake**
**2 teaspoons Japanese soy sauce (*shoyu*)**
**1 tablespoon sugar**
**¼ teaspoon salt**

■ If using bamboo shoot tips, wash and drain, then cut vertically into wedges, about 3 mm (⅛ inch) thick on the outside, while their inside looks like the teeth of a comb. If using bamboo shoot chunks, cut into triangular slices about 5 cm (2 inches) long and 3 mm (⅛ inch) thick.

■ Combine the stock, sake, soy sauce, sugar and salt in a small pan and bring to the boil. Drop in the bamboo shoots and simmer gently for 5 minutes, turning occasionally.

■ Leave to cool in the liquid, again turning the pieces from time to time so that they pick up the colour evenly.

# MUSHROOMS

## *Kinoko*

*JAPAN*

Serves 4

If using prepared *dashi-no-moto* instead of Japanese Soup Stock, omit the salt.

**8 medium mushrooms**
**150 ml (¼ pint) Japanese Soup Stock (see page 255) or light unsalted chicken stock**
**1 tablespoon sake**
**2 teaspoons Japanese soy sauce (*shoyu*)**
**2 teaspoons sugar**
**¼ teaspoon salt**

■ Wipe the mushrooms with a damp cloth and halve them lengthways.

■ Combine the stock, sake, soy sauce, sugar and salt in a small pan. Bring to a simmer, then add the mushrooms and cook, stirring occasionally, over a medium-low heat for about 2½ minutes.

■ Turn off the heat and leave the mushrooms to cool in their liquid. Drain and serve.

# desserts and drinks

# PLATTER OF TROPICAL FRESH FRUIT

In much of Asia meals end not with puddings and desserts, but with fruit. Sometimes it is just one glorious seasonal fruit, such as perfumed summer mangoes chilled in iced water, or it could be a collection of several fruits, all pared and cut into neat mouthfuls.

In Korea these neat mouthfuls sit on a common platter set in the centre of the table. Each piece of fruit is pierced with a small 2-pronged fork so that it can be picked up with ease and nibbled at will. In Thailand, where a whole school is devoted to the art, fruit comes carved in the most elaborate floral and geometric designs; you cannot even get a simple papaya in your hotel room without some slight hint of delicate fingers at work. In Japan, where the fruit is not tropical, the presentation is invariably stunning. I was once served a whole orange that had been peeled in one neat spiral and sectioned, then re-assembled so that the fruit looked whole. Alongside was a bunch of grapes – each one had been seeded and somehow loosened inside from its coarse skin. All I had to do was hold a grape to my lips and just suck in the smooth insides.

While I do not suggest that you spend all day carving fruit – enough effort is required to prepare the main meal – here are helpful hints on preparing tropical fruits that you may be unfamiliar with, yet are now often available here from good greengrocers and supermarkets.

## CUSTARD APPLE

This is a heart-shaped fruit that seems to be covered with a green alligator skin. It must be fully ripe when it is bought, which means that it should yield easily to the touch when pressed. Serve each person a whole chilled custard apple. You can easily split it open lengthways, using nothing but your hands. The inside is filled with white, creamy, sugar-sweet buds that often harbour smooth, black seeds. Ease your spoon into the custard-like pulp. The art of eating this fruit lies in knowing how to dislodge the seeds from the pulp while the buds are still in your mouth and then delicately spitting out the seeds while retaining your dignity.

## DURIAN

Dare I mention it! This is the fruit that is banned from hotels and aeroplanes because of its lingering odour. South-east Asians are always surprised when a Westerner can allow himself or herself to go near it, let alone eat it. I love it passionately and recommend it without hesitation.

It looks unprepossessing – large, green and full of murderous spikes, a football made by a dinosaur for a dinosaur. It needs to be cracked open with a hatchet wielded by a practised hand. Lying inside its five compartments are pale, off-white segments of the creamiest, smoothest texture imaginable. These segments are sweet in flavour, and the texture is the most heavenly blend of cream, bananas and flowing ripe brie.

In Indonesia the durian is considered to be an aphrodisiac and, the saying goes, 'When the durian comes in, the sarongs go up.' Might that induce you to try it?

## POMELO

This is best described as an extra-crisp, crunchy, flaky grapefruit. Once it has been peeled, its wedge-like sections can be separated and the papery skin on each wedge pulled off with ease. This makes it ideal for fruit plates and salads. Each peeled wedge can be flaked by separating all the individual 'buds' in it. In Thailand the 'flaked' version is used in everyday salads.

## WATERMELON AND BANANAS

Chunks of watermelon and sliced bananas may be added to any plate of tropical fruit that you wish to serve.

*Sweet, juicy and – at its best – smooth-textured and fragrant, a mango to me is the king of fruit. There are hundreds of varieties, each with its own taste, texture and colour. In Thai villages, baskets of mangoes are left to ripen under the bed. When the perfume becomes overwhelming, the household knows that the mangoes are ready to be eaten!*

*Mangoes sold by many shops in this country are hard and under-ripe. Smell the mango at its stem end, and if it seems to have the potential of being sweet, buy it. When you get home, wrap the hard mango in newspaper and put it in a basket or an open cardboard box. Do not refrigerate it. You can ripen several mangoes together in this way, wrapping each one separately in newspaper first. Examine your mangoes every day. They should eventually yield very slightly to the touch, but should not have black spots on them. You may now chill the mangoes in the refrigerator, or cool them in a bucket of iced water before serving.*

LYCHEES

Lychees have a red or reddish-brown, tough skin. The inside is white, translucent and glistening. Chill lychees before serving. Put a whole bunch in a bowl in the centre of your table and let people break off their own, peel and eat them. Or peel the lychees yourself and arrange them on a plate with other cut fruit. Do not remove the stone; that is the least people can do for themselves. The easiest way to eat lychees is to pop them whole into your mouth, remembering the stone.

MANGOSTEEN

In spite of its name, the mangosteen is not related to the mango. It is purplish or reddish-brown on the outside, the size of a tangerine and quite hard. There is a knack of cracking it open with a good twist, but I suggest an easier method. With a sharp knife, make a cut all around the equator. Now pull the top off like a cap. Sitting propped up inside a natural cup, will be 5-8 white, juicy, translucent segments – eat these with a spoon. They will be deliciously sweet, with a hint of sourness.

MANGO

The mango usually has two flatter sides. Cut a thick slice lengthways off each of these sides as close to the stone as you can. (Peel the remaining mango and devour it yourself, or cut into cubes.) The two mango slices make a serving: the pulp may now be scooped decorously out of the skin with a spoon. You could also cut a cross-hatch pattern in the flesh, making rows at about 1 cm (½ inch) intervals with a sharp knife cutting down to the skin, but not through it.

PAPAYA

A papaya should be very ripe and sweet. It should yield slightly to the touch and have a nice yellowish colour on the outside. Chill it first, then cut it in half lengthways. Scoop out the dark seeds. You may now cut it into long slices, or you may serve a whole half with a wedge of lime, or you may peel the papaya halves and cut them into cubes.

PASSION FRUIT
This wonderfully fragrant fruit looks like a wrinkled purple (or sometimes yellow) plum. Split it open and you will find crunchy seeds covered with a clear, gelatinous flesh nestling in the hollow. At their peak of ripeness, passion fruit have a sweet and sour taste that seems to combine the flavour of limes and berries. The easiest way to eat passion fruit flesh is with a teaspoon. The pulp may also be strained and served over ice cream.

PINEAPPLE
To choose a ripe pineapple, smell it; it should have a sweet aroma. Look at its colour, too – the yellower it is, the riper it will be. Feel the very top of the fruit, near the leaves – it should have a little give. To prepare a pineapple, peel it, then remove its 'eyes' with the tip of a knife. Either serve cut into wedges with the core removed – as they do in South-east Asia – or in rounds, with the central core taken out. Fresh pineapple is best served chilled.

RAMBUTAN
This is a large reddish-brown member of the lychee family. Its tough skin is covered with soft, red spikes. The white translucent flesh of the rambutan tastes a little like a lychee, but is much less juicy. In Thailand, rambutans are often presented half-peeled on a fruit plate to show off their interesting skins. Rambutans also have seeds in them.

STAR FRUIT
When this yellowish-coloured fruit is cut crossways into slices, each slice looks like a star – hence its name. Its flavour can be sour, sweet and sour, or just sweet, depending upon the type. It is exceedingly juicy. Slices of star fruit can be added to a plate of fruit served at the end of a meal. They can also be left on the table, along with herbs and lettuce leaves, to be nibbled upon at will during the course of a Vietnamese, Thai or Malaysian meal.

# PEARS POACHED IN A SAFFRON SYRUP

## *Zaafraani Nashpati* — *INDIA*

Serves 4-8

These pears, which I first made with the purest saffron from Kashmir, are heavenly. They turn a rich gold colour and are suffused with the heady aromas of saffron and cardamom – amongst the most prized spices in the world.

**200 g (7 oz) sugar**
**6 whole cardamom pods**
**¼ teaspoon saffron threads**
**3 tablespoons lemon juice**
**4 firm pears**

■ Put the sugar into a medium heavy-based saucepan with 450 ml (¾ pint) water. Add the cardamom pods, saffron and lemon juice. Heat gently until the sugar dissolves, then bring to a simmer.

■ Peel the pears, halve lengthways and remove the core; add each pear to the simmering syrup as soon it is cut, to avoid discoloration. Cover and cook gently for 20-25 minutes, turning the pears in the syrup from time to time.

■ Carefully lift the pears out of the liquid and arrange them in a serving dish in a single layer, cut-side down. Boil the syrup until it is reduced to about 250 ml (8 fl oz) and thickened slightly. Pour the reduced syrup evenly over the pears. Allow to cool before serving.

# SWEET WALNUT SOUP

## *Waiyou Hetao Tang* — *HONG KONG*

Serves 4

This recipe comes from a restaurant in Hong Kong that is renowned for its desserts. One of the specialities is hot, sweet soup. Machines in the back of the restaurant whirr busily, grinding sesame seeds to a fine paste for sweet sesame seed soup. One may order sweet red bean soup, or almond cream soup, or a sweet walnut soup. This particular soup may be served chilled in the summer.

**2 teaspoons cornflour**
**75 g (3 oz) shelled walnut halves**
**120 ml (4 fl oz) groundnut oil**
**3½ tablespoons sugar**
**120 ml (4 fl oz) single cream**

■ In a small bowl, mix the cornflour with 2 tablespoons water and set aside.

■ Bring a medium pan of water to the boil, then drop in the walnuts and boil for 10 seconds. Drain the walnuts and leave them in the sieve.

■ Heat the oil in a wok or small pan over a medium heat. Don't let the oil get very hot: the temperature should be around 160°C (325°F). Add the walnuts and immediately take the wok off the heat. Stir the walnuts for 5 seconds, then remove with a slotted spoon and place in a blender.

■ Add 250 ml (8 fl oz) water and blend until smooth. Pour the walnut mixture into a clean pan. Some of the mixture will cling to the blender, so pour in another 250 ml (8 fl oz) water and blend again for a few seconds. Pour this liquid into the pan as well.

■ Add the sugar, stir and bring slowly to a simmer. Give the cornflour mixture a stir and add that to the pan as well. Cook, stirring, for 30 seconds or until the soup has thickened slightly. Add the cream and heat through. Pour into Chinese soup bowls or other serving bowls and serve hot.

# APPLE OR GUAPPLE PIE

*PHILIPPINES*

Serves 4

The El Ideal Bakery in the Negros township of Silay makes some of the best pies in the country. A crumbly guapple pie is only one of its superb offerings. What is a guapple? It is a big, round, hard guava. To prepare a guapple, remove the seeds, coarsely chop the flesh, then – to give it the tartness it lacks – toss with lime juice, as well as the more usual sugar and cinnamon. While the bottom of the pie has a regular short crust, the top is all crumb. If you manage to find very hard guavas, do use them for this recipe; sweet, ripe guavas are not suitable. I have used apples instead. You will need 1-2 limes to provide 1½ tablespoons finely chopped rind.

FOR THE BOTTOM CRUST

**150 g (5 oz) plain flour, plus extra for dusting**

**40 g (1½ oz) chilled margarine**

**25 g (1 oz) chilled lard**

**about 2 tablespoons ice-cold water**

FOR THE FILLING

**150 g (5 oz) sugar**

**¾ teaspoon ground cinnamon**

**1½ tablespoons thinly pared and finely chopped lime or lemon rind**

**1 kg (2 lb) hard, sour apples (such as Granny Smith's)**

**1½ tablespoons cornflour**

FOR THE CRUMB TOPPING

**100 g (4 oz) plain flour**

**75 g (3 oz) sugar**

**75 g (3 oz) chilled butter**

■ First make the bottom crust. Sift the flour into a bowl. Cut the margarine and lard into small pieces and add to the flour. Using your fingertips, rub the fat into the flour until the mixture resembles coarse breadcrumbs. Sprinkle in just enough ice-cold water – about 2 tablespoons – to mix to a dough. Gather the dough into a ball, knead lightly and quickly, then form a ball again. Spread a sheet of greaseproof paper, about 40 cm (16 inches) long, on your work surface.

■ Put the ball of dough in the middle and flatten it slightly. Place another sheet of greaseproof paper on top. Now roll the dough from the centre outwards, keeping it between the sheets of paper, to a 25 cm (10 inch) round. Remove the top paper.

■ Lift the dough with the help of the lower sheet of greaseproof paper and invert it on top of a 20 cm (8 inch) pie plate or tin. Fit the pastry into the tin. Trim the edge, then press the prongs of a fork around the rim to finish neatly. Leave to rest in the refrigerator, while making the filling. Preheat the oven to 220°C (425°F) gas mark 7.

■ Next make the pie filling. Put the sugar, cinnamon and lime or lemon rind in a large bowl and toss to mix. Peel, core and quarter the apples, one at a time. As you cut each quarter, slice crossways into 5 mm (¼ inch) thick pieces and immediately add to the sugar mixture. Toss every now and then. Finally, add the cornflour to the bowl and toss again.

■ For the crumb topping, mix the flour and sugar together in a bowl. Cut the butter into tiny pieces and rub it in with your fingertips until the mixture resembles coarse breadcrumbs.

■ To assemble the pie, pile the apples and their juice into the bottom crust. Sprinkle the crumb topping over the apples. Bake the pie just below the middle of the oven for 10 minutes. Turn the oven temperature down to 180°C (350°F) gas mark 4. Bake for a further 40-50 minutes, until the pie is nicely browned on the top. Serve warm.

# COCONUT MILK CUSTARD

## *Sankhaya*

*THAILAND*

Serves 4

Many South-east Asian countries use coconut milk rather than milk to make custard. The results are superb. You may, if you like, top each custard with a sprinkling of desiccated coconut, though I prefer to serve them plain with nothing to impair the smoothness. Canned coconut milk, well stirred, is of the correct consistency for this custard.

This custard is cooked in a steamer. If you do not have one, you can improvise. Use a wok and place a rack, or steaming tray perforated with holes, inside. Alternatively, use a large pan with a raised trivet inside. It is important that the water stays below the trivet or steaming tray and that it is kept at a bare simmer so that the custard is not overheated, otherwise it will be filled with air bubbles.

**2 eggs**
**250 ml (8 fl oz) thick coconut milk (see page 258)**
**65 g (2½ oz) light brown sugar**

TO DECORATE
**desiccated coconut, sweetened or unsweetened (optional)**

■ Beat the eggs lightly in a bowl. Stir the coconut milk well and add it to the eggs with the brown sugar. Stir to mix.

■ Strain this mixture into a heavy-based pan or a double-boiler set over boiling water. Cook very gently, stirring all the time with a wooden spoon, until the custard has thickened enough to lightly coat the back of the spoon; do not allow to boil or the eggs will curdle.

■ Strain the custard into 4 custard cups, small heatproof bowls or ramekins. Cover lightly with upturned saucers or foil and steam very gently (see above) for 15-20 minutes or until the custard is just set. Allow to cool before serving.

# RICE PUDDING WITH CARDAMOM AND PISTACHIOS

## *Kheer*

*INDIA*

Serves 4

This is my mother's recipe for *kheer*, which she set in shallow half-baked earthenware bowls called *shakoras*. As a result, it picked up the delicious fragrance of freshly moistened earth. You could serve your *kheer* in individual custard bowls or, if you prefer, in one shallow serving bowl.

**1.1 litres (2 pints) milk**
**1 tablespoon long-grain rice**
**4 whole cardamom pods, bruised**
**2 tablespoons sugar**
**10 unsalted pistachio nuts, slivered**

TO DECORATE
**vark (optional, see below)**
**extra pistachio nuts**

■ Combine the milk, rice and cardamom pods in a heavy-based pan or cooking pot. Slowly bring to the boil. Lower the heat and simmer steadily until the milk is reduced to approximately 600 ml (1 pint); this may take about 1¼ hours. Turn off the heat.

■ Remove and discard the cardamom pods. Add the sugar and pistachio nuts, stir well, then leave to cool.

■ Stir the kheer again. Pour into a serving bowl. Decorate with vark, if using. Sprinkle a few more slivered pistachios on top of the vark. Cover and refrigerate until ready to serve.

*Vark is very fine real silver or gold leaf, traditionally used to decorate Indian desserts for special occasions. Each silver or gold leaf is layered between sheets of paper. To use it, you simply pick up the piece of paper and gently invert the vark on to the food to be decorated, taking care to ensure it does not disintegrate. Vark is edible. It is only available from selected Indian food shops.*

# CARAMEL CUSTARD FILIPINO-STYLE

## *Leche Flan*

*PHILIPPINES*

Serves 4

I have such a weakness for soothing, slithery milk desserts – especially for caramel custard. It is made particularly well in the Philippines where, as in Spain, it could be considered the national dessert. What do the Filipinos do differently? They never seem to use fresh milk, for one thing. Their love affair with canned American products continues unabated and, I must say, in this case works well. The dessert is rich, creamy and, as one of my daughters pronounced, the best ever.

All households in the Philippines seem to agree on the use of canned evaporated milk but seem to disagree on the number of eggs and whether they should be used whole or in part. One is apt to hear comments like, 'I make my *leche flan* with 3 eggs' with a retort such as 'You should really have my mother's. She uses 8 egg yolks. Hers is delicious.' This recipe calls for 3 whole eggs and 2 egg yolks, a very happy middle-ground.

In the Philippines caramel custard is served on special occasions with a topping of slivered *macapuno*, a mutant glutinous coconut. *Macapuno* in syrup is available canned from some South-east Asian grocers. If you find it, you might wish to give it a try. If you want to invert the custard on to a serving plate to bring it to the table, you should butter the mould lightly before pouring in the custard.

*With the arrival of the Americans in the Philippines during 1898 came a large military presence and vast stocks of exotic goodies such as canned evaporated and condensed milk, canned fruit, bottled mayonnaise, hot dogs, sweet bottled pickles and canned tomato sauce. It was considered a decided improvement to make the Spanish dessert flan (caramel custard) with evaporated milk instead of water buffalo milk.*

FOR THE CUSTARD

**3 large eggs**
**2 large egg yolks**
**75 g (3 oz) sugar**
**pinch of salt**
**750 ml (1¼ pints) canned evaporated milk**
**1½ teaspoons vanilla essence**
**butter, for greasing (optional)**

FOR THE CARAMEL

**75 g (3 oz) sugar**

■ Preheat the oven to 160°C (325°F) gas mark 3. Pour a 2.5 cm (1 inch) depth of hot water into a small roasting tin, large enough to hold a custard mould of 1.1 litres (2 pints) capacity or 4 individual moulds. Place this tin in the oven.

■ Put the eggs and egg yolks into a bowl and beat lightly, until evenly blended but not frothy. Add the sugar and salt and mix in. Heat the evaporated milk until it is very hot, but not boiling. Slowly pour the hot milk on to the eggs, whisking vigorously as you do so. Mix in the vanilla.

■ If you are intending to invert the custard when serving, grease the custard mould(s) with butter.

■ To make the caramel, put the sugar in a heavy-based frying pan or other wide heavy pan, spreading it evenly. Place over a medium heat. As the sugar melts and turns brown, tilt the pan around so that the sugar moves a little; do not stir. When all the sugar has caramelised, pour it into the custard mould, or divide it among the 4 individual moulds. Tilt the mould(s) around so that the sides are coated a little as well as the base. The caramel will harden: this is as it should be.

■ Now strain in the hot custard and stand the mould(s) in the roasting tin. Cook in the oven allowing about 1 hour for a large custard, or 30-40 minutes for individual ones. The custard is ready when it appears to be set and a knife inserted into the centre comes out clean.

■ Allow the custard to cool before inverting it on to serving plate(s), if you wish to turn it out. You may serve it warm – as I like to – or cold in the traditional way.

# ICE CREAM WITH CARDAMOM AND PISTACHIOS

## *Kulfi*

*INDIA*

Serves 6

This is Indian ice cream at its best. Milk is boiled down to a third of its original volume, then sugar, cardamom and nuts are added. The thickened milk is eventually frozen in special conical containers (or other freezerproof moulds). If you have an ice-cream maker, use it to make this ice cream and dispense with the need to stir it yourself during freezing.

Traditionally, kulfi is served with *falooda*, a transparent vermicelli rather like the Japanese noodles in a *sukiyaki*.

**1.4 litres (2½ pints) milk**
**4 cardamom pods**
**3 tablespoons sugar**
**1 tablespoon unsalted pistachio nuts, slivered**
**extra pistachio nuts, to decorate**

■ Put the milk in a heavy-based pan or cooking pot and bring to the boil. Lower the heat and simmer steadily until the milk is reduced to 500 ml (16 fl oz), stirring every few minutes; this may take up to 1½ hours. After the first hour, lightly crush two of the cardamom pods and add them to the milk.

■ When the milk is reduced to 500 ml (16 fl oz), turn off the heat and discard the cardamom pods. Add the sugar and nuts. Stir well.

■ Grind the seeds from the other 2 cardamom pods and add them to the milk. Leave to cool.

■ When cool, stir once, then pour the milk into a freezerproof bowl (or ice-cream maker, see above). Cover the bowl with freezer film or foil and place in the freezer. Place six 75-100 ml (3-4 fl oz) individual freezerproof moulds or empty yogurt cartons in the freezer to chill thoroughly. Every 20-30 minutes, take the kulfi out of the freezer and stir well to break down the ice crystals; it will get harder to stir as it thickens.

■ When the mixture becomes almost impossible to stir, divide it between the moulds; or pour into a pudding basin. Cover with foil and freeze.

■ To serve, run a warm knife around the inside of each container, or briefly dip the mould in warm water to loosen the kulfi, then invert on to serving plate(s). Scatter with pistachios to decorate.

# FLUFFY PANCAKES WITH SWEET SESAME-PEANUT FILLING

## *Ban Chan Kuay, Sweet Martabak*

*MALAYSIA, INDONESIA*

Serves 4

This thick sweet pancake, with its characteristic crumpet-like holes, is a popular street snack in both Malaysia and Indonesia. Its origins probably go back to the *appam* (or 'hopper', as the British called it) of South India. I found it very interesting that a similar pancake, cooked today by Muslim fisherwomen of the southern Philippines, is still called an *appam*. In former times the yeast for this dish was provided by fermented palm toddy. Today most people use either dried yeast or baking powder.

In the streets of Padang in Western Sumatra the filling often consists of butter, sugar, crushed peanuts and, would you believe it, chocolate vermicelli! In Penang in Malaysia the chocolate is left out and roasted sesame seeds are added to the peanuts. Both versions are very good.

To make these pancakes, you need a heavy cast-iron frying pan or an old-fashioned cast-iron crêpe pan. It should be about 15 cm (6 inches) in diameter, though a larger one would be acceptable. A lid is also required, though you can improvise with anything that fits.

Each pancake takes about 4 generous tablespoons of batter. To get a rough idea how much batter you will be scooping up each time, pour this amount of water into a small cup or ladle, then empty the cup or ladle and wipe dry.

These pancakes must be eaten hot. Since each pancake takes about 6 minutes to cook, I often have two pans going at the same time.

**225 g (8 oz) plain flour**
**2 teaspoons baking powder**
**¼ teaspoon salt**
**2 teaspoons plus 2 tablespoons caster sugar**
**1 large egg**
**300 ml (½ pint) milk**
**4 teaspoons vegetable oil**
**40-50 g (1½-2 oz) Roasted Peanuts (see page 223)**
**40 g (1½ oz) unsalted butter, softened**
**3 tablespoons roasted sesame seeds (see page 263)**
**2 tablespoons icing sugar (optional)**

■ Sift the flour, baking powder and salt into a bowl. Stir in the 2 teaspoons caster sugar and make a well in the centre. Beat the egg lightly, then pour it into the well with the milk and oil. Mix to a smooth batter. (Alternatively, you can mix the batter ingredients in a blender or food processor.) Cover and set aside for 2 hours or longer.

■ Crush the peanuts to a coarse powder in a mortar or a clean coffee grinder. Put the crushed peanuts, remaining caster sugar and the roasted sesame seeds in separate bowls near the hob before you start to cook the pancakes.

■ Set a cast-iron frying pan on a medium-low heat. When it is hot, put in ½ teaspoon butter. Stir the batter quickly, then scoop up a measure (see left) and pour into the pan. Cover immediately and turn the heat to low. Cook for 3 minutes or until bubbles appear on the surface.

■ Quickly spread 1 teaspoon butter on top of the pancake and sprinkle with 1 teaspoon sugar, followed by 1½ teaspoons sesame seeds, then 1 tablespoon peanuts. Cover again and cook for a further 2½-3 minutes or until the pancake is done.

■ Uncover and fold the pancake in half. Serve plain or dusted with 1 teaspoon icing sugar. Wipe the frying pan clean before making the next pancake. Make all the pancakes in this way, not forgetting to stir the batter each time.

*In a popular open-air restaurant on a high-rise rooftop in Penang, the food is served on green or orange plates. This is an Islamic nation and green signifies that the food is halal – that is, approved for Muslim consumption; orange plates may well have pork on them. This way, friends of different faiths can sit together and know instantly what foods they must not touch and which are safe to eat. You might wish to end the day on Penang's seafront, Gurney Drive. Here, calmed by the soft lapping of the waves and the cooling breeze, you can take a last bite from one of those gorgeous sweet pancakes, ban chan kuay, spongily light and stuffed with sesame seeds and peanuts.*

# CANDIED WALNUT HALVES

## *Hotoo Twikim* — *KOREA*

Serves 4

Fried candied walnuts are often served as after-dinner treats or snacks in China and Korea. This is the Korean version.

**4 tablespoons sugar**
**100 g (4 oz) shelled walnut halves**
**300 ml (½ pint) groundnut oil**

■ Put the sugar in a wide bowl or saucer. Bring a large pan of water to a rolling boil. Drop in the walnuts and boil rapidly for 20 seconds. Drain the walnuts thoroughly and toss with the sugar; it should cling to the nuts. Spread the walnuts out on a clean plate and leave them to cool off and dry for about 30 minutes.

■ Set a strainer over a bowl. Heat the oil in a wok or small frying pan on a medium-low heat to about 120°C (250°F). Add the walnuts and fry, stirring, for 5-6 minutes or until they begin to glisten and turn a soft brown colour. Do not let them darken or they will taste bitter. Immediately pour the oil and walnuts into the strainer.

■ Spread the walnuts out on a plate or tray, spacing them slightly apart. Allow to cool.

■ Tip the cooled nuts on to kitchen paper to absorb any remaining frying oil, changing the paper for a fresh sheet if necessary. Store the walnuts in a tightly lidded jar for up to 2 weeks until ready to serve.

# PEANUT CANDY

Serves 4

For this candy, which is made throughout South-east Asia, you need palm sugar. If you cannot get it, a good substitute is jaggery, sold by Indian grocers. It is sold in lump form and the best kind is crumbly and breakable, not hard as a rock.

**150 g (5 oz) shelled, raw, unskinned peanuts**
**2 teaspoons groundnut oil**
**175 g (6 oz) palm sugar, or jaggery**

■ Warm a medium heavy-based frying pan (preferably cast-iron) on a medium heat. Add the peanuts and dry-roast, stirring constantly, for about 3 minutes or until they begin to show signs of browning. Turn the heat down to medium-low. Continue to stir and cook for a further 6-7 minutes or until the peanuts are roasted.

■ Turn the peanuts on to a piece of kitchen paper and leave until cool enough to handle. Now rub off the papery skins with the help of the paper and blow them away, or pick out the peanuts; put them in a bowl. Wipe the frying pan clean.

■ Brush an 18 cm (7 inch) pie tin with 1 teaspoon of the oil. Break up the palm sugar into small lumps and put it into the frying pan, with the remaining 1 teaspoon oil and 2 tablespoons water. Place over a medium heat. When the liquid starts bubbling, turn the heat to low and let the palm sugar melt. Cook very gently, allowing 5 minutes for chewy candy; or about 8 minutes for hard, brittle candy. The palm sugar will become thicker as it cooks.

■ Take off the heat and add the peanuts to the pan. Immediately pour the mixture into the oiled pie tin, allowing it to spread evenly. Leave to cool, then pull, tear or break the candy into pieces.

# JAPANESE RICE WINE

## *Sake*

*JAPAN*

Japanese habits are changing. It is now considered chic to drink whisky with a meal, and it is quite common to have beer, but sake, the indigenous rice wine, remains the national drink. Famed as the mythical drink of the gods in ancient times and limited to exclusive consumption by nobles and priests through the Middle Ages, today sake is available to the masses even in cardboard cartons that are sold out of slot machines just like Coca-Cola.

Sake is colourless, like vodka, though much less potent. Its alcoholic content can range from 15 to 17 per cent for the general market, and up to 20 per cent for some very special varieties. At weddings and banquets it may be served cool, straight out of specially ordered cedar casks, rather like beer out of barrels. These days, it may also be served chilled. Chilled sake is being promoted quite a bit now in Japan to lure back the infidels who have been seduced by the fashionable white wines of France.

The most common way to drink sake, however, is not cooled or chilled, but warmed. Warming releases its aromas and allows the alcohol to enter the bloodstream with a more pronounced sense of urgency. Sake that has been warmed once is not considered good for drinking any more as its aromas have been dispersed. (It is, however, good for cooking.) It is for this reason that only small quantities of sake are warmed at a time. Servings, too, are small as the entire amount – a few thimblefuls – is supposed to be drunk at one go, before it has a chance to cool off. It is considered polite to serve one's neighbours when their glasses are empty and to let them do the same for you. It is not quite the done thing to serve oneself when in company. Sake can be drunk through every course of a Japanese meal.

Once a bottle of sake has been opened, it behaves rather like wine and it is best to consume it all. You may, if you have to, keep it for up to 2 weeks in a cool place or in the refrigerator, but its life is limited.

For heating and serving, sake bottles and cups are sold by many oriental shops. If you do not wish to buy a set, you can easily improvise. For drinking, use the smallest liqueur glasses in your possession; the size will probably be just right. For heating and serving, use any pretty glass or ceramic bottle of roughly 300 ml (½ pint) capacity. Fill it with sake. Half-fill a medium pan with water and stand the bottle of sake in it. Heat the water gently. The sake should be very warm but not hot. Aim for a temperature of around 54°C (130°F). Heat several batches, one after the other, as you need them. By the way, the word for 'cheers' is *kampai!*

# GINGER TEA

## *Salabat*

*PHILIPPINES*

Serves 4

Ginger tea in some form or other is drunk nearly everywhere in the Far East. It is meant to be very good for coughs and colds and is also a digestive. In the Philippines it is often offered at breakfast and with midday snacks or *merienda*.

**3 x 2.5 cm (1 inch) cubes fresh root ginger**

**4-5 teaspoons honey, or light brown or demerara sugar, to taste**

■ Peel the ginger and chop it coarsely. Put it into a small pan with 1 litre (1¾ pints) water and the honey or sugar. Bring to the boil. Turn the heat to low and simmer gently for 15-20 minutes. Strain and serve.

■ You may also serve this tea cold.

# GINGER COFFEE

## *Kopi Jahe*

*INDONESIA*

Serves 4

Indonesians grow their own coffee and one of the ways they drink it is very sweet, with a strong ginger flavour. It is quite easy to make such coffee at home. Whether you drink the instant version or use a filter, all you have to do is prepare a ginger broth and make your coffee with that instead of water. (It is not advisable to make this coffee in an electric coffee maker.)

**2.5 cm (1 inch) cube fresh root ginger**

**instant or fresh ground filter coffee, enough for 4 cups**

**brown, demerara or white sugar, to taste**

■ Peel and coarsely dice the ginger. Put it into a pan with about 4¼ teacups water. Bring the water to the boil, turn the heat to low and simmer gently for 15 minutes. Strain.

■ If you are making instant coffee, put about 1 teaspoon coffee (or to taste) into each cup and pour the hot ginger broth over it. Stir to mix. If you are using a filter, measure out enough coffee for 4 people and put it into the filter. Pour the hot ginger broth over the coffee and let it filter through.

■ Hand the sugar round separately when you serve the coffee.

# reference

# MENUS

There is no reason why you should feel compelled to put together meals with dishes from just one country. However, in case you want to, here are typical menus from each country. In each case the first menu is for a simple family meal, the second for a more elaborate dinner party. I have also included a couple of suggestions for menus of mixed origin.

## *Simple Thai Menu*

Hot and Sour Prawn Soup (*page 24*)
Minced Chicken Stir-fried with Basil (*page 97*)
Greens with Garlic and Oyster Sauce (*page 173*)
Plain Rice

## *Elaborate Thai Menu*

Chicken, Prawn and Fruit Salad (*page 41*)
Fish Steamed with Lemon Grass (*page 64*)
Easy Beef Curry (*page 134*)
Plain Rice

*Dessert*
Fresh Fruit Platter (*page 233*) or
Coconut Milk Custard (*page 239*)

## *Simple Japanese Menu*

Fermented Bean Paste Soup with Bean Curd (*page 33*)
Breaded Pork Cutlets (page 148)
East-West Sauce (*page 216*)
Plain Japanese Rice (*page 191*)
Green Beans with Sesame Dressing (*page 161*)

## *Elaborate Japanese Menu*

Green Beans with Sesame Dressing (*page 161*)
Stuffed Mushrooms (*page 48*)
Grilled Mackerel with Sweet Soy Sauce (*page 56*)
Asparagus (*page 228*)
Plain Rice

*Dessert*
Fresh Fruit (*page 233*)

## *Simple Indonesian Menu*

Whole Grilled Fish, Sour and Spicy (*page 60*)

Cauliflower and Carrots with a Coconut Dressing (*page 166*)

Plain Rice

*Dessert*

Fresh Fruit (*page 233*)

---

## *Elaborate Indonesian Menu*

Spicy Chicken Kebabs with Peanut Sauce - *Satay* (*page 90*)

Beef Chunks Cooked in Coconut Milk (*page 129*)

Spiced Mushrooms in a Packet (*page 182*)

Plain Rice

Prawn Wafers - *Krupuk* (*page 40*)

*Dessert*

Fresh Fruit Platter (*page 233*)

---

## *Simple Malaysian Menu*

Rice Noodles in a Coconut Curry Soup (*page 211*)

Bean Sprouts with a Spicy Coconut Dressing (*page 163*)

---

## *Elaborate Malaysian Menu*

Squid in Chilli and Garlic Sauce (*page 45*)

Spicy Prawn and Cucumber Curry (*page 71*)

Perfumed Rice with Vegetables Nonya-style (*page 200*)

Aubergines in a Thick, Hot, Sweet and Sour Chilli Sauce (*page 156*)

*Dessert*

Fluffy Pancakes with Sweet Sesame-Peanut Filling (*page 233*)

---

## *Simple Korean Menu*

Stir-Fried Pork with Red Pepper (*page 145*)

Seasoned Spinach (*page 179*)

Plain Japanese or Korean Rice (*page 191*)

Cabbage Pickle (*page 226*)

---

## *Elaborate Korean Menu*

Savoury Egg Custard with Prawns and Mushrooms (*page 118*)

Marinated and Grilled Beef Strips - *Bulgogi* (*page 124*)

Stir-Fried Courgettes with Sesame Seeds (*page 167*)

Plain Japanese or Korean Rice (*page 191*)

Cabbage Pickle (*page 226*)

*Dessert*

Fresh Fruit Platter (*page 233*)

---

## *Simple Vietnamese Menu*

Pork and Crab Soup (*page 27*)
Easy Beef Kebabs (*page 125*)
Plain Rice
Green Salad (with Lettuce or Baby Spinach, Mint and Basil)

---

## *Elaborate Vietnamese Menu*

Savoury Pork and Crab Toasts (page 38)
Aromatic and Spicy Beef Stew (*page 132*)
Smoky Aubergines in a Lime Sauce (*page 157*)
Kohlrabi Salad (*page 174*)
Plain Rice

*Dessert*
Fresh Fruit Platter (*page 233*)

---

## *Simple Hong Kong Menu*

Sesame Noodles with Chicken and Vegetables (*page 208*)
Lamb with Spring Onions (*page 142*)
Plain Rice
Braised Broad Beans (*page 162*)

*Dessert*
Fresh Melon

---

## *Elaborate Hong Kong Menu*

Bon Bon Chicken (*page 112*)
Glazed Gingery Spareribs (*page 149*)
Fish Fillets with Black Bean Sauce (*page 57*)
Salad of Cucumber, Carrots, Celery and Ham (*page 172*)
Plain Rice

*Dessert*
Sweet Walnut Soup (*page 238*)

---

## *Simple Philippines Menu*

Pork Cooked in a Pickling Style (*page 145*)
Plain Rice
Mangetout Stir-fried with Prawns (*page 178*)

*Dessert*
Caramel Custard Filipino-style (*page 240*)

---

## *Elaborate Philippines Menu*

Mackerel 'Cooked' in Lime Juice (*page 47*)
Glorious Seafood Soup (*page 28*)
Lamb Stew with Olives, Potatoes and Peppers (*page 138*)
Plain Rice
Mangetout Stir-fried with Prawns (*page 178*)

*Dessert*
Apple or Guapple Pie (*page 238*)

---

## *Simple Indian Menu*

Marinated Grilled Chicken (*page 106*)
Moong Dal (*page 187*)
Cauliflower with Ginger and Garlic (*page 170*)
Rice with Spinach (*page 199*)

*Dessert*
Fresh Fruit (*page 233*)

---

## *Mixed Menu*

Hot and Sour Prawn Soup (*page 24*)
Aromatic and Spicy Beef Stew (*page 132*)
Stir-Fried Courgettes with Sesame Seeds (*page 167*)
Plain Rice

*Dessert*
Fresh Fruit (*page 233*)

---

## *Elaborate Indian Menu*

Wholewheat Samosas (*page 50*)
Fresh Coriander and Yogurt Chutney (*page 224*)
Sea Bass in Green Chutney (*page 66*)
Chicken Moghlai (*page 107*)
Cauliflower with Ginger and Garlic (*page 170*)
Basmati Rice with Spices and Saffron (*page 194*)
Tomato and Onion Relish (*page 224*)

*Dessert*
Kulfi (*page 243*)

---

## *Elaborate Mixed Menu*

Chicken on a Skewer - *Yakitori* (page 88)
Fish, Shellfish and Bean Curd Stew (*page 70*)
Green Beans and Carrots with Ginger and Chillies (*page 158*)
Plain Rice
Ginger Tea (*page 247*)

*Dessert*
Caramel Custard Filipino-style (*page 240*)
Candied Walnut Halves (*page 245*)

---

# CHICKEN STOCK

Makes about 2.75 litres (5 pints)

Good chicken stock is needed for many recipes in this book, so it is useful to keep a supply handy in your refrigerator or freezer. Here are a few tips:

■ Whenever you poach a chicken breast, strain the liquid and save it. Use it when small amounts of stock are needed.

■ Save all chicken bones and carcasses and store in the freezer; they can be added to the pot when making stock.

■ When cooking stock, maintain it at a low simmer or it will turn cloudy; it should bubble only very slightly. Skim the stock frequently as it cooks, especially during the first 30 minutes.

■ Sometimes a little salt can be added to the stock at the end of the cooking time to bring out its flavour. You should leave out salt when making stock for use in Japanese recipes.

■ Before freezing stock, boil it down to half its original quantity so that it occupies less space in the freezer. It can easily be reconstituted later.

■ Pour cooled, de-greased stock into ice-cube trays and freeze. When frozen, the cubes can be transferred to freezer bags. You will then be able to use small quantities of stock as and when you need them.

■ Frozen stock can be defrosted quickly in the microwave.

**1.5 kg (3 lb) chicken necks, wings, backs and bones**
**1 kg (2 lb) chicken pieces, such as legs**
**2 spring onions**
**2 thin slices fresh root ginger**
**salt (optional)**

■ Wash the chicken pieces and put them into a large pan. Add 3.4 litres (6 pints) water and bring to a simmer. Maintain the stock at a low simmer; do not let it boil. For the next 30 minutes, keep removing the scum that rises to the surface.

■ Trim the spring onions, discarding the green part. Add the white spring onion to the stock with the ginger slices. Partially cover the pan and cook the stock for a further 3-4 hours, maintaining the heat at a bare simmer.

■ Strain the stock through a sieve lined with a double layer of dampened muslin into a bowl. Season the stock with a little salt if required. Stand the bowl in a large basin or sink of cold water to cool it quickly. Pour the cooled stock into containers, cover and refrigerate. Remove the fat from the surface once it has solidified. You can now freeze the stock.

# BEEF STOCK

## *Nuoc Pho*

*VIETNAM*

Makes about 2.25 litres (4 pints)

Good beef stock requires both meat and beef bones. The bones provide body, but the depth of flavour comes from meat. Ideally you should use equal quantities of bones and meat, though you can save money by using more bones. I freeze odd bones from roasts, until I decide to make stock.

If you are starting from scratch, ask your butcher for soup bones (marrow bones are best) and get him to saw them into smaller pieces. As far as the meat is concerned, you may use brisket, removing it after about 2½ hours when it is tender. Or you can use stewing beef and leave it in for the entire cooking time. Some people like to use shanks, cut up of course, as they provide both meat and bones. Take the meat off the bone after 2½ hours and let the bones cook on.

Although it is usually best to salt stock once the cooking is completed, in this recipe I add a small quantity of salt earlier just to give the meat a little flavour. The brisket may be cut into thin slices for use in salads and soups.

This stock recipe is from Vietnam, but if you season it with salt to taste rather than fish sauce, you can use it for any recipe in this book that calls for beef stock. If you do not have a large enough pan for the stock, use 2 pans.

**100 g (4 oz) onions**
**7.5 cm (3 inch) piece fresh root ginger**
**1.75 kg (4 lb) beef marrow bones, in smaller pieces**
**1.5 kg (3 lb) beef brisket or stewing beef**
**5 cm (2 inch) cinnamon stick**
**2 whole star anise**
**1 teaspoon salt**
**2 tablespoons fish sauce, or extra salt to taste**

■ Preheat oven to 230°C (450°F) gas mark 8. Peel the onions. Put the onions and unpeeled ginger in a small baking tin and roast in the oven for 20-30 minutes, until browned.

■ Meanwhile, put the bones and meat into a very large pan. Add 5 litres (8 pints) water and slowly bring to a simmer. Keep the stock at a low, steady simmer. For the next 15 minutes, keep removing the scum that rises to the surface.

■ Add the onion, ginger, cinnamon, star anise and salt. Partially cover the pan and cook very gently for approximately 2½ hours until the meat is tender. Take out the meat. (Once cooled, it can be refrigerated for use in other dishes.)

■ Continue to simmer the stock gently, partially covered, for a further 2-2½ hours. Add the fish sauce a little at a time, to taste; the stock should be slightly under-seasoned.

■ Strain the stock into a large bowl through a sieve lined with a double layer of dampened muslin. Stand the bowl in a large basin or sink of cold water to cool quickly. Pour the cooled stock into containers, cover and refrigerate. When the stock is cold, remove the solidified fat from the surface. The stock may now be frozen, as for Chicken Stock (see left).

# JAPANESE SOUP STOCK

## *Dashi*

*JAPAN*

Makes 1 litre (1¾ pints)

The Japanese make their basic stock out of fish and sea kelp. The most common fish used for stock is bonito, a member of the mackerel family. It is sold in Japan in a dried, filleted form that looks rather like a piece of smooth, hard, petrified wood, and in fact needs to be shaved with a plane. The delicate, curled shavings are at their best when they are freshly done and when they are a pale pinkish-brown colour. The finest of Japanese food establishments would consider using no other, just as the best French restaurant would always make its stock from scratch. The discriminating Japanese housewife does not shave her own bonito, but she can go into any good market and get it shaved for her on the spot. The average Japanese, on the other hand, either buys packaged bonito shavings, which come in plastic bags or boxes, or uses instant soup stock (*dashi-no-moto*) which is available in granular form.

The other ingredients used in good *dashi* – and for vegetarians it is often the only ingredient – is *konbu*, a special kelp sold in the form of large, dried leaves. Only sections of it are used at a time. The kelp needs to be of good quality. Its flavour is said to reside on its surface, so it is never washed, just wiped lightly with a damp cloth. This kelp should never be boiled vigorously; it is either soaked overnight or allowed to simmer very gently.

Whether you will be able to get shaved bonito (*hana-katsuo*) and the right kelp (*dashi-konbu*) is another matter. Do make an effort, as their flavours are the purest. If you cannot, use instant *dashi-no-moto*, though it is very often salted. As a last resort, you may use very light, unsalted chicken stock.

**25 g (1 oz) piece kelp (*konbu*)**

**25 g (1 oz) dried bonito shavings (*hana-katsuo*)**

■ Wipe the kelp lightly with a damp cloth and put it into a medium pan. Pour in 1 litre (1¾ pints) water and very slowly bring to a simmer over a medium-low heat. If you are using the stock to make clear soup, remove the kelp just before the water comes to the boil. If you are using the stock for anything else – such as Fermented Bean Paste Soup with Bean Curd (page 33), noodles, sauces or for cooking vegetables – let the kelp barely simmer for 10 minutes without ever letting the water come to the boil.

■ Remove the kelp, then add the bonito shavings. Immediately take the pan off the heat. Do not stir. Within the next minute or so, the bonito shavings will sink to the bottom. Strain the soup through a sieve lined with a piece of dampened muslin.

■ While stock for clear soups is best freshly made, all other Japanese Soup Stock may be made ahead of time and refrigerated for up to 3 days. To reheat, bring slowly to a bare simmer.

■ Japanese Soup Stock is generally seasoned with a little salt and/or soy sauce when it is used for clear soups.

*I learned the correct way to make authentic dashi when I visited Ecole Technique Hôtelière Tsuji, the largest school training professional chefs in Japan. First, a hunk of wood-like bonito was quickly rinsed and dried. Odd bits of dried skin and dried blood were scraped off. Just before the stock was made, the bonito was shaved with a plane that was affixed to a box. The shavings fell neatly and conveniently into a drawer!*

# INGREDIENTS

Asian cuisines depend for their distinctive flavours on some special ingredients. It is worth making the effort to seek these out from larger supermarkets and specialist food stores. Some ethnic food suppliers operate a mail order service (see page 265 for details). For the recipes in this book I have suggested substitutes for those ingredients which may be difficult to find; in such cases the authentic ingredient is always given first, followed by the suggested substitute.

AGAR-AGAR This is a vegetarian gelatine made from a type of seaweed. It is available from Japanese, Korean and Chinese grocers in powder, flakes and sticks. The sticks, which look like uneven clear noodles, can be melted and used just like ordinary gelatine but in this book they are only needed for a few salads. For these recipes, you should first soak the sticks in cold water until they are soft but retain a slight crunch. Drain, then cut them into the size you require. They may now be added to any salad and dressed.

ANCHOVY PASTE This is the best substitute I can think of for the various types of shrimp paste used in South-east Asia. Most of the better supermarkets and delicatessens sell it.

BAMBOO SHOOTS Sadly, we cannot usually obtain fresh bamboo shoots in the West and must make do with canned ones. Good canned bamboo shoots should be creamy white and crisp with a clean refreshing taste. Look for the better brands, which are generally of excellent quality. You can buy canned bamboo shoots in rather large hunks, which may then be cut up into cubes of the desired size, or you can sometimes buy the cone-shaped and very tender bamboo shoot tips, which are usually cut into comb-like wedges. Some canned bamboo shoots come ready sliced. Try to get the chunks instead if possible.

All bamboo shoots that come out of a can have a faint tinny taste. To rid them of this, wash in fresh water and drain before use. Any bamboo shoots that are unused may be covered with clean water and stored in a lidded jar in the refrigerator for 2-3 days. In order to keep the bamboo shoots fresh, the water should be changed every day.

BASIL Many different types of fresh basil are used in South-east Asia. Each country – sometimes each province within a country – has different names for these. There is sweet basil (*bai horapha* in Thailand); holy basil with thin purplish leaves (*bai kaprow* in Thailand) and lemon basil (*bai manglak* in Thailand). Ordinary basil and fresh mint are our best substitutes for the highly aromatic South-east Asian basils.

BEAN CURD This is made of soaked, mashed and strained soya beans and takes the form of white, milky, custard-like squares. Bean curd is sold in selected supermarkets, Chinese grocers and healthfood shops. It can be soft (silken tofu) or firm. For the recipes in this book, use firm bean curd. Bean curd squares are sold packed in water. If you are not using them immediately, put them in a bowl, cover with fresh water and refrigerate, changing the water every day.

BEANS, LONG Also known as asparagus beans and yard-long beans, these can indeed be very long. In the Far East they come in two colours, pale and dark green, the dark being the crisper of the two varieties. Long beans are sometimes available from Asian food stores. For cooking, they are generally cut into smaller lengths and then used just like French beans. The best substitute is, indeed, French beans.

BEAN SAUCE, BLACK Commercially prepared sauces made of fermented soya beans are used throughout Malaysia and other parts of South-east Asia. They can be very thick, filled with crumbled beans, or smooth and somewhat thinner. Use any bottled or canned black bean sauce that is available. Once you have opened a bottle you should store it, tightly closed, in the refrigerator.

BEAN SAUCE, YELLOW Like black bean sauce, this is commercially prepared from fermented soya beans, only it has a very pale brown, almost yellowish colour. It can be smooth but I like to use the kind that has whole or halved beans in it, usually labelled as 'crushed yellow bean sauce'.

BEAN SPROUTS These are crisp sprouts grown from the same mung beans sold in Indian stores as whole *moong*. They can now be bought fresh in supermarkets and healthfood stores as well as Indian and Chinese grocers' shops. Look for crisp, white bean sprouts. When you buy fresh sprouts, rinse them in cold running water, then put them into a bowl of fresh water, cover and refrigerate. If the beans are not used by the next day, you should change the water again.

It is considered proper to 'top and tail' bean sprouts before using them. This means pinching off the remains of the whole bean at the top as well as the thread-like tail at the bottom, and requires a lot of patience. The sprouts do indeed look better after this treatment, but I have to admit that I very rarely bother with it. Canned bean sprouts are available, but I never use them as they lack crunch.

BLACK BEANS, SALTED These are salted, spiced and fermented soya beans, sold in plastic bags. They need to be rinsed slightly to remove any excess salt, then chopped before use. They are also available in cans as 'black beans in salted sauce' – whole black beans usually floating in liquid. Lift these beans out of their liquid, chop them and use as the recipe suggests.

BONITO STOCK See *Dashi*

BONITO, DRIED Known as *katsuo-bushi* in Japan, this fish of the mackerel family is filleted and dried until it becomes as hard as wood. It is then shaved with a plane rather like a piece of wood. These shavings are an essential ingredient in Japanese soup stock. The shaved flakes are sold in specialist shops as *hana-katsuo*.

CANDLENUTS Called *kemiri* in Indonesia and *buah keras* in Malaysia, these nuts are used in curry paste to give it thickness and texture. As they are not easily available in the West, a reasonable substitute would be plain cashew nuts (unsalted, and not roasted) or macadamia nuts, both of which are sold in healthfood shops and selected supermarkets.

CARDAMOM PODS These are available pale green, creamy white, or black. The small green-coloured pods have the most aromatic black seeds inside them and are the best type to buy. The whole pods are used to flavour curries, rice dishes and Indian desserts. If green cardamoms are unavailable, opt for the creamy white pods; these are less aromatic but an acceptable substitute for the green variety.

CASHEW NUTS These nuts travelled from the Americas via Africa and India all the way to China. For the recipes in this book they are used in their raw form as a substitute for candlenuts. (In fact all so-called 'raw' cashews have been processed to remove the prussic acid which they contain in their natural state.)

CASSIA BARK This is often called Chinese cinnamon, and is one of the ingredients of five-spice powder. Cassia bark resembles cinnamon and has a similar flavour, but it is thicker and coarser, with a stronger taste.

CHILLI BEAN SAUCE This reddish-brown, hot and spicy sauce is made of soya beans, red chillies and other seasonings. It is used in the cooking of Western China and is sold in jars in larger supermarkets and Chinese grocers. Yu Kwen Yick is a good brand.

CHILLI OIL This is an orange-coloured oil that acquires its heat and its colour from red chillies. Small amounts of chilli oil can be added to dishes as they are being cooked – to pep them up a bit. Many Chinese restaurants have small bottles of chilli oil on the table for those who wish to season their own foods further. Chilli oil can be bought from any Oriental grocer, but you can easily make your own (see page 216).

CHILLI PASTE, THAI The Thai chilli paste (*nam prik pow*) is made by frying shallots and chillies together, then combining them with sugar and tamarind until the seasonings have the consistency of a thick jam. *Nam prik pow* is sold by Thai grocers and selected supermarkets. It is available in different strengths – hot, medium and mild – ask the shop assistant for help if you are unsure of the labelling. If you cannot obtain Thai chilli paste, you could substitute one part each of chilli powder and sugar mixed with two parts vegetable oil, though you won't obtain the same flavour.

CHILLI POWDER This is made by grinding dried hot red chillies to a powder. Both mild and hot forms are widely available. You can add as much or as little chilli powder to a dish as you like, depending on how hot you like your food.

CHILLIES, DRIED RED These can be small and thin, or long and fat. The small variety is the most easily available. When used for making a spice paste dried chillies are usually soaked in water before being ground with other spices.

CHILLIES, FRESH GREEN AND RED Chillies originated in Mexico, then travelled via Africa and India all the way to China and Korea. The East has adopted them with a passion almost unmatched in the countries of their origin. There are hundreds of different kinds of chillies, varying in their intensity of heat. Red chillies are ripened green chillies, and tend to have a slightly different flavour as they sweeten during ripening. However, their intensity can be exactly the same. In general, long, thin chillies are inclined to be hotter than short, plump ones. Red chillies are used in hundreds of South-east Asian curry pastes not only for their heat but also for the colour they impart to the sauce. When I cannot obtain fresh red chillies, I find that a combination of our more common sweet red pepper with paprika and chilli powder makes the best substitute.

Chillies are a very rich source of iron and vitamins A and C. As they vary tremendously in size, shape and heat, it might take a little experimenting to find the chillies you like best. To store fresh red or green chillies, wrap them first in newspaper, then in plastic, and place in the refrigerator; they should last for several weeks. Any that begin to soften and rot should be discarded at once as they tend to infect the whole batch. Chillies may also be washed, dried and then frozen whole in plastic containers. Hot chillies must be handled carefully. When you are cutting them, be careful not to touch your eyes or your lips with your fingers or they will sting. Wash your hands thoroughly afterwards. As a precaution, you may prefer to wear rubber gloves when preparing chillies.

Chillies are used for their taste and heat, but also to provide a decorative element to many South-east Asia dishes. Sometimes they are sliced into rings, at other times into slivers, and often they are cut to resemble flowers.

*To make chilli flowers* Cut off a tiny piece of the very tip, leaving the stem attached. Make four lengthways cuts in the chilli, starting from a little below the stem and going all the way down to the tip. You should now have four sections still attached at the stem. Remove all the seeds and soak the chillies in cold water until they open into flowers.

CHINESE CABBAGE There is great confusion about what Chinese cabbage is. To me, Chinese cabbage is the very chunky, pale green, long, wide-ribbed cabbage that is generally about 13 cm (5 inches) or more in diameter. Its leaves resemble those of the vegetable sold as Chinese leaves, tapering away from the base in much the same way. They are, however, much wider and have greater flavour. This is the vegetable that is used to make the Korean cabbage pickle called kimchee. If you cannot get it, use Chinese leaves, which are widely available, as a substitute.

CHINESE CELERY This resembles Italian flat-leafed parsley. It is larger and coarser and its thin stalks have a distinct celery flavour. Celery stalks, finely diced, and celery leaves can be used as substitutes: follow the directions in individual recipes.

CHINESE CHIVES These are a member of the onion family. The leaves of Chinese chives are flat and have a pronounced garlic-like flavour. During the season in which the plant is budding, buds – still attached to their stalks – are also sold by Chinese grocers. These add a wonderful touch to stir-fried dishes. Ordinary chives can be used as a substitute, and you can include their young buds as well when available.

CHINESE LEAVES This is an exceedingly slim version of Chinese cabbage (see above).

COCONUT, FRESH When buying coconut, look for one that shows no signs of mould and is free from cracks. Shake the coconut. If it has a lot of water in it, it has a better chance of being good. People generally weigh a coconut in each hand and pick the heavier.

To break open a coconut, use the unsharpened side of a cleaver or heavy knife and hit the coconut hard all around its equator. You can hold the coconut in one hand over a large bowl to catch the coconut liquid while you hit it with the other. Alternatively, you can rest the coconut on a board while you hit it, then rush it to a bowl as soon as the first crack appears. Some people like to drink this coconut water; I do. This liquid is not used in cooking but it is a good indication of the sweetness and freshness of the coconut.

You should now have two halves. Before proceeding any further, cut off and taste a small piece of coconut flesh – it should have a sweet flavour. If it is lacking in sweetness, this can be endured, but if it is at all rancid or mouldy you must discard the coconut. Now remove the tough outer shell by slipping a knife between it and the flesh, then prising the coconut flesh out. Sometimes it helps to crack the halves into smaller pieces to do this.

The coconut flesh is covered with a thin brown skin. If your recipe calls for grated fresh coconut, remove the skin with a vegetable peeler or knife, cut the flesh into small cubes and put these into a food processor or blender. Process until you have the semblance of grated coconut. You can freeze what you do not use. Grated coconut freezes very well and is useful to have to hand.

As a substitute for grated fresh coconut you can use unsweetened desiccated coconut which is sold in most healthfood stores. To obtain the equivalent of 50 g (2 oz) of grated fresh coconut, soak 25 g (1 oz) desiccated coconut in 4 tablespoons water for 1 hour.

COCONUT MILK This is best made with fresh coconut but is also available canned or can be prepared using powdered coconut milk, unsweetened desiccated coconut or blocks of creamed coconut. No coconut milk of any sort keeps well – this includes canned milk after it has been opened. Even if you refrigerate it, it generally does not last more than a few days.

*Using fresh coconut* First prise the flesh off the shell as described above. Whether you also peel off the brown skin depends on the dish you are preparing. If it needs to look pale and pristine, remove the skin; if not, leave it on. Grate the coconut flesh in a food processor or blender as described above.

To make about 350 ml (12 fl oz) coconut milk, fill a glass measuring jug to the 450 ml (¾ pint) level with grated coconut. Turn into a blender or food processor, add 300 ml (½ pint) very hot water and blend for a few seconds. Empty the contents of the blender into a muslin-lined sieve placed over a bowl. Gather the ends of the cloth together and squeeze out all of the liquid. For most of the recipes in this book, this is the coconut milk that is needed. If you leave this milk to stand for a while, cream will rise to the top. That is why I recommend stirring the coconut milk before using it. If just the cream is required for a recipe, spoon it off the top.

*Canned coconut milk* is available from most Chinese and Indian grocers but the quality varies. I particularly like one of the brands made in Thailand – it is white, creamy and quite delicious. As the cream tends to rise to the top in a can as it does in fresh coconut milk, always stir it well before using it. Sometimes, because of the fat in it, canned coconut milk tends to become very grainy. To rectify this you can either whizz the coconut milk for a second in a blender or beat it well. I find that whereas you can cook, say, a fish in fresh coconut milk for a long time, canned coconut milk, which behaves differently, is best added towards the end of the cooking time.

*Powdered coconut milk* You can buy packets of powdered coconut milk from Oriental grocers and supermarkets. Their quality varies from good to poor, the poor ones containing hard-to-dissolve globules of fat. I like a Malaysian variety. Directions for using the powder are given on the packet. To use the powder in any of the recipes in this book calling for coconut milk, mix an equal volume of powder and hot water and then stir well until the powder dissolves. If unwanted granules or globules remain, strain the milk before using it. I find that it is best to add coconut milk made of powder towards the end of the cooking period as it tends to separate easily when heated.

*Using unsweetened desiccated coconut* Put 350 g (12 oz) desiccated coconut into a pan. Add 600 ml (1 pint) water and bring to a simmer. Now pour the contents into a blender or food processor and blend for 1 minute. Strain the resulting mixture through a double thickness of muslin, pushing through as much liquid as you can. You should get about 600 ml (1 pint) coconut milk.

*Using creamed coconut* This is available in block form, and can also be turned into coconut milk. I do not advise you use it if you need a large quantity of coconut milk, but if you require just a few tablespoons, it is ideal. Simply mix equal quantities of creamed coconut and hot water. The thick coconut milk that will result should be added to dishes only at the last moment.

CORIANDER, FRESH Also known as Chinese parsley and cilantro, this is the intensely aromatic equivalent of our parsley – used throughout the eastern half of Asia. Generally just the delicate, fragrant, green leaves are added to dishes to impart flavour, or used as a garnish. In Thai curries, however, the white root is sometimes ground in as well, and in China the stems are dried and put into sauces. The best way to keep a bunch of coriander fresh is to stand it in a glass of water so the roots are immersed, cover it with a polythene bag and refrigerate the whole thing. Break off the coriander leaves as you need them.

CORIANDER SEEDS These are the round beige seeds of the coriander plant, sold both whole and ground. You can grind the whole seeds yourself, then put them through a fine sieve to make powder.

CUMIN SEEDS Cumin was brought into South-east Asia by Arab and Indian traders. Sometimes the seeds are used whole, though in this region they are generally ground with the spice paste for curries.

CURRY LEAVES These highly aromatic leaves are used in many areas of South-east Asia. In Indonesia, where they are known as *daun salaam*, they are always used in their fresh form. They are not easily available fresh in the West, however. You could use the dried leaf, but I think a better substitute is the Indian curry leaf (*kari patta*) which is sometimes available both fresh and dried. Fresh curry leaves may be frozen flat in a polythene bag or plastic box.

*DASHI* This is Japanese soup stock. The most common kind is made with a combination of shavings from dried bonito fillets and a dried kelp (*konbu*). (See recipe on page 255.)

*DASHI-NO-MOTO* This is instant dashi, available in granules and generally salted. It is sold under many brand names. The *dashi-no-moto* I use requires 2 teaspoons of the granules to be mixed with 450 ml (¾ pint) hot water to make a basic Japanese stock. To season this stock for soup, I suggest you add 1 tablespoon sugar, 3 tablespoons Japanese soy sauce (*shoyu*) and 2 tablespoons sake. Simmer gently for a few minutes until the sugar dissolves.

EVAPORATED MILK Available in cans, this is milk which has been condensed but not sweetened. It is popular in Malaysian and Filipino cooking.

FENNEL SEEDS These seeds look and taste like aniseed, but they are larger and plumper. Indians often serve roasted fennel seeds at the end of a meal as an aid to digestion and as a mouth-freshener. To grind fennel seeds, put a few tablespoons into a clean coffee grinder or spice grinder and grind as finely as possible. Store in an airtight container.

FISH SAUCE Known as *nam pla* in Thailand, *nuoc mam* in Vietnam and *patis* in the Philippines, fish sauce is used in these countries much as soy sauce is used in China. A thin, salty, brown liquid made from salted shrimp or fish, it has a very special flavour of its own. It is obtainable from Chinese and Far Eastern grocers and selected supermarkets. You can, if you must, use salt as a substitute or improvise by mixing 1 tablespoon water with ½ teaspoon salt, ¼ teaspoon soy sauce and ¼ teaspoon sugar, though the flavour won't be as good.

FIVE-SPICE POWDER A Chinese spice mixture, this contains star anise, fennel, cloves, cinnamon and Sichuan peppercorns. It is sold already ground by Chinese grocers and many supermarkets. To make it yourself, combine 2 whole star anise, 1 teaspoon whole fennel seeds, 1 teaspoon whole cloves, a 5 cm (2 inch) stick of cinnamon or cassia bark and 1 tablespoon Sichuan peppercorns. Grind as finely as possible in a clean coffee grinder or spice grinder and store in a tightly lidded jar.

FUNGUS, BLACK Also known as *moer* mushrooms and cloud ears, this tree fungus is a speciality of the Sichuan province of China. It is sold in Chinese grocers' shops in the form of little, dried, curled up, black chips. These need to be soaked in warm water for about 20-30 minutes before use. On soaking, they enlarge considerably. At this stage you should feel with your fingers for their little hard 'eyes' and snip them off. Rinse the pieces of fungus well as they tend to be gritty. They add a pleasant, chewy texture to dishes.

*GAI LAN* This is the Chinese name for a wonderful member of the cabbage family. Deep green in colour, *gai lan* is close in taste to broccoli, but it has no head. It is basically all leaves with tasty stems and small flowers. It is usually available in Chinese grocers' shops, where it may be labelled in Cantonese as *kai lan*.

GALANGAL Known as *laos* and *lengkuas* in Indonesia, *langkuas* in Malaysia and *kha* in Thailand, this ginger-like rhizome has a very distinct earthy aroma of its own. Unfortunately, it isn't widely available in its fresh form in the West, though you may be lucky enough to find it. Dried sliced galangal is more readily obtainable from some Chinese and East Asian grocers. This needs to be soaked in water before use. It is then usually ground with other spices to make curry paste. Approximately 3 slices dried galangal is equivalent to a 1 cm (½ inch) cube of the fresh form. Ground dried galangal – usually called laos powder – is also obtainable.

GARAM MASALA An Indian spice mixture which is generally sprinkled on to foods towards the end of cooking to impart a final aromatic flavouring. It may also be used as a garnish. Garam masala usually contains cardamom, cinnamon, cumin, cloves, black peppercorns and nutmeg, but there isn't a standardized recipe. It is available ready-ground from supermarkets and Indian grocers, or you can grind your own spices using a spice grinder or clean coffee grinder.

GARLIC This is widely used in large quantities in South-east Asian cooking. There are pink-, white- and purple-skinned varieties – the purple-skinned variety is generally considered to be the best. In South-east Asian recipes, garlic is very often sliced, fried into crisp chips and either scattered over foods as a garnish or tossed in with them for added flavour. Garlic is also a component of many spice pastes.

*GHEE* This is butter that has been clarified so thoroughly that you can even deep-fry in it. As there are no milk solids left in it, *ghee* does not need refrigeration. It has a nutty, buttery taste. All Indian grocers sell *ghee* and I find it more convenient to buy it ready-prepared. If, however, you need – or want – to make your own, put 450 g (1 lb) unsalted butter in a pan over a low heat and let it simmer very gently until the milky solids turn brownish and cling to the sides of the pan or fall to the bottom. The time this takes will depend on the amount of water in the butter. Watch carefully towards the end of the heating period and do not let the *ghee* burn. Strain the *ghee* through a triple layer of muslin. *Ghee* which you have prepared yourself is best stored in a refrigerator.

GINGER, FRESH ROOT You almost cannot cook without fresh ginger in the Far East. This rhizome has a sharp, pungent, cleansing taste and is a digestive to boot. Its brown skin is generally peeled, though in Chinese cookery it is sometimes left on.

When a recipe calls for finely grated root ginger, it should first be peeled and then grated on a fine grater so it turns into pulp. If a recipe requires a 2.5 cm (1 inch) piece of ginger to be grated, you will find that it is easier to grate that length from the larger knob, so saving you from grating your fingers.

When buying ginger, look for pieces that are not too wrinkled. Ginger should be stored in a cool, dry place. It can be stored buried in fairly dry, sandy soil. This way small portions can be broken off as they are needed, while the rest of the knob generously keeps growing.

HOISIN SAUCE This is a thick, slightly sweet, smooth Chinese bean sauce with a light garlic flavour. It may be used in cooking or as a dip. It is sold in bottles by Chinese grocers and most supermarkets. Once opened, store tightly sealed in the refrigerator.

HOLY BASIL (*bai kaprow*) See *Basil*.

JAGGERY A form of raw lump cane sugar. You should look for the kind that crumbles easily and is not rock-hard. It can be bought at Indian grocers. This is the best substitute for the palm sugar that is used in South-east Asia.

JAPANESE SEVEN-SPICE SEASONING See *Shichimi*.

KAFFIR LIME The wonderfully fragrant leaves and rind of this dark-green knobbly fruit are used a great deal in South-east Asian cookery. Kaffir limes are highly aromatic and there is no real substitute for their flavour. If you are lucky enough to obtain fresh leaves, you should tear them in half and strip out their coarse centre veins before using them. Any leaves that you are not using immediately can be stored in a plastic bag in the freezer. Whole kaffir limes may be frozen as well. Both leaves and rind are sometimes available dried; use these if you cannot find the fresh version. Whole kaffir limes, the leaves and dried rind are sold by Far Eastern and some Chinese grocers. You may have to ask for help in locating the rind, which may be labelled in Thai as '*piwma grood*'.

*KOCHU CHANG* A spicy paste made with fermented soya beans and red chillies, this is a very common seasoning in Korea. You can improvise by using the recipe on page 218.

*KOKUM* Various souring agents are used in Indonesian cookery. *Asem candis*, the dried skin of a mangosteen-like fruit, is very popular in Western Sumatra. As it is hard to find in the West, I use the Indian *kokum*, which is very similar.

*KONBU* This green, calcium-rich, dried kelp used for making stock (*dashi*) in Japan is sometimes sold as *dashi-konbu*. It resembles large long leaves and is available either folded up or cut into small pieces.

*Konbu* (sometimes called *kombu*) should never be washed as its flavour resides near the surface. It should be wiped with a damp cloth just before use. *Konbu* may be allowed to simmer gently but must never boil vigorously. It is obtainable from Japanese and some Chinese grocers where its price is generally a good indication of its quality.

*KRUPUK* These tasty Indonesian wafers can be served with most meals. They are available in different flavours, though the base ingredient is usually tapioca. When dried, they are hard and brittle. When fried, they expand and turn very crisp. They are obtainable from Far Eastern and some Chinese grocers. Once a packet has been started, any unused wafers should be transferred to a tightly lidded jar.

LEMON GRASS Known as *sereh* in Indonesia, *serai* in Malaysia and *takrai* in Thailand, lemon grass is a tall, hard, greyish-green grass often used in South-east Asian dishes for its distinctive aroma and flavour. It is available in many supermarkets and ethnic grocers. Usually only the bottom 15 cm (6 inches) are used and the straw-like top is discarded. The lemon grass may be used whole, its bulbous base first bruised with a hammer or other heavy object, or it can be sliced.

Lemon grass is fairly hard. To slice it, first cut off the hard knot at the very end and then slice crossways into paper-thin slices. Even when lemon grass is to be ground to a pulp in a blender it needs to be sliced thinly first or it does not grind properly. Lemon grass is best stored with its bottom end in a little water. This prevents it from drying out. You can also freeze stalks of lemon grass.

In South-east Asia, lemon grass is always used fresh. Fortunately, fresh lemon grass is increasingly available here from larger supermarkets and Oriental grocers. However, we sometimes have to make do with the dried form. If necessary, I buy dried sliced lemon grass and then soak it before use: 2 tablespoons dried sliced lemon grass is roughly equivalent to 1 fresh stick. As its name suggests, lemon grass has a citrus flavour and aroma. You can use lemon rind as a substitute, though it is nowhere near as good as the real thing.

LIME AND LIME JUICE There are several varieties of lime in East Asia and are they are frequently used in cooking. The Philippines have the very small *kalamansi* lime which is squeezed over foods and makes excellent limeade. There is the kaffir lime of Indochina with its unmatched aroma, and then there is the lime that we know in the West, though here it is generally found in a smaller size. If you really cannot get limes, use lemons as a substitute.

MINT You will find various sorts of mints in South-east Asian markets and vegetable stores. They are used in cooking and are also nibbled at on the side during meals. In Vietnam, mint leaves are added to morsels of food along with other herbs just as they are about to be eaten. Only fresh mint can be used.

MIRIN This sweetened sake is an essential ingredient in Japanese cookery, though it is sometimes difficult to find in the West. You can, however, make a reasonable substitute by combining equal parts of sake and sugar and then cooking them gently until the sugar dissolves and the liquid is reduced by half. I have tended to use this combination in my recipes instead of mirin. If you have access to a Japanese grocer, do try to get the real thing.

*MISO* A Japanese paste made from fermented soya beans, *miso* also contains other fermented grains. Among the *misos* easily available in the West is *aka-miso*, a reddish-brown variety. *Miso* can usually be found in healthfood shops. Sometimes it is labelled according to its colour – 'red', 'brown', 'yellow' or 'white'. In Japan, where *miso* is used a great deal, it is available in almost every shade and texture. It can be used for soups and stews, it can be lathered on to vegetables such as aubergines before they are grilled, and it can also be used in the preparation of pickles and dressings. To make soup, *miso* needs to be dissolved in water and then strained. It should never be allowed to boil vigorously.

MOOLI See *Radish, white*.

MUNG BEANS, WHOLE These yellow beans with green skins are sold in supermarkets, healthfood stores and Indian grocers.

MUSHROOMS Hundreds of different varieties are sold throughout East Asia, from tiny pinheads to large meaty mushrooms. A few Asian mushrooms are available in the West, but generally only in their dried or canned forms. (See also Fungus, black.).

*Dried Chinese mushrooms* These are available in selected supermarkets and Chinese stores. Price is generally an indication of quality. The thicker the cap, the meatier the texture. Dried mushrooms need to be soaked in warm water before they are used. The texture of the stalks remains hard, even after soaking, so they need to be cut off. The soaking water has a good flavour, so it is worth saving. Strain it through muslin or a fine sieve to remove grit and add to stocks or use to cook vegetables.

*Straw mushrooms* Smooth and meaty, there is nothing quite as delicious as a fresh straw mushroom. I eagerly await the day when they will be as commonly available in the West as they are in the East. Meanwhile, we have to make do with the canned variety. Drain these before use, then rinse and use according to the recipe.

MUSTARD SEEDS, BLACK AND YELLOW Black mustard seeds are used in Indian cooking, and in curry pastes in some parts of South-east Asia. The seeds are tiny, round and dark reddish-brown (rather than black) in colour. They can be bought from Indian grocers. Yellow mustard seeds may be substituted for the black ones.

NOODLES Noodles probably originated in the Far East. They are sold both dried and fresh, made of wheat or rice, and there are literally hundreds to choose from.

*Fresh Chinese egg noodles* These are usually sold in plastic bags in the chilled section of Chinese grocers. A 450 g (1 lb) quantity usually serves 4-6 people. If you intend using smaller portions, divide the noodles as soon as possible after purchase, wrap well and freeze what you are not going to use that day; the rest can be refrigerated until you are ready to cook them.

The best way to cook fresh egg noodles is to put them into a large pan of boiling water. As soon as the water comes to the boil again, add a teacup of fresh water. Repeat this about three times or until the noodles are just tender. The noodles can now be drained and used as the recipe suggests. Frozen egg noodles defrost quickly and easily when dropped into boiling water: just stir them about at first to ensure that they separate.

*Dried Chinese egg noodles* When fresh noodles are not available, use dried ones. Put them into a large pan of boiling water and cook them as you would fresh noodles.

*Fresh rice noodles* These are white, slithery and absolutely delicious. In South-east Asia they are available in all sizes and shapes. They generally stay fresh for just a day. Many do not need to be cooked at all; others should be heated through very briefly. Unfortunately, these noodles are hard to find in the West.

*Dried rice noodles* We usually have to make do with dried rice noodles in the West. For most of the recipes in this book, buy *banh pho* or any other flat rice noodles, soak them for about 2 hours or until soft, then cook them very briefly in a large pan of boiling water. Drain and rinse the noodles in cold water before using as the recipe suggests. *Banh pho* is the noodle to use for making the Vietnamese noodle soup called *pho*.

*Rice vermicelli* Several recipes in this book call for rice vermicelli. These are very fine noodles which closely resemble cellophane noodles but are longer. Rice vermicelli are, of course, made from rice, whereas cellophane noodles are made from mung beans.

*Cellophane noodles* Also called bean thread or transparent noodles, these are made from ground mung beans. Chinese grocers sell them dried. They are very fine and white in colour, and should be soaked for 10-15 minutes before use.

*Udon* These are white, slightly rounded or flat Japanese wheat noodles. They can be bought in the West only in their dried form. Cook them as you would Chinese fresh egg noodles, but then rinse them under cold running water.

OILS For most of the recipes in this book, I would recommend using groundnut (peanut) or corn oil. If the oil is used for deep-frying, it can be re-used. Skim off all extraneous matter with a slotted spoon or a Chinese mesh skimmer and then drop a chunk of ginger or potato into it and let it fry: this will absorb most of the unwanted flavours. When it is cool enough to handle, strain the oil through a sieve lined with a double thickness of muslin. Let it cool completely, then store in a bottle. When re-using, mix half old oil with half fresh oil.

Olive oil is used only in the Philippines because of its Spanish heritage. See also *Sesame oil*.

OYSTER SAUCE A thick, brown, Cantonese-style sauce made with oysters, this is salty and slightly sweet at the same time. It is used to flavour all sorts of dishes from vegetables to noodles. Once opened, a bottle of oyster sauce should be stored in the refrigerator. It is obtainable from supermarkets.

PALM SUGAR This is a delicious, raw, honey-coloured sugar used in many parts of South-east Asia. It comes in lump or fairly flowing forms. The best substitutes for it are either Indian jaggery or brown sugar.

PAPRIKA This is not generally used in South-east Asian recipes, but when I cannot find fresh red chillies I use paprika instead to give dishes their traditional colour.

PEANUTS Raw peanuts can be obtained at supermarkets, healthfood stores and ethnic grocers. For roasting and crushing peanuts, see page 223.

PEPPERS, RED AND GREEN Cooked foods in South-east Asia are often garnished with strips of fresh hot red and green chillies. Since this tends to make the dishes even hotter than they already are, I frequently substitute strips of sweet red and green peppers. The curry pastes of this region often require a pounded paste made from fresh red chillies. If these are unobtainable, the best substitute is a combination of sweet red pepper, water and paprika.

PRAWNS Raw prawns are used for most dishes in this book. For instructions on preparing them, see page 15.

After you have prepared them, it is a good idea to wash prawns with salt to remove any sliminess and refresh them. To do this, put the peeled prawns in a bowl. Sprinkle a tablespoon or so of coarse salt over them and rub them lightly, then wash them in cold water. Repeat once more, making sure that all the salt is washed away.

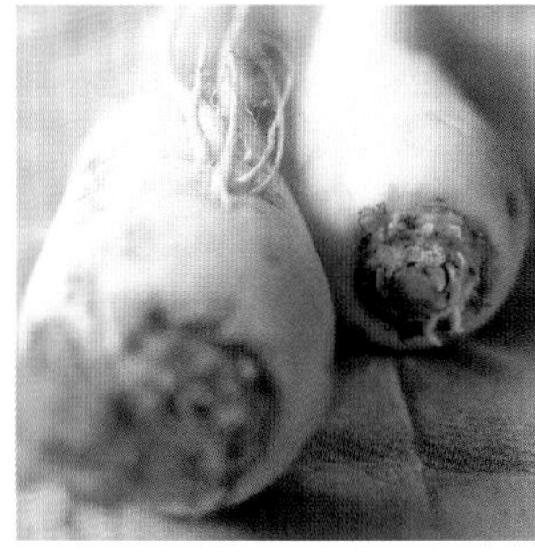

RADISH, WHITE Also known as *mooli or daikon*, this very large, long radish resembles an elongated parsnip. It can be as much as 7.5 cm (3 inches) in diameter. It has a relatively mild peppery taste and is used in Far Eastern salads, as well as soups and other cooked dishes. *Mooli* is particularly popular in Japan. This vegetable should always be peeled before it is used.

RICE This is the staple in most parts of the Far East. Each country, sometimes each province within each country, favours its own special rice. For the purposes of this book, two types of rice should suffice: long-grain for all the dishes from India, Indonesia, Malaysia, Vietnam, Thailand, the Philippines and Hong Kong; and Japanese short-grain for Japanese and Korean dishes. For special Indian meals, you may like to buy basmati rice, which is a wonderfully fragrant long-grain variety. Rice is generally washed before use. For directions on cooking rice see pages 190-1.

In some regions of Indochina, such as northern Thailand, glutinous rice is the staple. The grains are short and opaque. Directions for cooking glutinous rice are on page 191.

RICE PAPER, VIETNAMESE This is the thin translucent wrapper used to make Vietnamese spring rolls. It generally comes with the markings of the mats on which it was dried still imprinted on it. It needs to be dampened slightly in order to become soft. Rice papers are available in various sizes from selected Oriental grocers.

RICE WINE, CHINESE Several rice wines are used in Chinese cookery, the most common being Shao-Hsing. This is whisky-coloured with a rich sweetish taste. A reasonable substitute is dry sherry.

SAFFRON This is the whole stigma of the autumn crocus, which is available dried in the form of strands or threads. Look for a reliable source for your saffron as it is very expensive and there can be a great deal of adulteration.

SAKE This is the renowned Japanese rice wine used for both cooking and drinking. It is generally served warm as a drink. Sake is available from many good off-licences and Japanese grocers. Once opened, it must be refrigerated and used within 2-3 weeks. For more information, see page 246.

SESAME OIL Oriental sesame oil is made from roasted sesame seeds. It therefore has a golden colour and a deliciously nutty taste and aroma. It is not used for cooking as such. Small amounts are added to dressings and foods just to give them a sesame flavour and sometimes a sheen. Store sesame oil in a cool place away from the light, but not in the refrigerator or it will turn cloudy.

SESAME PASTE Chinese and Japanese sesame pastes are made from roasted sesame seeds and are darker in colour than Middle Eastern sesame paste (*tahini*). If you cannot get the former, use the latter. All sesame paste has oil floating on the top. You need to mix the contents of the jar or can thoroughly before using it. The paste can be very hard initially but softens up on mixing. Sesame paste is available from ethnic grocers; *tahini* is sold at most healthfood shops and selected supermarkets. Store all types of sesame seed paste in the refrigerator.

SESAME SEEDS You may use either the white seeds or the beige ones for all the recipes in this book calling for sesame seeds.

*To roast sesame seeds*, set a small cast-iron frying pan over a medium-low heat. When it is hot, put in 1-3 tablespoons of sesame seeds. Stir them around until they turn a shade darker and give out a wonderful roasted aroma. Sesame seeds do tend to fly about as they are roasted. You could turn down the heat slightly when they do this, or cover the pan loosely. Remove the seeds from the pan as soon as they are done. You may roast sesame seeds in advance, cool, then store in a tightly lidded jar. They will last for several weeks kept this way, though they are best freshly roasted.

SHALLOTS These are used in large quantities in South-east Asian dishes. Shallots are ground into curry pastes, sliced into salads and fried into crisp flakes to be used both as a garnish and as a flavouring.

*SHICHIMI* This Japanese seven-spice seasoning is also sold as 'seven-spice red pepper' ('*shi-chimi togarashi*'). Available only from Japanese grocers, it contains a coarsely crushed mixture of red pepper, a special Japanese pepper called *sansho*, roasted sesame seeds, roasted white poppy or hemp seeds, white pepper and tiny bits of orange peel and seaweed. Use my easy Sesame Seed Seasoning as a substitute.

*To make Sesame Seed Seasoning*, set a small cast-iron frying pan over a medium-low heat. When it is hot, put in 1 tablespoon sesame seeds, 1 tablespoon Sichuan peppercorns and 1 small dried hot red chilli. Stir these around until the sesame seeds turn golden brown. Allow the mixture to cool, then grind it together with ¼ teaspoon salt in a clean coffee grinder or mortar until you have a fairly smooth powder.

SHRIMP PASTE This paste made of fermented shrimp is used as a seasoning throughout South-east Asia. It comes in many forms ranging from a grey watery paste to crumbly brown blocks. South-east Asian grocers sell an array of shrimp pastes.

To make your own substitute for the thin grey shrimp paste, buy a can of 12 anchovy fillets in oil, drain well, then blend them with about 1½ tablespoons water.

There is really no substitute for the blocks, which are known variously as *blachan* and *terasi*, although I have used anchovy paste in desperation. When *blachan* or *terasi* are used in uncooked dishes, they need to be roasted first. To do this, break off the amount you need and either hold it over a low gas flame with a pair of tongs, turning it around until it is roasted, or spread it out on a piece of foil and grill it. You could, if you like, fry it in a tiny amount of oil instead.

SICHUAN PEPPERCORNS Reddish-brown, highly aromatic pods, these are very slightly larger than ordinary peppercorns. They are available from Chinese grocers and selected supermarkets. Store them in a tightly lidded jar.

*To roast Sichuan peppercorns*, set a small cast-iron frying pan over a medium-low heat. When it is hot, put in the peppercorns. Stir and fry until they release their fragrance. They might smoke a little, but the smoke will be highly aromatic. To grind roasted Sichuan peppercorns, allow them to cool, then put them into a spice grinder, clean coffee grinder or mortar and grind until you have a powder.

SOY SAUCE Many different soy sauces are used in East Asia. Not only do countries have their own brands of soy sauces but regions, towns and even individual villages within these countries sometimes proudly boast of producing their very own. All soy sauces are made from fermented and salted soya beans. They range from salty to sweet, from light to dark, from thick to thin, and have many different textures. Dark soy sauces tend to be thicker than the light ones and generally add a dark colour to the dish to which they are added. Light soy sauce tends to be thinner and saltier.

Since soy sauces vary so much in their saltiness, it is always advisable to use slightly less than the amount required in the recipe – you can always add more later.

*Kecap manis* is a thick, very sweet – indeed, syrupy – soy sauce used in Indonesia. If you cannot find it, you can make an approximation of it yourself by combining 250 ml (8 fl oz) dark soy sauce with 6 tablespoons treacle and 3 tablespoons brown sugar, and heating them gently together in a pan until the sugar has dissolved.

Japanese and Chinese soy sauces have very different flavours. Hence, it is best to use Japanese soy sauces (sold in healthfood shops as *shoyu*) when called for, and Chinese soy sauces as required. The quality varies, so seek out a good brand. The best-known Japanese soy sauce is Kikkoman.

STAR ANISE This attractive flower-shaped pod consists of the fruits and seeds of an Oriental evergreen tree. It is an important spice in Chinese cooking and has a decided aniseed flavour. It is one of the ingredients in Chinese five-spice powder and is used whole in Chinese-style braised dishes. Store star anise pods in a tightly lidded jar to keep them fresh.

TAMARIND This is a bean-like fruit of a tall tree. When ripe, the beans are peeled, deseeded and packed in lumps or bricks. Tamarind is sold by South-east Asian and Indian grocers.

*To make your own tamarind paste*, break off 225 g (8 oz) from a brick of tamarind and tear it into small pieces. Put them into a small glass or stainless steel bowl, cover with 450 ml (¾ pint) very hot water and set aside for 3 hours or overnight. (You could achieve the same result by simmering the tamarind in the water for 10 minutes.) Set a sieve over another glass or stainless steel bowl and empty the tamarind and its soaking liquid into it. Push down on the tamarind with your fingers or the back of a wooden spoon to extract as much pulp as you can. Put whatever tamarind remains in the sieve back into the soaking bowl. Add 120 ml (4 fl oz) hot water to it and mash a little more. Return it to the sieve and extract as much more pulp as you can. Retrieve the pulp that clings to the underside of the sieve.

This quantity will make about 350 ml (12 fl oz). Any leftover tamarind paste may either be refrigerated for up to 2-3 weeks, or it can be frozen.

TURMERIC Many South-east Asian countries use fresh turmeric. It is a rhizome not unlike ginger but smaller in size and more delicate in appearance. Many Indian stores sell it. Even though the ground turmeric available in most supermarkets is adequate, use fresh turmeric whenever possible. A 2.5 cm (1 inch) piece is equivalent to about ½ teaspoon ground turmeric. Like ginger, it needs to be peeled and ground. This grinding is best done with the help of a little water in an electric blender.

VINEGAR There are probably as many vinegars in the East as there are soy sauces, with every district in every country producing its very own brand. China, for example, has red, black and white vinegars. The Philippines have a pale, slightly milky vinegar made from palm toddy, and Japan is proud of its very mild rice vinegars.

To simplify matters, I have specified distilled white vinegar almost all the way through this book. Occasionally, I have stipulated Japanese rice vinegar where it is an important ingredient. If you cannot obtain it, make your own version by combining 3 parts distilled white vinegar with 1 part water and ¼ part sugar.

WATER CHESTNUTS Dark-skinned and chestnut-sized, these grow in water. They are sold fresh only by some Chinese grocers. The inside flesh is deliciously crisp and white. Canned water chestnuts are not really comparable, but may be used in cooked dishes.

YELLOW BEAN SAUCE See *Bean sauce, yellow*.

# SPECIALIST SUPPLIERS

There are now many oriental grocers throughout the UK, and the chances are that you may well have one in your local town. Most major supermarkets now stock an excellent range of Asian foods too. Here is a selection of specialist oriental food stores, including mail order suppliers.

WING YIP,
395, Edgware Road, Cricklewood, London NW2
Tel: 0208 450 0422

WING THAI,
13, Electric Avenue, Brixton, London SW9
Tel: 0207 738 5898

LOON FUNG SUPERMARKET,
39, Gerrard Street, London W1
Tel: 0207 437 7332

TUNG HING,
41, The Vale, Acton, London W3
Tel: 0208 743 5171
(also mail order)

THE SPICE SHOP,
1, Blenheim Crescent, London W11
Tel: 0207 221 4448
www.thespiceshop.co.uk
(also mail order)

WING YIP,
Oldham Road, Ancoats, Manchester M4
Tel: 0161 832 3215

WING YIP,
375, Nechells Park Road, Nechells, Birmingham B7
Tel: 0121 327 6618

# INDEX

*Page numbers in italic refer to the illustrations*

# ACKNOWLEDGEMENTS

There were, literally, hundreds of people who helped me through this enormous project. I would like to express my gratitude to all of them, especially to:

HONG KONG: Willy and Mimi Mark, Grace and Kendall Oei, Mrs Audrey Fung, Priscilla Chen, Margaret Leeming, Hong Kong Tourist Association, Irene Ho

PHILIPPINES: Mila Rodriguez, Sandra Cahill, Reynaldo Alejandro, Sandy Daza, Glenda Barretto, Ruby and Buddy Roa, Doreen and Willy Fernandez, Ruska Gamboa, Ramon Hofilena, Doctora Fe Elseyer, Tina Lapres, Philippines Department of Tourism

VIETNAM: Biche Lombatière, Indrajit Ghosh, Ram and Shangri-La Gopal, Richard G Tallboys, Thuy Pellissier, Lîu Thanh Nhàn, Mrs Vuong, Ngùyên, Van Y, Ministry of Information

MALAYSIA: Zainal Arshad, Puan Rashidah, Lim Suan Har, Hasna Abu Bakar, Ahminahbi, Mrs Zaidah Ahmed, Lim Bian Yam, William Chan and the Nyonya Heritage Museum, Zainal Aziz, Penang Development Corporation, Tourist Development Corporation of Malaysia, Boon Cheong

THAILAND: Pieng Chom Darbanand, Chompunute and Akorn Hoontrakul, Duangmarn Mekswat, Chalie Amatyakul, Chai and Daeng Jongmu, Kruamas Woodtikarn, Mrs Ubol, Mrs Boonyoun, Tourism Authority of Thailand

INDONESIA: Sri Owen, Mrs Sanuar, Amri Yahya, Jonqui and Sian Januar, Martini Jufri, Usman and Rosalina Beka, Risnawati Agus, Lastri Krisnarto, Department of Tourism, Cri Murthi Adi, Muriel Peters

KOREA: Mrs Han Chung Kyu, Mrs Choi Sang In, Sang Kyung Lee, Dr Park Hun-Seop, Chilwon Village, Korea National Tourist Corporation, Mrs Han Chung Hea

JAPAN: Professor Shizuo Tsuji and the staff of the Ecole Technique Hotelière Tauji, Keiko Okamoto, Tawaraya Inn, John J. McGovern, Tsuruya Ryotei, Japan National Tourist Organisation, and Professor K. C. Chang at Harvard University, Boston, USA

The publishers would also like to thank Magimix for supplying equipment for photography.